THE MANAGERS

THE
MANAGERS
Corporate Life in America
BY DIANE ROTHBARD MARGOLIS

William Morrow and Company, Inc.
New York   1979

For RJM

Library of Congress Cataloging in Publication Data

Margolis, Diane Rothbard.
    The managers.

        Bibliography: p.
        Includes index.
        1. Middle managers—United States—Case studies.
I.Title.
HF5500.3.U54M37   658.4'3'0973   79-13274
ISBN 0-688-03537-X

Printed in the United States of America.

This book is based on eighty-one in-depth interviews with managers and wives of managers. At first I concentrated upon the most salient feature of corporation managers' life patterns: their transiency. It is not hard in suburbia to find transient managers to interview. One has merely to mention an interest in talking to people who have moved a great deal, and suggestions come rolling in: "You ought to see Barbara Woodward [1]—she's moved fifteen times in fourteen years." "Have you met Bob Hardy? He's had two transfers a year for the past three years." "You know, you should talk to some real estate agents—they really get to deal with transients. Tom Moore told me he just sold a house to some guy who got transferred out again a week before the closing. His furniture was already on the van and he had to tell them to send his stuff to California instead of Connecticut."

For a while I followed such leads. I spoke to champion transients to find out what their lives were like; I spoke to top executives of corporations to learn something of the reasons for transfers; and I spoke to a couple of real estate agents to get the views of local businessmen on their prime customers. After seventeen such interviews it became clear that most corporation managers were not transferred as frequently as were the ones I was interviewing and that transiency was just one of several ways in which the relationship between the corporation and its managers governed the lives of managerial families.

A more systematic, less biased sampling technique was in order. So I chose a "*Fortune* 100" corporation and a suburban town some thirty miles from corporate headquarters. The managers who worked for that corporation and lived in that town, as well as their wives, were individually interviewed. When this phase of the study began in the spring of 1973, 39 such couples were living in the town. During the year at least 1 member of all but 4 of the couples agreed to be interviewed, resulting in 64 interviews—30 with men and 34 with women.

The interviews lasted anywhere from one to four hours, with two hours the usual duration. They tended to be discursive. In fact, some of the men complained at the end of their interview that it had rambled. They were not able to catch any theme.

There was, of course, a theme, and also some direction. The managers and their wives were encouraged to talk about their careers, the communities they had lived in and their participation in those communities, their transfers, their aspirations, their friendships, their attitudes toward the corporation, their ways of adjusting to the transfers, and their family backgrounds. Later, when I analyzed the transcripts, I concentrated upon those responses that were repeated from couple to couple. These responses, the patterns of life for corporation managers and their families, provided the focus for the study.

The year after the managers were interviewed, I undertook another study, one that investigated the differences between men and women as they worked in local political organizations. This gave me an opportunity to interview another group in town, members of the Town Committees of the Republican and Democratic parties.[2] They were roughly similar to the corporate managers in age, income, and educational background, but they were very different in most other respects. The managers worked for a giant corporation. Most of the Town Committee members were either self-employed or worked for small, local companies. The Town Committee members were residentially more stable and more deeply involved in the affairs of their town. Although the purpose of the second set of interviews was different, some of the topics covered were the same. The contrast between the two groups elucidated the social effects of the managers' corporate employment. In the first two parts of this book those contrasts are implicit; in the third they are made explicit.

levels, colonial reproductions, or Cape Cods. These have been built for and bought by the newly arriving corporation managers.

Notes on the Method

Essentially this is a case study, with the inherent advantages and disadvantages of that genre. The method was chosen because it suited the purposes of the study. I began with no precise hypotheses that could be translated into items for a large survey-questionnaire. Instead I started with some general ideas of what I might find—ideas chiefly about transiency and its effect on local politics. Like most of the town committee members I interviewed a year later, I thought transient managers played an active, but poorly informed, role in their communities.

Fortunately, case studies and small samples permit a great deal of flexibility. The researcher can easily drop lines of inquiry that turn out to be barren and pick up emergent threads that promise to be fruitful. This I did as soon as I learned in the early interviews that the only clear patterns to emerge were tendencies on the part of managers, first, to trivialize all political issues, and second, to be alienated from all things political. Then the question turned to why. What was it about the managers' corporate attachments that separated them both in thought and in activity from the democratic political process? The answers did not come together until, with analysis of the transcripts, I began discovering persistent patterns; but even during the interview stage I suspected that the answers would lie in the special life-style requirements the managers had to meet, and I was able to concentrate my questioning in those areas.

Another advantage of this method is that it permits long interviews in which it is possible to take the time and ask the questions necessary to make sure that the interviewer understands the respondent's meanings and values. That was important, for my perspective differed from that of the managers and their wives. Much about their lives that was incomprehensible to me seemed reasonable and worthwhile to them. I had to keep asking questions in an attempt to see events from their vantage point.

For all their advantages, case studies and small samples have at least one serious flaw: to generalize from them is to take a great leap into uncertainty. There is no way of knowing whether the experiences reported, the feelings expressed, or the social structures and relationships revealed are typical or idiosyncratic. However, similarities between the early interviews, which were with people who lived in a number of suburban towns and worked for several other corporations, and the later set of sixty-four interviews afforded some confidence that the second group was not eccentric. A further check was provided by the similarities between what was learned in this study and the findings of other studies of corporation managers and their families.[4] (Both similarities and differences will be discussed in the text and in the notes.)

In order to gain as much precision as possible, the words *one, hardly any, a few, some, not many, many, most, almost all,* and *all* will be used to specify definite proportions when referring to the GPIers. The words and the numbers they represent are as follows:

	Couples	Men	Women
one	1	1	1
hardly any, a few	2–7	2–6	2–7
some, not many	8–14	7–11	8–13
many	15–21	12–17	14–20
most	22–28	18–23	21–27
almost all	29–35	24–29	28–33
all	36	30	34

ACKNOWLEDGMENTS

Every book begins with the twin notions that the book should be written and that the author is equal to the task. Although the latter assumption is especially critical, many writers cannot remember its roots. But I, a woman who came of age in the nineteen-fifties, can mark with ease the moments when the idea took shape, for they came after my first thirty years, the ones during which I grew to believe, along with almost everyone else, that any woman committing the hubris of serious intellectual activity would be visited with the nemesis of a loveless life. So my first thanks are owed to Betty Friedan and other women of my generation and older, most of whom I have never met, who argued in their work and in their ways that creativity in mind as well as body is possible for both genders.

They sent me back to school. There men were most influential. Richard Sennett was the first to suggest this book. It was in the lounge of the sociology department at New York University, and he was commenting on a paper I had written for his course in urban sociology. I was surprised at his ambition for that little paper, but he seemed confident.

Before this was a book, it was a dissertation. As my adviser, Dick Sennett guided with a light hand and a quick mind. Always he was encouraging, but at several critical junctions where I was lost, he pointed the way with brilliant precision and such an uncanny rightness that virtually all the directions he suggested worked. Others at N.Y.U., especially Wolf Heydebrand and Patricia Cayo Sexton, deserve much thanks. Wolf helped me to understand the many problems in my method and kept me from becoming too entangled in the miles of tapes on which the interviews were recorded, and Pat's insightful criticisms have, I hope, prevented the book from bearing some of the faults that were in the dissertation.

My attempts to make sense of the diverse phenomena reported here rest on the formulations of seminal thinkers. My debts to C. Wright Mills, Max Weber, Georg Simmel, Ferdinand Toennies, and others are noted in the text. There is one, however, whose own work did help to mold my thoughts, but whose guidance was more personal than that. When this book was just a term paper, Dick Sennett suggested that I send it to David Riesman and again, when there were a few chapters written, Dick showed them to him. Professor Riesman responded with insightful criticisms and suggestions for directions further study might take. The book and I have profited from his generous interest.

There was interest, too, from my friends. John K. Jessup, Eunice Jessup, Joan Larned, Sandy Mintz, Walter Mintz, and Eugene Katz all read the dissertation and commented with kind hearts and critical minds. Two friends, W. Stewart Mac-Coll and Helen Littauer, deserve special thanks. From the beginning, when even the term paper was but an idea, Stew was there as someone with whom I could explore emerging patterns and try out interpretations. As pastor of The Wilton Presbyterian Church, he ministered to a congregation made up in large part of corporation managers and their families. Because he approaches his own work with an unsurpassed sense of responsibility and concern, he approached my work with the same qualities. There is hardly an idea in the book that was not honed against Stew's strong sensibilities. And Helen: at a time when the failure of local officials to enforce the town's regulations left me without a quiet place in which to work and threatened my faith in community, she lent me a room, a desk, and, most important, an ear. Heart of graciousness that she is, Helen insisted all the while that I was doing her a favor. Later, Helen read the final draft and her close reading and impeccable taste sheltered me again—this time against my own clumsy expression.

Other favors came from the many men and women whose

words form the substance of this study, but who cannot be thanked by name without retracting the anonymity they were promised. They gave unstintingly of their time, their thoughts, their hospitality, and their experiences. No doubt some will feel their generosity badly repaid by an interpretation they neither like nor share. I hope, nevertheless, they will see in these pages an accurate reflection of the world they know and an understanding that is as concerned as it is critical.

Many others gave assistance of a practical sort. First, there were the patient and careful typists: Sibyl Martin, who prepared the transcripts; Babbie Agnew, who suffered through the dissertation; the typing pool at the University of Connecticut; and especially Cynthia Conti, who typed the final draft. John Knauth helped me deal with tape recorders; and a small grant from New York University covered the expenses of the first transcripts. Ruth Mandel and Marilyn Johnson at the Center for the American Woman and Politics at Rutgers University have let me use in this work some of the data from the study of men and women in local political parties that the Center sponsored. They have waited patiently for the completion of that other study while I finished this one.

I have left for the last thanks to my family, for words are poor conveyors. My mother and father, though they sometimes feared the threatened nemesis, gave me the determination and the education that was there to build on when finally my world had changed and I was ready to proceed. As this study grew from term paper to book, my sons Harry and Philip grew from boys into men. Each in his own way so exceeds my hopes and imaginings that I often wonder at the paltriness of my dreams and the foolishness of my fears. Both were perceptive readers and good editors of this manuscript. But the best editor, teacher, and proof against the nemesis is my husband, Dick. Where other men might have railed, he rallied; where others might have groused, he gloried. No petulant or passive bystander to my metamorphosis, he was my foundation and my mentor. Through clear explanations and painstaking corrections, he helped me find my voice.

Tradition demands a disclaimer: the faults of the book rest solely on the shoulders of the writer. Sometimes, reading other acknowledgments, I've wondered how true that is. In this case I have no doubt. All my helpers implanted or tried to bring out the best that is in me. If some of the worst shows through in spite of their efforts, or if the best is not good enough, chalk it up to my frailties, at least one of which is a certain incorrigibility.

CONTENTS

. . . this nomadic civilization . . . is altering human nature so profoundly, and throws upon personal relations stress greater than they have ever borne before. Under cosmopolitanism, if it comes, we shall receive no help from the earth. Trees and meadows and mountains will only be a spectacle, and the binding force they once exercised on character must be entrusted to Love alone. May Love be equal to the task.

—E. M. FORSTER, *Howard's End* (1921)

CHAPTER 1

Introduction

A question sociologists should try to answer, C. Wright Mills has advised, is:

> What varieties of men and women now prevail in this society and this period—in what ways are they selected and formed, liberated and repressed, made sensitive and blunted? [1]

This is a study of one variety of men and women in our society: corporation managers and their wives.[2] The managers' work at the corporation will be examined to discover the effect of that work upon them and their families in the world outside the corporation. How did corporate requirements shape them as husbands and wives, as parents, as friends, as citizens? How did the corporation liberate or repress, make sensitive or blunt? Though managers and their wives, in general, are not the type of men and women who prevail in this society at this period, the lives of the persons I interviewed were dominated by a social institution that does prevail.

In an era that has witnessed the erosion of most major social institutions—the family, the church, the educational system, and even the nation-state—the global corporation has prospered and triumphed. It appears to follow the laws of a new economics but there is no generally accepted theory to explain it. In his seminal work on the subject, *The Dual Economy*, Robert T. Averitt wrote, "the old economics is not so much wrong as out of date." It explains the workings of what Averitt calls the "peripheral economy" but it does not account for the corporations in the "center economy." The latter is far more powerful. Averitt describes corporations in the center economy:

> The center firm is large in economic size as measured by number of employees, total assets, and yearly sales. It tends toward vertical integration (through ownership or informal control), geographic dispersion (national and international), product diversification, and managerial decentralization. Center firms excel in managerial and technical talent; their financial resources are abundant. Their cash flows are large, particularly during prosperity. Center managements combine a long-run with a short-run perspective. Short-run considerations are entertained at the lower levels of the managerial hierarchy, while long-run planning is the prerequisite of top management. Their markets are commonly concentrated. Taken together, center firms make up the center economy.[3]

I can add little to what Averitt and others have said about the economics of the center firm. My interest is in the center firm's sociology, and my question is: What varieties of men and women does the center firm require for its functioning, and how are these persons shaped to corporate specifications?

This is hardly the first time a social scientist has set out to study corporation managers. Their character, their life-style, their effect on the American culture, and their position in the power structure have all been subjects of scholarly analysis and popular commentary. It may be well here to review those earlier approaches and to indicate where mine agrees and where it differs.

One way of looking at corporation managers has been to probe their psyches. Over the past quarter century the men who manage giant corporations have been described as "other-directed," "conformist," "security-seeking" "organization men."[4] Most recently they have been called "gamesmen" who are "lacking in passion and compassion; cool . . . intellectually interested . . . emotionally cautious . . . and protected against experience." They are, in short, thought to be "fine-tuned instruments . . . [who] never question the basic system [nor] concern themselves with the social implications of what they [do]." [5] I agree. My question is: How did they get that way?

Some commentators, more interested in social signs than in managerial psyches, have found a broad metaphor in the manager's character: they see the manager as a symbol of either the best or the worst in our society. On the one hand, managers have been hailed as the organizers and stewards of a new age of affluence. On the other, they have been deplored as the forerunners of an age of material plenty but cultural emptiness. Among the first of the sanguine heralds was John Kenneth Galbraith. In 1958 he argued that we had achieved a "great and unprecedented affluence," and that the technology organized by large corporations had delivered "the comparatively small corner of the world populated by Europeans" from want.[6] Behind that technology was the "technostructure," the technicians and managers who possessed and organized the knowledge that had made a surfeit of goods possible.[7] Daniel Bell [8] and Alvin Toffler [9] were two who followed and elaborated upon Galbraith's message.

Not all were so optimistic. David Riesman, William H. Whyte, and Philip Slater, to name a few, worried about the cultural vacuity, the tyranny of groups, and the loneliness that appeared to accompany affluence. With titles such as *Eclipse of Community*, *A Nation of Strangers*, *The Pursuit of Loneliness*, *We, the Lonely People*, and *Abundance for What?* they and others announced that the living conditions of the managers and the plenitude they created were mixed blessings.[10] These authors perceived a variety of flaws. Some, such as Slater, saw human needs for engagement and belonging frustrated by the anonymity of life in large cities, the mobility of persons, the instability of family ties, and the rapid changes in institutions. Others, such as Riesman and Whyte, thought that freedom and individuality were being submerged in the group. No matter the emphasis, managers stood as the epitome of our time. They were said to be the most affluent, the most lonely, the most transient, and the most desperately dominated by the group.

Even so, no alarm would have been sounded had it not been for a tradition that developed early in these discussions of the managers and that turned the tone to that of either hosanna or jeremiad, depending on whether the writer was in Galbraith's camp or Whyte's. The tradition they established was to assume that the manager was both ruling agent of our present and harbinger of our future. A characteristic description of the manager was Andrew Hacker's: The giant corporation, he observed, was a "prototypical" institution, "typical not of what exists now but rather of that which will be at some future time." [11] Managers, he explained, had "become objects of widespread attention" because they were "the waves of the future." [12]

Such a notion—that the social arrangements of the giant corporation today are the social arrangements for all of us tomorrow—goes hand in hand with another prevailing idea: that the corporation is like Frankenstein's monster—a wonder run amok, no longer under control of the people who created it. That notion runs to fatalism. A basic premise of this book, however, is that human beings have the capacity to exercise choice; the institutions they create need not take them in directions they abhor. Unless we want it that way, the managerial life-style does not necessarily portray our future.

Nor is it characteristic of our present. The center economy is powerful. In 1973 it received 92.5 percent of gross private investment in the United States and collected 83.5 percent of all sales. Yet it accounted for only 3 percent of all businesses in the United States and employed only a small percentage of the work force.[13] In 1964, even while he was arguing the prototypicality of the corporate world, Andrew Hacker noted that the "100 largest manufacturing corporations employ less than 6 million persons out of the total labor force, and the 500 largest provide jobs for only about 4 million more."[14] The increase over the decade hardly signifies the "take-over" Hacker predicted. By 1974 the 100 largest manufacturing corporations employed fewer than 9 million persons and the 500 largest provided jobs for only about 7 million more out of a total labor force of 88 million.[15] Moreover, only a fraction of those jobs were in the managerial or technical category. The current assumption that work will become increasingly managerial is similar to assumptions made a half century ago that the assembly-line worker was or would be typical of industry. In fact, assembly-line workers never represented more than 5 percent of the work force.

Again, we are not, most of us, affluent. In 1971, the median income of American families was $10,285, and fewer than 26 percent earned as much as $15,000.[16] Sixty-six percent of American families had less than $2,000 in liquid assets; more than 12 percent of the population lived below the poverty line.[17] (Patricia and Brendan Sexton, Richard Parker, and others have sufficiently exposed the myth of affluence; the point need not be belabored here.)[18]

Nor is our nation now any more transient than it ever was. The oft-quoted statistic that each year 20 percent of the population moves means neither that every American moves once in five years nor that American communities experience a complete population turnover every five years. Transiency rates vary from community to community. Even in the highly transient counties of Fairfield, Connecticut, and Westchester, New York, there are towns where as many as 72 percent of the 1965 population were still living in the same house in 1970, and there is no town in which at least 47 percent of the 1965 population did not stay on until 1970.[19] This suggests not "a nation of strangers," but a nation part transient and part stable.

We have always been so; transiency is not a new phenomenon. From his study of Boston and from other studies of transiency, Stephan Thernstrom concluded:

> Over the span of a century and two-thirds, there was no clear, long-term trend toward either increased or decreased population mobility in the United States. . . . High rates of population movement in the United States were not a product of the automobile age, nor even of the industrial age. Nor does the opposite assumption—that the fluid chaotic nineteenth century may be contrasted with the more ordered and settled twentieth century—find any support here. The migratory impulse seems to have been surprisingly strong and uniform over a period of almost 170 years.[20]

If we are no more transient a society now than before, what accounts for the cries of loneliness and loss of community? Thernstrom suggests an answer. Although transiency rates have been more or less constant over the past century and a half, there has been

> a major shift in the *kinds* of men who were most transient. In the nineteenth- and early-twentieth-century America, persons on the lower rungs of the class ladder were far more likely to move than those of higher rank. . . . Soon after World War I, however, there was a fundamental alteration of this historic pattern, . . . [there was] a reversal of the long-established pattern in which the tendency of men to remain rooted in the community varied directly rather than inversely with socio-economic rank.[21]

In other words, movers were once the invisible poor, but now they tend to be the conspicuous affluent. Unlike the sporadically employed laborer who moved to find employment of any kind and whose transiency had for so long gone unnoticed, the manager gives the impression of a whole nation suddenly on the move.

If the manager's transiency gets noticed it is partly because he lives in the same suburbs as his publicists. Vance Packard explained how transiency came to his attention in his introduction to *A Nation of Strangers*:

> When my wife, Virginia, and I moved to New Canaan twenty-four years ago it was a semi-rural town and I soon knew most of the people living within a mile of us. In recent years almost all the old neighbors have moved and many dozens of new houses have sprung up near us, many of them occupied by high mobile managerial and professional families. One house close by, for example, has been occupied by four families in five years. My wife and I make stabs at inviting newcomers in, and there are still a few standbys left in the neighborhood, but today I wouldn't even recognize half of the people living within five hundred yards of our house. Virginia and I feel increasingly isolated. . . . Personal isolation is becoming a major social fact of our time.[22]

Thus is born the myth of a modern malaise.

Why write another book about a myth? First, because every myth has a nucleus of reality and it is that nucleus about which we write: corporation managers *are* isolated, and when their numbers multiply in a town, that sense of isolation can spread to the rest of the community. Second, because it is not the personal isolation of the managers that is at issue here but their concomitant moral and political isolation. Third, and most important, because through the lives they lead managerial families bring into sharp relief the values of the center economy. They are its human products.

In short, the values managers represent differ from the traditional values of our society. The old values are embedded in pluralist democratic theory which in turn relies on a strong, independent middle class. The new values both challenge these assumptions and compel us to reexamine them. The very concepts of class and democracy may have to be revised in light of the manager's position in society.

Managers' incomes are high; but aside from the material plenty that income buys, managers do not enjoy most of the benefits that once came with success and affluence. They have the price of admission into the middle class, yet their lifestyles stand out in sharp contrast to the older middle class that is still made up of professionals and independent businessmen. The old middle class is stable. Indeed, residential stability is one of the most cherished prizes of success. Corporation managers are transient. Not to be offered a promotion and the transfer that goes with it is a sign that the manager has leveled off, that he has failed. The old middle class has an important place in the community; its members are the local leaders and doers. Managers and their wives have no time, energy, or interest for activities outside their families or the corporation. The middle class is said to be the backbone of democracy. Except for an occasional visit to a polling booth, transient managers are separated from the democratic process. That stems in part from their close identification with the corporation. This in turn blinds them to the possible conflicts between their own interests and those of their corporation and renders other issues irrelevant. Moreover, managers lack property and the security that comes with it. Andrew Hacker has explained property's importance to the old middle class:

> Property is—to mix metaphors—both a hedge and a pedestal. It is a hedge in the sense that it provides an area of freedom for the property owner. Inside this hedge—small or large—the owner is free to do as [he] likes in [his] own holding. Property is also a pedestal, in that it gives its owner an extension of his personality, something more to stand on than his own two feet.

Men and women with property automatically have more power—and usually more prestige—than those without it. . . . The small middle class in the eighteenth and nineteenth centuries was a propertied class. Rugged individualism and the Protestant ethic were created for this secure and independent group.[23]

Democracy, too, was created for this group. Indeed, the personal qualities and political system that were necessary for early capitalism and still are necessary for the peripheral economy are quite different from the qualities and politics demanded in the center economy. Democracy came with the need to break up the feudal estate system. Persons had to be free to migrate and free to sell their labor. That freedom was no boon to the first laborers cast from rural field to urban factory by the English enclosure laws, but over the centuries it has brought a standard of living higher than any previously experienced to a majority of the populations of Western nations. Along with economic betterment have come opportunities for greater political autonomy and expression; but corporation managers, though they share in the economic improvement, seem to have been left out of the political advancement.

Three themes—elitism, pluralism, and "elitist-democratic theory"—have dominated our thinking about Western democracies. No matter which we follow, it seems clear that managers have no active role in the polity. Classic elitist theorists [24] argue that democracy is either a fantasy or a fraud: all governments are necessarily oligarchies, for out of any mass a few will always rise to rule. Among elite theorists there are some who have predicted that the technologists and managers of giant corporations will become the modern elite.[25] From the dominance of their institutions their power will spread to political arenas. But these theorists seldom make clear just which positions or talents would be the springboard for power.

Some, like C. Wright Mills, believe only top managers will form an elite; most think power will spread to lower ranks in the corporate hierarchy. From the present study I can make no statement as to the political strength of top managers, the chief executives who Mills thought made up part of a triumvirate power elite that also included a small group of political and military leaders; [26] for, with the exception of two corporation presidents and three vice-presidents, most of whom were interviewed during the preliminary phase of this study, possible members of that elite were not included. As for the managers who were interviewed—those at middle levels of the managerial hierarchy—they were part of no political elite. They made only the short-run decisions at the corporation and their voice was heard nowhere else.

According to the pluralists, the voices of these managers should have been heard in their local communities.[27] The actively participating citizen is the mark of a democracy, and the local government is its medium. It is the place where face-to-face association is possible for all citizens and thus where direct self-government and political expression not limited to the vote can occur. According to some, local governments (and voluntary associations) provide both a training ground for political expression and a necessary buffer between the individual and the state.[28] It was there that Alexis de Tocqueville and James Bryce found the engaged citizenry from which they drew a picture of a vigorous nineteenth-century American democracy.[29]

That view provided Americans with a self-image that remained untarnished until surveys of political participation and voting behavior, begun in the 1930s, forced a reassessment. Those surveys challenged the belief that democracy in general and American democracy in particular was based on an informed, rational, and active citizenry. They suggested

instead that voluntary association membership was not characteristic of the majority of Americans,[30] and that the voter,
far from making an informed and deliberate decision among
two or more choices, was predisposed to vote one way or
another long before the start of a campaign. As Lazarsfeld
showed in *The People's Choice*,[31] a voter's decision could be
largely predicted from two or three social characteristics
rather than from campaign infiuences. Because this is true,
prediction has become a national pastime played with some
precision at election time, and the newly discovered image
of the apathetic citizen has led to some revamping of traditional theories of democracy.

The authors of *Voting*,[32] a successor to *The People's Choice*,
recovered from the shock of discovering a less than ideal
electorate by posing a Panglossian revision of democratic
theory, one often referred to as elitist-democratic theory.
Apathy, they and others of their persuasion claimed, was not a
danger to democracy; in fact it could be an asset. The democratic system could be viable only if the majority of voters
were not too deeply involved in politics. Apathy, in this best
of all possible worlds, thus became a sign of stability, modera-
tion, open-mindedness, and even contentment among the electorate.[33]

Countering this view, the English scholar W. G. Runciman suggests that there are two possible senses of apathy:

> In the first sense, the apathetic voter is one who may scarcely
> care as between Conservative and Labor policies, or Repub-
> lican and Democrat, but who would nevertheless be prepared
> to be active in defense of both of them against a serious ex-
> tremist challenge to the system as such. In the second sense,
> the apathetic voter is one who is quite indifferent to the rules
> and forms of a democratic system, but who will vote happily
> for Stalin or Franco or Perón if this is the easiest thing to

do. . . . It . . . may be the sort of apathy of the Weimar electorate, many of whom had been indifferent to the existing parties until they turned to vote for Nazism.[34]

Managers and their wives were driven toward an apathy of the second sort by the demands the corporation made upon them. Early capitalism and the peripheral economy require democracy; the center economy does not. The firms of the peripheral economy are grounded in a specific geographic place, as are local governments, while center economy firms have "no necessary inescapable base in a specific area," [35] they are place-free. Their managers must be equally place-free and ready to move on short notice. The peripheral economy demands individuality, autonomy, and independence. The center economy requires conformity, cession of responsibility, and dependence. The first are characteristics appropriate to citizens of a democratic society; the second are not.

Early capitalism broke up the unitary dominance of the feudal system, creating a pluralism of interests and competing institutions that made democracy possible. The center economy pulls back toward unitary control and thought. A basic social change that came with the industrial revolution was the separation of the spheres of an individual's life. In the peripheral economy individuals work in one place, learn in another, sleep in another, and play in yet another—all with different co-participants and under different authorities. Every institution captures something of the time and interest of its members, but none dominates. This fulfills many of the conditions necessary to free citizen activity. Corporation managers also work in one place and sleep in another, but their work gives them little time to do anything else. The corporation is in competition with the managerial family and any other social attachments the manager might make; it demands long hours of work, relinquishment of any claim to a personal product that may result from one's work, and frequent transfers. Because of their association with the corporation, managers and their wives lack familiarity with local issues and the structures of local governments; they have no opportunity to develop acquaintances and friendships with others who are active in local government; and, having accepted an economic role that cedes to others control over most of their waking hours, as well as the right to choose where they shall live and when they shall move, managers are equally uncaring and unprotective of their rights as citizens. They are typified by a manager in this study who said:

> I'm satisfied if my taxes are reasonable, and I get services and good schools for my children. . . . I really don't care if ninety percent of the town voted for Hitler or whatever in terms of their politics if it doesn't impact on the kinds of things that are important to me and what I want out of this community.

This is apathy of Runciman's second sort—the apathy of citizens interested in the services of government but not in its processes. I will argue that it is an apathy bred by the powerlessness corporations impose upon their managers.

The corporate values that managers exemplify are reflected in the manners they display. We need Mills again to make this point clear:

> When people cherish some set of values and do not feel any threat to them they experience *well-being*. When they cherish values but *do* feel them to be threatened, they experience a crisis. . . . But suppose people are neither aware of any cherished values nor experience any threat: That is the experience of *indifference* which, if it seems to involve all their values, becomes apathy.[36]

The managers in this study exhibited the words and manners of indifference. There is hardly a single study of corporation

managers in which their smoothness, their polish, and their
cool veneer are not remarked. Indeed, the most notable characteristic of the managers I interviewed was their mannerly
lack of intensity. Nothing seemed to matter very much. No
values seemed to be deeply held. There appeared to be no
connection between the managers' beliefs or even their descriptions of their own experiences and their emotions. Their
characteristic mode was trivialization. Their response to virtually every social issue was "Ridiculous!"

The plan of this book follows the career of that trivialization of once cherished values. It begins at the corporation,
moves to the family, and ends up in the community. Each
of the three parts into which the book is divided corresponds
to one of the three main social settings of the managerial lives
—the corporation, the family, and the community. In the first
part we look at how the corporation selects and forms those
persons it needs for its functioning, and how it eliminates
those who do not fit. Training and weeding out is a long
process. It can last as many as fifteen years—which might
seem a season far too long to be called a training period.
Yet so many practices common to initiations or to religious
conversions continue through the first and second decades of
a manager's time with his corporation that those years can
best be thought of as an initiation. Chapter 2 reviews a typical
career. Accepted and familiar characteristics of corporate
employment—long hours, frequent business trips, transfers
—emerge as critical techniques to cut managers off from
competing social structures such as their families and communities. Chapter 3 explains how those who do not fit are
eliminated, while those who do are tied ever more tightly to
the corporation. In Chapter 4 we look at the way the corporation turns what might be a simple economic exchange

into a relationship between a powerful organization and its powerless employees. As training continues, the manager's needs for identity, self-worth, legitimacy, and security become translated into terms only the corporation can satisfy. Without knowing it the manager has exchanged self-will and self-interest for dependency. Chapter 5 shows how, out of the plethora of conflicting values in our complex society, the manager learns to honor those that advance corporate interests and to ignore others. At last he becomes the finely tuned, nonconflicted instrument the corporation needs.

In Part II we turn to the family. We see how the corporation simultaneously reduces the force of its major institutional competitor and blunts the feelings of all members of the family, especially the father/husband. Through him, and to win him, the corporation stages competitions that it invariably wins. There seems to be no other way for most managers to bear the responsibility of having been the instrument through which their loved ones have been hurt than to deny that any harm has been done, and to pressure family members to join in that denial. The corporate family adjusts, and reveals both a sturdy practicality and a pattern of disengagement and detachment, a sealing off of individuals from consciousness of their own emotions.

Part III takes us into the community, and here, because the manager's community life is so marginal, we introduce the Republican and Democratic Town Committee members. Chapter 7 compares their two worlds, showing the world-*creating* activities of the Town Committee members as contrasted with the world-*using* activities of the managerial families. In Chapter 8 we contrast the friendship patterns of the two groups, emphasizing the difference between those that are grounded in community and those that float in space. Finally, in Chapter 9, by comparing the political activities of the two groups, we glimpse the meaning of the center economy as it pertains to the possibilities of local democracy.

Chapter 10, the concluding chapter, attempts to draw these themes together in an essay on the well-trained manager versus the public interest.

PART 1

AT THE
CORPORATION

CHAPTER 2

The Making
of Managers

Here is one manager's detailed description of his years at
Global Products, Inc. Al Corelli was in sales. A man in merchandising might have spent most of his time at headquarters;
one in production, personnel, or finance might have moved
neither so far nor so fast; but, in general, this man's career
was typical:

> Right now I'm a regional sales manager. I've been in the sales
> area for the entire twelve years. I started out as a sales repre-
> sentative in Cleveland. The salesman is basically calling on
> retail stores, trying to get them to display your products and
> price them properly. So my job was to make sure they order
> it, and make sure they order more than they need. Make sure
> it's priced right, and on the shelf right, enough space. Yeah,
> cover up your competitor when you can. I spent almost two
> years there.
>
> The next level I went to was account manager. I had to
> move to Columbus, and I had accounts there and in Dayton.
> There I called on the buyers, the guys who make decisions for
> the chains. You're really dealing across a desk instead of in
> the stores, although I still retained some retail responsibilities
> but very little.
>
> I spent on the account manager job, I think it was a year
> and a half, and then I became a sales supervisor and my re-
> sponsibility was for the Syracuse area, so I traveled around
> upstate New York a great deal. That job was supervising
> salesmen to make sure the salesmen were trained properly
> to cover retail stores and get our products displayed. That's
> about the first level of management. I was there about a year.
>
> Then I went on the same job to Philadelphia, with a bigger
> market. I spent about a year there doing the same thing, but

there I had people who had headquarters accounts reporting to me too. I didn't have the large customers, I had the smaller customers. I had about nine men and three of them had accounts, so I got involved in supervising accounts, supervising men who had accounts, which was another experience. GPI is a series of experiences. I was there about a year and a half, which seems to be the magic number.

I was moved then to headquarters into what they call a staff assistant, who is kind of in training for district manager. It gives everybody in headquarters an opportunity to see how this guy thinks. He does some jobs that are questionable. Analysis, administrative detail work that really nobody wants to do but somebody has to do. And in the process of doing these jobs which are really not very important, it gives all the people who are important an opportunity to look at this guy and see how he thinks. I wasn't there that long, only for half a year as it turned out.

Usually it was supposed to be like a year or a two-year duty, so I came in and started to do my thing and before you knew it they needed a district manager and they said, "Corelli, you're it!" So that was kind of nice. We were living in Portchester then. We had bought a home and everything, because the guy I replaced had been there two years. There's no way of knowing, and neither was I given any indication that it would be a short time. They told me it would probably be a year or two years and before you knew it somebody quit and a guy in Texas got promoted and they offered me the Texas district. And I was happy to go because that's what I wanted, a district manager's job.

That was another new experience because that's a broker territory, strictly brokers. I was district manager in Texas for about fifteen months and then I went to San Francisco and was district manager there. I had a district sales force there. I covered basically northern California and a little bit of Nevada. I had Lake Tahoe and that area up there, but I really didn't get up there that much. My basic business was in the Bay Area and Sacramento; that's where my direct sales

force was. I was there for two years and then I came to headquarters again as region manager.

Region manager is the guy who supervises the district
managers.

In his twelve years with GPI, Corelli had held eight different positions. Each was in a different part of the country
from the one previous, each therefore required his family to
move, and each presented Corelli with new and more demanding training. Through that training he had changed from
the innocent tyro he presumably had been twelve years earlier
to the seasoned corporation man he was when interviewed.
Though Corelli spoke of his career dispassionately, as an
orderly and uneventful stepwise progression, those years of
climbing the corporate hierarchy were for him, and for most
managers, an all-consuming experience culminating in a transfer to headquarters.

Corelli was the son of a semiskilled factory worker. As
was the case with nearly all the managers, his career path
was determined by his blue-collar origins. These were not men
born to be chief executives. Corporate leaders are generally
chosen from the ranks of the upper class and the upper middle
class, from among those who have attended select preparatory
schools, elite colleges, and a handful of leading business
schools.[1] There is at the corporation a noticeable difference
between the career paths of such men and the paths of ordinary graduates of state universities or denominational colleges.

To illustrate what a difference one's background could
make, a manager in finance told a story about a Harvard
Business School graduate he knew:

> You know the degree is worth something when you see who
> the people are that get ahead. Like there was one fellow whom
> I thought was extremely bright and then I found out that
> he went to Harvard Business School. I said, "Gee, he doesn't
> impress me as being a guy who went to HBS." Normally they

have an air about them and this fellow just didn't have it. You were able to talk to him. He just didn't put you down all the time. The others tend to get a little bit snippy once in a while. But this fellow was struggling along in his capacity and finally (I don't know if he made a conscious decision but I have to think that he did) he became area director for contributions to Harvard Business School. And Harvard picks this up right away and has him put his picture in our weekly paper. Well, I have to tell you this, from that day forward his career has just taken off. He jumped twice and has got quite a responsible position now in one of the new divisions. You know it can't be coincidence—it just can't be. There he was for three years and nobody knew the poor guy existed; he was doing a good job but all of a sudden, once it became generally known, he just took off. You know, when you read your bulletins on people who are getting the promotions, well, Ivy League schools and a Harvard MBA are just so prominent; they're the people who are really getting the promotions.

Without such credentials a manager's chances of reaching the top are slim. That is so, management experts argue, not because the leaders of industry are snobbish exclusionists, but because the managerial job is amorphous; training for it has more to do with learning attitudes and values than with the actual learning of knowledge and skills.[2] According to Rosabeth Moss Kanter, "Conformity pressures and the development of exclusive management circles closed to 'outsiders' stem from the degree of uncertainty surrounding managerial positions." Bureaucracy, many contend, reduces uncertainty, yet within large corporations the higher the rank the greater the number of situations where people, rather than impersonal procedures, have to be relied upon. Thus it is that the higher the rank the more likely the position will be open only to individuals whose social backgrounds match the elite backgrounds of those already in the highest places.[3]

Which is not to say that the highest ranks are the exclusive preserve of those with elite backgrounds. There are too few of the latter to fill all of the former. However, if the elite socialization necessary to a captain of industry has not been part of a man's upbringing, he will have to make up for the lack with much effort and decades of resocialization, so that eventually he will think, feel, and act like those raised to command.

Because some of the highest positions at a corporation must be filled by those from lower classes, most managers are treated as if they are in training for the top. And because as he rises in the corporation his work becomes less predictable and therefore less easy to control by rules, a manager's training is not simply a matter of learning skills, but one of learning a corporate attitude, of taking on corporate values as his own. It is an initiation.

The Initiation

Initiations are not peculiar to giant corporations. They are found in every society as processes by which an individual assumes a new status. Rites of passage, the tribal ceremonies that induct an adolescent into adulthood, are the prototypical form of initiation. Generally they include a series of ordeals during which the initiate is critically altered. The processes whereby people are inducted into specialized occupations in industrial societies are analogous to rites of passage.

Through both the tribal and the industrial initiation new members are indoctrinated into their social roles: they learn new languages; they share new values with other group members; they assume new identities; they develop new associates and new loyalties; and they internalize new emotional responses. Thus, through initiations, social institutions shape new members into the institutional mold. Cloning not being possible, initiations are the way older members and leaders can replicate themselves.

There are, of course, important differences between the initiations of preindustrial and industrial societies. In their transport from one kind of society to the other, initiations have lost their apparent ceremony, some of their intensity, and they have become more drawn out. They have also become more varied. In primitive societies there are, in addition to the rites of passage marking adult status, only one or two other initiations into specialized secret functions such as those of the hunter or the shaman. In societies with extensive divisions of labor, on the other hand, a large number of specializations offer individual intiations.

In the army it is basic training; in medicine, internship; and for lawyers there is a period called clerkship. At the corporation there is no name for it. Managership is a new kind of employment and giant corporations are a new kind of social institution. Their ways are changing and are not yet standard enough to be codified and named. Some corporations, but not GPI, have training programs. These are part of, but not the entire, initiation. The conditions that characterize an initiation can often extend through a manager's entire career. Such a long initiation period is unique to the corporation.

Though all specialized roles require training, they do not all require initiations. In most cases the simple acquisition of a new skill is all that is required. At giant corporations, for example, blue-collar workers need not endure initiations. Unlike managers, their exchange with the corporation is strictly economic—duties and wages are precisely specified in advance. But between the manager and the corporation, reciprocity is more subtle; it is a social and political exchange.[4] The blue-collar worker works *for* the corporation; the manager, as a result of his initiation, becomes a part *of* the corporation. The corporation, like all social institutions, has no existence outside the successive generations of people who, as members of the institution, give it life. It is because managers, if they become top executives, will be the life of the corporation that they must undergo an initiation. They must learn to think for the corporation; the corporation's interests must become their own.

Given these goals, it is not surprising that many aspects of a corporate initiation are comparable to those of religious conversions. Peter L. Berger and Thomas Luckmann have described the ingredients that go into those total transformations they call "alternations":

> A "recipe" for successful alternation has to include both social and conceptual conditions, the social, of course, serving as the matrix of the conceptual. The most important social condition is the availability of an effective plausibility structure, that is, a social base serving as the "laboratory" of transformation. This plausibility structure will be mediated to the individual by means of significant others, with whom he must establish strongly affective identification. . . . The plausibility structure must become the individual's world, displacing all other worlds, especially the world the individual "inhabited" before his alternation. This requires segregation of the individual from the "inhabitants" of other worlds, especially his "coinhabitants" in the world he has left behind. Ideally this will be physical segregation.
>
> . . . Such segregation is particularly important in the early stages of alternation (the "novitiate" phase). . . .[5]

That is the "recipe" for "alternations." But, as Berger and Luckmann point out, socializations to work roles are only partial transformations. "They build on the basis of primary internalizations and generally avoid abrupt discontinuities within the subjective biography of the individual." It is not necessary that the trainee abandon or repudiate all alternative realities. A reordered emphasis is all that is usually required. For example, the army recruit who has been taught not to kill in his primary socialization has also been taught to be loyal, obedient, and patriotic. During basic training the latter lessons will be reinforced enough to enable the recruit to overcome the former. Similarly, in the development of the manager the values of primary socialization seldom need to be repudiated or replaced. Instead, out of the plethora of often contradictory values and interpretations of reality that mark an industrial society, the junior manager will be guided toward a world view in which some values assume absolute priority while others are allowed to atrophy.

In the process, most of the ingredients of an "alternation," usually in a modified form, will be present. The corporation itself is the laboratory; the manager's boss, or rather, succession of bosses, is the significant other; and the combination of long hours, business trips, and transfers serves to segregate novitiate managers from the inhabitants of other worlds.

The Transfer

A transfer is a change of job within the corporation, usually a promotion, which involves a move from one corporate location to another. As the managers step from job to job, their families follow, living in many communities. A corporation transfers its managers for several reasons. The most apparent is that it has a position to be filled at one location and a person who is able to fill it at another. A vice-president (of another corporation), who was interviewed during the preliminary stage of this study, described the following series of transfers:

> We have somebody in the Philippines we're going to replace. This situation has triggered five moves. The man in the Philippines is being let go because he's not doing the job. A man in

Hong Kong will be moved to the Philippines. A man in Singapore will go to Hong Kong. One in Thailand will be transferred to Singapore and a man somewhere else in Asia, we haven't decided who yet, will replace the man in Thailand.

Although not all locations are so exotic, the chain effect is a common characteristic of transfers.[6] When a large corporation recruits only for lower positions and fills its higher positions through internal promotions, it is not unusual for one transfer to trigger a half dozen or so more. Most giant corporations think of their "personnel pool" not as scores of separate bodies each at a different facility, but instead as a single entity encompassing all corporate salaried employees. When a position needs to be filled in one location, the supervisor does not restrict himself to those already stationed there, but instead he sends a message to a central personnel office where a computer is programmed to find those ready to fill the opening, no matter where they are stationed. A GPI manager explained the process:

I guess obviously an opening has to appear. Normally someone leaves a position and they're looking around for someone to fill it. Then the supervisor will ask for the file of people who are ready for that individual position and they will send the cards to him. Then the ones who will make the decision will screen the cards and pick two or three people that they seem to like and they will interview these three people and choose from them.

At the simplest pragmatic level that is all there is to a transfer: a job has to be filled and the most qualified manager at the corporation is chosen to fill it. Geographical considerations are irrelevant. Yet, in terms of the manager's training, geography—the need for a man to move through several locations—is critical. Corporate spokesmen readily acknowledge the use of transfers "to broaden the man's experience, season him, [and] groom him for future and greater responsibilities." [7] They are not generally as aware of or as outspoken about the process by which transfers play a key role in the psychological initiation of managers.

That process points to the emotional and ideological changes that are meant to occur in the manager during his acculturation to the company. Not only do transfers separate managers and their families "from the inhabitants of other worlds," but they are, among all the components of a corporate initiation, the most ritualistic. They have the clearest symbolic overtones.

Arnold van Gennep, the turn-of-the-century ethnographer who coined the term "rites of passage," distinguished in those ceremonies the recurring themes of death and rebirth:

> The life of an individual in any society is a series of passages from one age to another and from one occupation to another. . . . Progression from one group to the next is accompanied by . . . ceremonies whose essential purpose is to enable the individual to pass from one defined position to another.
>
> [The] dramatic representation of death and rebirth . . . is suggested or dramatized in rites of puberty, initiation, pregnancy and delivery. . . . The "logical idea" behind these [ceremonies of] . . . transition from one state to another is literally equivalent to giving up the old life and "turning over a new leaf." [8]

At the corporation, with its many transfers, death and rebirth are played out not just once, but often as the leitmotif of the initiation. From the moment that the man first becomes aware of stirrings at the corporation (when he is called to some distant location for an interview), a transfer carries with it overtones of both birth and death. His announcement to his wife that a transfer is in the offing is similar, especially in the early years of his career, to her announcement of a pregnancy. There is the exhilaration of an approaching new life somewhere else, the joy of success, and the reward of promotion; and there is the excited planning for the happy event. Betty Corelli, the wife of the manager whose career took the family to eight different places in twelve years, told how she felt about her moves:

> Each move was in a sense like going out to the next adventure. I hated leaving but then I was excited about going.

It is only later, when there have already been several moves, that the husband's announcement of yet another transfer calls forth a rueful response. Then the excitement of new places, of finding a new house and decorating it, of growing familiar with a new community and meeting new people, is overpowered by the sadness of leaving, with its emptying of the home and its partings from friends and neighbors.

A woman who was interviewed during the initial phase of the study, one who had been moved fourteen times in as many years, said:

> Just moving gets to be quite a chore, especially when you do it every eleven months or so. Once you know you're going to go, you live geared to the fact that you're going to go. You don't participate in anything that's going on in town. You say, "Well, why should I get involved in town politics, why should I care about the town taxes? I won't be here anyway to pay them." And you say, "Why worry about making too many friends? I won't be here." I know that every time we have actually known that we were going to have to move, you get yourself ready to move by shutting off what you've got. You turn off and start thinking in terms of "This is where I am going" and start thinking, "I am moving and this is where I am going to live." And right away you have to start cutting the ties where you are.
>
> My daughter said to me that this is one of the things she always did when we moved: she began thinking about all the bad things she was leaving and all the good things about

where she was going to go. You get yourself into that, you're going to go and actually once you know you're going to go, the sooner the better, because it's sort of something that's hanging over your head all the time then.

Many people approaching death have noted that others tend to shun them. Persons about to be transferred reported the same sort of withdrawal. The woman continued:

If people know you're going to move, they themselves start to disengage themselves from you, too. It's very noticeable that when people find you're going to move, you find them backing off. You'd think they'd say, "Gee, we haven't much time left together, let's do this and let's do that." But that's not what happens at all. You start finding out that they're not there anymore. They're busy. And they're busy with things they know they're going to be doing without you so they start doing them without you even before you've left. You notice it and it's just a feeling you get. It's not just all of a sudden, slice, you're cut off. But you do notice people starting to draw back. And the kids, I know, would say that they couldn't get any friends to come and play. The other kids would suddenly be busy with somebody else, even though they'd always been with them. Their friends were starting to find somebody else because after all, "she's leaving."

The similarity between death and transfers highlights precisely that quality of the transfer which makes it such an important ingredient in the indoctrination of the manager. The transfer separates people. In this, the first transfer is most critical, for it is the one that removes the manager and his family from the places and persons of his primary socialization. It calls a halt to the daily conversations (and the possible criticism of his new behavior) that might reinforce early training, and it leaves the young manager open to new ideas and values. Away from the people of his youth, he can develop into a corporation man without the need to defend his changing self.

Through the initiation the small-town or ghetto youth is transformed so that he no longer resembles the people of his early years. They might be proud of his "success" but they are also likely to be resentful as he becomes different from them. If he were to stay in his hometown there would be a daily tug-of-war over him between the corporation and the members of his primary community. The first transfer makes possible a circumvention of such difficulties.

Beyond that, the first move teaches the young couple that they can live successfully without the people and communities that nurtured them. Release from old associations seemed to the GPI managers and their wives to represent a newly found independence. Actually, however, most men and women did not become autonomous; instead they transferred their needs for security, nurture, and community from family and friends to the corporation. Partly because they were so taken up by their nascent careers and partly because they were so closely associated with the corporation that it could readily fill the gap left by their initial separation, the men reported no feelings of either anxiety or release as a result of the first transfer. Their wives, on the other hand, pointed to the first move as the most difficult and also the one which made all subsequent moves easy. One young woman said:

> It was a big move for us to move east, but now it doesn't seem like anything at all and now I would go to Florida or the Philippines or anywhere my husband wanted to go, and he would be willing to, too. Our first big move was going to New Jersey and after that it wasn't a big hassle.

Another made more of the difference between her reaction and her husband's:

> I don't find moving difficult now. At first I did because we had

> lived all our lives, both of us, in Detroit, and when he took this job I don't think we realized, maybe he did and I didn't, what it would involve. I think the first move was the hardest, moving from Detroit to Battle Creek only three hours away and we could get in often, but just breaking the family ties was difficult for me. It wasn't for him. I guess it never is for a man; they're not as close to their families as women are. After that I really got to enjoy it, meeting people and seeing the country and traveling around. But it took a while to adjust to it and each move had its adjustments because it's a new situation, but we've always made friends and I've enjoyed it.

After the first move, subsequent transfers serve to prevent the man and his family from developing extracorporate relationships. Human associations take time to develop. Although transients become adept at striking up instrumental relationships—friendships geared to mutual help or to parallel play —they seldom in adulthood develop the feeling or caring relationships they enjoyed in high school. The prevention of deeply felt relationships outside of the corporation was not recognized by any of the managers or corporate officers as one of the functions of transfers. In other organizations that transfer their personnel, however, it is an acknowledged purpose of the transfer. Herbert Kaufman in his study of the U.S. Forest Service notes that the Service would transfer rangers who became too closely involved with their communities. In addition, it moved its men regularly to prevent any community attachments that might compete with loyalty to the Service:

> Transfer of personnel is treated in the Forest Service as a device for "the development, adjustment and broadening of personnel"; consequently, men are deliberately moved a good deal, particularly during their early years in the agency. The Service does not merely wait until vacancies occur; it shifts

men to replace each other in what looks like a vast game of musical chairs . . . the impact of rapid transfer is more profound than training alone; it also builds identifications with the Forest Service as a whole. For during each man's early years, he never has time to sink roots in the communities in which he sojourns so briefly. . . . He barely becomes familiar with an area before he is moved again. Only one thing gives any continuity, any structure, to his otherwise fluid world; the Service. . . . Loyalties to the agency are so well nurtured that they offset competing loyalties to other groups and symbols.[9]

When it was suggested to some of the managers that their transfers at the corporation might have had the same motive as transfers did in the Forest Service, they were surprised. Nonetheless, when talking about their community activities, most of them mentioned their transfers as one reason they had not become involved in their communities. One man explained:

I've never been a joiner. I think you'd have to say, though, that there hasn't been one community I've lived in while at Global Products where I expected to establish any roots. Not one. I fully expected to progress out of an assignment, and that would mean a move. After you've been in a place, say a year, you finally begin to understand what it has to offer and you can begin to pick and choose what you want to do and you really are just getting settled at that point. I guess we were only in two places, Chicago and Syracuse, for as much as two years.

A woman gave a similar explanation of her husband's lack of participation in community activities:

My husband has never gotten involved in the community. He was never here. We were either moving in and he was getting established or we were moving out and he was already gone.

He hardly lived anywhere for a full year. It takes about a year to get settled in before you can get terribly involved. So he almost never was active in the community. The few places where we were there more than two years or a little bit longer, he got involved. He was always very involved with the family but spreading it out beyond that, no. After all, when you move so much, you have to give a lot more to your family because you have to help the children get established and help them find their level and their friends. As for myself, I was a Girl Scout leader in California.

Many found friendships not much easier to form in a short time than community attachments. A manager talked about his loneliness:

Superficially you might not be alone but realistically you are. Superficially people may be friendly with you because you are a neighbor and you'll probably be invited to a local neighborhood party or something like that.

It's hard to say what makes a relationship superficial. I've never been anywhere long enough for me to sit back and analyze it. I think you can generally see if someone is genuinely interested in you. At this point, I'm not sure I have a close or even a semiclose relationship with any of the men here.

Men at the corporation were aware that the social and emotional difficulties caused by transiency had been the subject of adverse criticism in recent years. Combining their faith in the benevolence of the corporation with a belief, quite prevalent in the sixties and early seventies, that the discovery and analysis of any problem is tantamount to its solution, many considered transfers to be already a thing of the past. The remarks of a manager in his early fifties were typical:

Talking to younger people you'd have a different set of situations than you would have talking to me, because the times have changed. I find now, for example, that people are reluctant to move where that was not the case fifteen or twenty years ago when we started this rat race. I find that big corporations, specifically GPI, are much more reluctant to move people now. Not just expense-wise, although that's important these days, but because I do think it upsets people. They don't seem to think it's as necessary as it used to be.

A man about a decade younger concurred:

I'd have to say we're doing a better job in Global Products now, of not moving people around as much. I think that there's a couple of reasons. You could say that it's expensive to do that and we're in an austerity year, or have been for the last couple of years. But I think it's beyond that. I think that there's managers now like myself who were moved around a lot who have decided that it didn't make any sense, not only for themselves but for the organization. There was no continuity. Nobody was there in a job long enough to really understand it, let alone make it move forward. For instance, we have now a forty-three-year-old group vice-president who also sits on the board of directors who, by his own admission, was never in a job long enough to understand it or really know it. He is the ultimate product of that system. Very successful, very bright, but he's concerned that he doesn't know how to manage anything because he's never spent any time long enough in one place to do that. The corporation has finally said, "Hey, we've got to slow something down; we're not learning from our mistakes, plus nobody really has had to live with their mistakes."

Nonetheless, by 1978 there was no firm evidence that the rate of transfers had declined or that managers were any less willing to take a transfer that enhanced career opportunities. On this score accounts in the popular press based on isolated instances of managers' resistance to transfers have tended to contradict evidence from more careful studies that corporations continue to demand transfers and that managers continue to be willing to move.[10] In the next chapter we shall return to the question of the necessity of transfers. That necessity, coupled with the transfer's value as a device in the ideological development of managers, suggests that the practice is unlikely to go away.

Long Hours

If transfers break up extended family and community relationships, long hours spent at work warp relationships within the nuclear family. Extensive corporate demands upon the young manager's time separate him not only from his friends and neighbors but from his wife and children as well. Of course, isolating the man from others is not the ostensible purpose of overwork at the corporation. As in the case of transfers, isolation is a seemingly unintended by-product. Nonetheless, the excessiveness of work at the corporation, along with its frequent absurdity and arbitrariness, points to its function as part of the initiation.

How much did the men at GPI work? Not many reported as few as fifty hours a week. More commonly, the men put in from sixty to seventy hours. Most left for work around seven thirty in the morning and did not return home for eleven or twelve hours. Usually they brought back with them two or three more hours of work. This homework typically involved catching up on correspondence or on business periodicals and trade journals, but occasionally it included report writing or communications with fellow workers. One man reported regularly receiving business-related telephone calls until eleven o'clock at night.

An average manager's Monday-through-Friday time chart might look like this:

Commuting to and from work	10 hours
Working at desk or in conference and group meetings	40 hours
Business lunches and dinners	8 hours
Homework, reading periodicals, etc.	12 hours
Total work time	70 hours [11]

In addition most managers traveled. Many reported being out of town regularly from Tuesday through Friday.

Weekends were different. Most managers thought of weekdays as corporation time and weekends as family time. If they wanted to spend more time with their families during the week, they slept less or skimmed more quickly through their periodicals. On weekends, though, except for the four to eight hours of work they generally brought home, their time belonged to the family.

Beyond GPI and their families, few of the men had other interests. A couple were hunters. One had a basement filled with decoys he had carved, and in the fall he rose at dawn and went to nearby lakes to shoot ducks before work. The other hunter chased bigger game on weekend jaunts. Two carried into adulthood their schoolboy interest in basketball; a few others were weekend tennis players. As for the rest, none seemed to have any deep or developed avocations. There was among them not one camera buff, not one Sunday painter, not one amateur musician, although two collected antiques. By and large, these were not the men around whom the currently burgeoning leisure-time industry is being built. They did not flit from hobby to hobby seeking ways to fill empty hours. They had few empty hours. And that was the way it had to be if by the end of their initiation the corporation were to become their supreme interest.

Nowhere was this so apparent as in their role as citizens

and community members. To be sure, one man was a member of Fairtown's Democratic Town Committee, another was president of the neighborhood association in his subdivision, an additional three were once members of the Jaycees. But that was the extent of the GPIers' community participation. Although most of the men said they thought they should be more active, they all explained their default in terms of the demands of work. One said:

> I think it would be very tough to attend a meeting, particularly when you travel. Because that would be kind of unfair to your wife, to come home and say, "Well, I'll see you, I'm going to a meeting." That would be very tough. I won't always be traveling, and when I'm not traveling, I think I'll have more time to devote to that and it's something I think I'd enjoy.

A woman whose husband had joined a GPI subsidiary in his late forties, after working for smaller firms in the Midwest, compared his current situation with his previous activities:

> He was on the finance committee of the school board in Indianapolis but he doesn't have time now. He'll vote, hopefully, if he's in town, but I don't think now he'd have time for the meetings. If he had a job where he was home every night at five o'clock, he would be a very active person. I can remember when Jimmy was small and Bob was basically working then eight to five and not traveling. He was gone to meetings every night then.

Travel and long hours were not all that inhibited participation. Many of the men felt that too deep an involvement in community activities would be disapproved of at work.

When asked what their corporation's attitude was toward community participation, half the men answered that GPI had no attitude. The other half thought the corporation had a position, but they were not united on what it was. Some believed the corporation encouraged only top executives to participate. Others felt that the corporate message was ambiguous. One of them explained:

> There's a corporate policy—they encourage you, okay? Now there's another theory and I thought it was a pretty good one, you know, being maze-bright or maze-dull, okay? To be maze-bright in a situation like this, you sort of suspect—if you're going to be successful in a corporation you've got to devote a lot of time to being successful in a corporation. Then, fine, they like to see you as president of the American Red Cross in your community, but they don't want you to devote that much time to it. So the object is to join the organization, get to be president, and do as little work as you possibly can and hang on for as long as you possibly can, and devote the time to GPI as a corporation. Whereas the maze-dull individual would take them seriously and he'd be in there slugging away helping them raise money every year and he'd be a worker and never get into the executive branch of the organization where he could just slough off and not really do anything for them.
>
> So I would tend to agree that this is what GPI is really encouraging their people to do—go through the ranks of an organization outside as fast as you can and not really devote that much time to it. They want that time for GPI.

The managers understood corporate priorities and adopted them as their own. They stayed away from community affairs and devoted their time and energies to GPI. Only a few men complained about the exclusive demands the corporation made on their time. One finance manager granted the corporation the right to call upon him for extra hours, if absolutely necessary, but when such requests seemed arbitrary, he grumbled:

> There are certain times of the year where financial people have to work Saturdays and Sundays. Like I have to work Good Friday. Because of the nature of finance, there are

times in the year when it has to be done and people in finance look on it almost like a cop who has to work on Christmas day.

It's different when it's not warranted, when it's somebody's whim. They say, "Gee, I'd like to see something by tomorrow," and it's five o'clock. They don't even think of you as a person sometimes. It's not as if he's deliberately treating you like a machine—he just doesn't know any better. For instance, if they want you to go on a trip or something and you say, "Geez, it's Easter Sunday," they'll say, "Oh, yeah, I guess so, I guess you'll want to be home, huh?" They never even think, "He wants to be home with his family on Easter Sunday." They just say, "Do this." It doesn't even enter their mind that they're infringing on you.

The idea of corporate infringement had not, in fact, entered the minds of most GPIers—at least it seldom came up in the interviews. When it did, a wife, not a manager, was usually the one airing a grievance. Yet two key aspects of overwork at the corporation were its frequent meaninglessness and its intrusion into all spheres of a managerial family's life.

Overwork, indeed overwork to the point of exhaustion, is part of many initiations in industrial societies, but generally it is required only briefly as part of an initial training period. In the army, recruits are forced through long marches during basic training. Medical interns and residents endure work schedules that "sometimes require them to put in 100 hours of duty a week, including on occasions fifty hours or more without a break." [12] Such overwork has the effect of lowering the novice's resistance, of making him submissive. It has much the same effect that seclusion, flagellation, or intoxication has on the adolescent initiate in tribal societies: it anesthetizes him. As Arnold van Gennep notes, "The initiate's anesthesia is an important factor in the rite of initiation. . . . The purpose is to make the novice 'die,' to make him forget his former personality and his former world." [13] In the case of soldiers and doctors, what needs forgetting is former aversions—to killing or to mutilation.

At the corporation, overwork is rarely extreme enough to induce stupefying exhaustion, nor is the desired alteration in attitudes so drastic. What is to be accomplished is not a total change in the young man's values or attitudes but merely their reordering. The priority of the corporation must be established. For that to happen, exhausting workloads are less strategic than work situations that put the corporation into competition with other institutions or persons who might lay claim on the man. These competitions, which always have the appearance of accidents, are in fact intentional enforcers or tests of the man's loyalty to the corporation.

However, they are seldom viewed as such by commentators on corporation life. On the contrary, the conflicts occasioned by the corporation's work demands are considered to be not an integral part of the organization's training program but pathological aberrations. Wilbert Moore, for instance, distinguishes between "routine managers" and "leaders." The latter, he claims, are "dangerous [men] at the corporation," in part because in the exercise of their leadership they are likely to stage competitions for subordinates' energies and loyalties on noncorporate turf.

> Under the guise of leadership, . . . the leader who extracts heroic performance from his followers may be thereby interfering in their normal involvements in all sorts of nonoccupational but proper uses of time and energy. His leadership may involve imperialistic forays into neighboring territories and consequent border disputes. [14]

Such an analysis overlooks two aspects of the corporation's "imperialistic forays into neighboring territories." First, the corporation seldom loses more than one or two border disputes over a single man without shortly thereafter severing its relationship with him; and second, such forays are not a rarity at the corporation, but a common occurrence.

True, few men or their wives complained about "infringements." But that indicates not that the complainers were rare victims of unusual bosses playing "leader," but rather that only a few still recognized territories that ought to have been inviolable. What set such men off from the rest was the continued vitality, for them, of the worlds of their primary socialization. In general, they tended to be more deeply religious than the rest and to have avoided transiency. They also, as a rule, were earning less and were in a less advanced position than were other men their age.

The family has a sacred place in the American scheme of things and it cannot be openly attacked. Instead, competitions between the family and the corporation must have the appearance of accidents. Business trips scheduled on religious holidays, last-minute demands for seemingly unnecessary reports when an anniversary dinner or a child's birthday party is scheduled, requests for information as the young manager is about to leave for home at the end of the day—these do not have the appearance of planned contests. Indeed, the superior who makes such demands may be unaware that he is staging a contest. Moreover, if the conflict is brought to his attention and if the young manager chooses the claims of family over those of the corporation, the supervisor is likely to acquiesce and withhold overt disapproval. After all, in this culture he must at least give lip service to the prior claims of the family. Some other time, however, in some other context, perhaps at the young manager's yearly evaluation, the boss will question the young man's "attitude." The complaining finance manager, Bob Hogan, described the process:

The man who works from nine to five is the man who will

make his $14,000 a year and no more. And he might really be brilliant in some respects and still make only $14,000. Because the company, as it starts promoting you, does indirectly say to you, "You owe me more than nine to five. You owe me Saturdays and you owe me nights and you owe me weekends." They don't say it directly but you get that message. Four thirty in an afternoon an executive will say, "Gee, I'd like to see the, ah, the K, P, and L lines for the last five years on Global Products measured against the profit plan. Can I get that first thing in the morning?" It's now four-thirty and he wants it by nine. You have a choice. You can tell him, "Well, by the time I get in at nine it won't be ready till noontime." He might say, "Okay." But he gave you the message, see, the message was there. "I'd like it first thing in the morning." You've got to know that the guy means around nine o'clock—he doesn't mean around noontime. Now you make a choice. You've got to make a choice. He's not telling you to stay. Some of them do but let's say the subtler ones— it's usually subtle.

Now the man who resists, who says, "I'll have it by noon," will be labeled "uncooperative," "not willing to extend himself for the corporation," and I think he would be considered "not dependable." Then when a promotion comes up and he's being considered, they'll touch bases and ask all around about him. Then somebody will say, "You know that guy; what do you know about him?" And the one who asked you to stay will say, "Oh, he's got a lousy personality. Every time I see that guy he's got a frown on his face. Am I going to have to put up with him again?" That'll kill you right there. There's a man who has an opinion about you. You can make a choice but you're not making it in a vacuum, you know damn well what you're doing to yourself. They won't fire you but you'll get bypassed when promotions come up.

The man who chooses family over corporation is failing the test, and the family that puts too much pressure on the man is failing, too. In that crucial moment, when the young manager phones his wife to announce that his boss wants him to stay late, he must show his strength and withstand the expression of her disappointment. Eventually her complaints will be muted. Hogan explained that process, too:

> What happens is this. You fit your family around the corporation. You do it this way. You say, "You always have to be available and if I'm called on then everything revolves around it." I do it and then the family life adjusts. They adjust their life or their recreation to the corporation. The family will change its style. It will learn to be less hurt about the canceled weekend. Maybe I shouldn't say it that way. It will get like a punching bag. When the husband says, "I have to take a trip," or "I have to work the weekend" and we cancel the weekend or we cancel the dinner or we cancel going out, and the family says, "Okay, take one more belt, I'm a punching bag anyway, so just hit me again." And it hits and it hurts, but they take the role that I'm here to get kicked around. Maybe it doesn't hurt any less but it sort of takes the guts out of the family and stuffs it with cotton. The family gets kicked around and then it sort of says, "Kick me around."

Of all the ways the corporation establishes its dominance over the family, perhaps the most insidious is through the work the manager brings home with him. Then he is "home," but not with the family. The wife is forced to hush the children and train them that they are "not to disturb Daddy while he has work to do." By turning the manager into a father and husband who is there but not available, the corporation can create a subtle wall of rejection between the man and his family that will strain family relationships. Then, the corporation can become the most satisfying world to him, and all other worlds can lose their importance.

CHAPTER 3

Pruning and Preserving

Up or Out

The managerial staff of most large corporations is, like an exquisite garden, always being perfected. According to the season and the changing plans of the presiding executive, new stock is added and old stock discarded; budding winners are identified and nurtured while weak specimens are pruned. A successful staff requires constant cultivation.

In this, corporations are unlike most other institutions, especially those where difficult initiations are demanded. In the army, for instance, or in the medical profession, recruitment is very nearly a guarantee of a full career. There is, to be sure, some fall-off during initiations—some tribal youths and marine recruits die during their ordeals; some men are found unfit during basic training—but transformation, not weeding, is usually initiation's primary function. Not so at the corporation, where there are no firm guarantees of long-term employment and where screening is as much a function of the initiation as is indoctrination.

Two metaphors of upward movement have dominated our thinking about careers in large organizations. One is a ladder, the other an escalator. In the first, men are imagined to be climbing from rung to rung, each advance achieved through fierce competitive struggle coupled with strain and self-denial. The second image is benign. Once a man has successfully mounted the bottom tread he is believed to be moved effortlessly onward and upward. Both analogies are partly accurate.

What those who subscribe to the escalator metaphor recognize is the inexorable upward movement of careers at the corporation. What they overlook is the difficulty many riders have in staying on at all. What holders of the ladder image recognize is the competitiveness and insecurity of careers at large corporations. What they misinterpret is the exact nature of that competition. While some men dream of executive suites, most have more moderate aspirations and would be satisfied with security. If they desire promotions, it is because promotions are the customary, and frequently the only, means of survival.

Like schoolchildren, managers want to be promoted not because they are ambitious but simply because they must keep up. And like a school, the corporation is a training institution, and learners must pass through its grades. Most positions, in addition to their importance in the producing and merchandising process, have an instructional component as well. As Corelli said, "GPI is a series of experiences." In order for each year's new crop of men to get their turns at each experience in the series, all positions must be periodically vacated.

Unlike a school, however, the corporation has no formal series of experiences, nor are the job durations standardized. Instead, a man's progress is determined by the current needs of the corporation and by his superior's estimate of his readiness to fill those needs. Movement should be upward and should occur about once every two years, and a supervisor should see to it that those under him "develop"; but a young manager can never be sure that what *should* happen *will* happen.

Such uncertainty explains in part why so many young men sacrifice their families in order to avoid offending their superiors. The uncertainty is deepened by another characteristic of the corporation. Its hierarchy is shaped like a pyramid and the number of positions decreases at each higher level. Thus the uncertain but short tenure at each level is coupled with a narrowing of opportunity at every rise. If at the university the motto is "Publish or perish," at the corporation it could well be "Move up or move out."

In no instance are these slim alternatives so clearly demonstrated as when a manager wishes to reject a promotion. It doesn't happen often in the corporate world. In fact, were promotions not so often linked to transfers, they might not be rejected at all. As it is, they are often greeted as a mixed blessing, because although the promotion might always be desired, the transfer is occasionally dreaded. And sometimes a manager refuses a promotion. What happens then?

Almost every manager interviewed mentioned two conditions under which it was possible to reject a transfer with no more jeopardy than the slight slowing of a career. Assuming that the manager's job was not being eliminated, if he could convince his superiors that the new job would not further his career, it was likely that he would receive an understanding response; because the reason he refused established his desire to advance. Again, if at the moment the transfer-promotion is offered some member of the manager's family were suffering from a serious but temporary medical problem, an especially difficult pregnancy, for instance, the man could refuse to transfer and his superiors would probably understand. A number of the men cited instances in their own careers when they had turned down a transfer for one of those two reasons with no serious slowing of their progress.

But what about other reasons for turning down a move? What if the man and his family just wanted to stay put because they liked it where they were? When these questions were asked, most of the men spoke of a recent change in corporate policy—from stern reprisal to relative leniency. Yet, there was some confusion, since they all recognized that most positions in the corporation could be held only temporarily. Maintaining that a "good man" would not be hurt by refusing to transfer, Jim VanDyke, the fifty-year-old manager who was quoted in the preceding chapter as one who thought transfer practices had eased, explained why, at the same time, no one could stay in one position for long:

> The nature of the business still dictates the transfers. Once they make the decision, invariably they transfer. I think maybe it's got a little heavier weight now in the decision process than it did before. But the key fact, the ultimate thing, is the needs of the business. They dictate that we need to make this move and we make it. If we want this particular guy to make this move, then we're going to insist that he make it. There are things we can do to make that insistence. There's a threat here and there perhaps and we can sweeten up the pot a little bit. There's numerous cases where a good guy's career is just cut off. There are good people still out in the field, very good people who have refused to transfer. Maybe they didn't get hurt the first time. But as they started to say no with some degree of frequency, a number of factors came into play. You don't want to talk to a guy like this that's negative. As time progresses, as his longevity increases, he gets the so-called ladder increases that everybody gets. He starts working himself way up in the salary range. The job is where we stretch in the salary range. Before you know it, the guy who's been in place on the same job for any length of time has worked himself up to the top of what we're willing to pay for that particular job. A couple of other things happen at that point. If the guy is older, maybe we want a younger guy in the hierarchy. He's at the top of the dollar, which is costly versus getting a younger guy. He's no longer available to build the organization. We can't make use of this wealth of experience the guy's got. So he starts to become more of a block, more of a con than a pro, more of a problem than an asset. At the same time he's becoming unhappy. Even though *he* made the refusal to move. He's got to be hit psychologically by seeing all these younger guys move around him, become his boss or his

boss's boss. The new boss—this young guy who's made all these moves—knows the older guy real well, which makes the older one vulnerable. The more the higher guy knows about you and your day-to-day operations, the more vulnerable you are. Jesus, nobody's perfect. So he's got the job security problems as these younger fellows keep going around him and up. So if the question is, "Do you have an up-or-out problem?" I think the answer has got to be, "Yes."

The Terms and the Technique

When initiates are compelled to be "maze-bright," when the organizational message is expressed in obscure language, one can usually find basic contradictions between the institution's stated values and its actual priorities. The discrepancy at GPI between what was being said about transfers and what was really happening is a case in point. The men at GPI were encouraged to believe that GPI was a benevolent corporation, one that would not make untoward demands on its managers. So, when asked about the corporate transfer policy, most of the men at first said something to the effect that a "good man" could not be hurt by refusing to transfer. But, on reflection, nearly all could remember stories of "good men" who *had* been hurt by refusing a transfer-promotion. For example, one manager at first told about a district manager in Minneapolis who was "happy right where he is" and didn't want to transfer:

> He could be the district manager in Minneapolis for another twenty-five years and if he continues to do the right job, I don't see any reason why he wouldn't be.

But then, after some thought, he added:

> We'd rather not have that situation because it really ties down a development district. Minneapolis is really a development

district for us. It's for young guys who are moving through to get their feet wet at being district manager in a smaller-type district where if something went wrong the impact wouldn't be that great.

And that reminded him of what happened to a "very bright young" regional manager:

There was a fellow, twenty-eight to thirty-five years old, who was a regional sales manager for a division. In the reorganization we went from thirty regional managers down to fifteen, and he was one of the people who won out in the reorganization, in the sense that he was made a region manager—the youngest to get one of those prime jobs. But he left the organization because it meant he'd have to move and he didn't want to leave that area of the country.

The president of GPI, underscoring the greater importance of being acquiescent to corporate demands as opposed to performance capabilities, and at the same time providing an example of ambivalent corporate language, had this to say on the subject of transfers:

We wouldn't fire a man for refusing to transfer, but we would begin to watch him more closely.

As VanDyke said, "Jesus, nobody's perfect." Watch anyone closely and critically enough and a case can be made against him. So GPI does not have a policy to fire a manager for refusal to transfer, at least not immediately at the time of his refusal. But because his refusal subjects him to close scrutiny and makes him vulnerable in the other ways described by VanDyke, a manager who consistently refuses transfers is not likely to remain with GPI.

When the subject turned to job security and the ways in which the corporation trimmed its ranks, the language managers used became especially murky. Even the wives spoke in euphemisms when the reorganization was discussed. Here is what one woman had to say (italics are mine):

> On a personal level we have seen happen at Global Products in the last couple of years a very real tightening of the belt. They just recently went through a whole reorganization and many people were *looking for jobs*. They had a desk and a telephone and they were *told to look*. A lot of people *left of their own volition* because they weren't happy with what was going on. They all ended up pretty good, but a lot of men ended up with lesser jobs. But nobody was left without a job, which was great. They did have to *cut down on the amount of people working* and the people ready for retirement, they *retired early*—gave them a nice package deal which my husband said was really very generous.

Her husband said:

> Most people found a place for themselves, or they found a place for most people. Nobody was *let go* that I know of. They indicated to a number of people that they *weren't going to go any further in the corporation* and they'd be smart if they *looked around while they still had a job* and *got a job somewhere else*. They didn't *summarily fire* anybody. Global Products doesn't do that. Big companies *don't like to fire* people. But some good people *got hurt and left the company or resigned as a result of pressure*.

The corporation never "summarily fires anybody," because "big companies don't like to fire people," yet "many people were looking for jobs" and the company did "cut down on the amount of people working" as a result of the reorganization. How, without firing anybody, does the corporation make room each year for a new crop of business- and engineering-school graduates, and how does it tighten its belt during reorganizations? Bob Hogan, the man who could tell the difference between a legitimate request for weekend or evening work and an invasion into noncorporate territory, translated some of the corporate lingo. He explained the processes by which the corporation gets "good people" to resign "as a result of pressure":

> They don't fire you but they say to you, "You've done a wonderful job and we really want to promote you but we don't have an opening right now and we'd like to put you on special studies where you can move into another job whenever it opens, at a moment's notice." On special studies, you can end up rehashing a study on the feasibility of producing some product in the Philippines, a study which has been done seven times already. And they say to you, "Here, it's been done seven times already, see if you can find a better way." Then you drive yourself through that for a while. But you're going to give it three to six weeks and then you're going to go. Because whenever you come up with something on a special study you can't get anybody to talk to you about it. Because they'll say, "Try something else" or "Show it to this guy" or "Show it to that guy." After a while you have to be dumb not to know that all you're doing is make-work.

> Or they trap you. What they do is they feed you the rope if they want to get rid of you. They'll get very critical of the due date that something comes in on, and they'll keep track of you on a log. And finally they'll turn around and say, "You've never been on time with a report." And you'll say, "Well, I'm only one day late." And they'll repeat, "Never been on time." And you'll say, "But Joe Blow has always been a week late." But they'll say, "You've never been on time."

> Or they'll turn around and they'll keep interviewing you or reviewing you. "Gee, your work isn't very good." So when they let you go, "Oh, yes, you've had four specific interviews and you've never improved from the first interview to now."

> So if you refuse to work nights and weekends, or you refuse to transfer, you get yourself into a certain category. And when you're in that category you're not going to move but they're not going to fire you because you're doing a decent job. But they're never going to give you anything because you're a

nine-to-five guy. Now, if a hotshot comes and they say, "Where are we going to put him?" then they point to you and say, "Ah, there's the guy; let's give him his job." And they get supercritical or put you on special studies. They've got ways.

Legitimations

The corporation has its ways and they are oblique. But why? Why do the executives of one of the largest corporations in the world have to be so circumspect? A district sales manager offered an explanation:

Big companies don't like to fire people, especially when they have no cause, because they'll get sued—for defamation of character, loss of position in the community, loss of standing. Having been fired without just cause, right reasons, you can sue an employer for that. Not if you have a layoff because of business conditions, but if you fire someone without any reason. Your reasons have to be pretty definitive. You have to have a written file on the individual. You've got to show that you identified to that individual the fact that they weren't doing their job, try to help him to do it. It gets very sticky and we try to stay away from these circumstances. Because that individual can find many people who have done what he's done. Global Products tries to stay away from anything that has to do with that type of action. GPI can be taken to court.

Most of the men agreed that "GPI bends over backward to avoid legal battles." That avoidance, however, is prompted not by fears of defeat but by a reluctance to bring personnel policies into open discussion. What the corporation stands to lose in court is not its case but its reputation with its personnel. According to Berger and Luckmann, the key requirement for an institution that must initiate its members is a self-legitimating belief system:

> The most important conceptual requirement for alternation
> is the availability of a legitimating apparatus for the whole
> sequence of transformation. What must be legitimated is not
> only the new reality, but the stages by which it is appropriated
> and maintained. . . .[1]

In terms of its managers and their careers, the corporation
is made legitimate by its appearing to be a meritocracy. In
order to be able to attract worthy neophytes and to continue
to command the loyalty of its managers-in-training, the corporation must engender an aura of fairness and a sense that
those who are worthy will be rewarded. The corporation must
appear to "let people go" only if they fail to do their jobs.
However, the work that managers must do is not so difficult
nor the recruitment process so faulty that incompetence is
often the cause of a firing. More likely, men will be told that
they "won't go any further in the corporation" because they
balk at the extras.

But those extras lack legitimacy. They run counter to the
interests of the family, and in this society the family must be
respected and protected—rhetorically, if not in fact. Because
most extras interfere with a manager's normal involvements
in all sorts of nonoccupational but proper uses of time and
energy, especially his family, they cannot be directly demanded, and refusal to accede to them cannot be open
grounds for dismissal. The fuzzy corporate tongue is thus a
protection from confrontations in and out of court which
might bring into question the corporation's legitimacy and
help spread sensitivities and perspectives like Hogan's.

Off the Beaten Track

Men who refuse the extras are not always eased out. Some find
a comfortable niche, a side alley at the corporation, a place
where their skills are rewarded and they are safely out of the
way of traffic on the main road to the top.

Frank Auslander was one. When interviewed, he expressed a rare independence. About transfers, he said:

> No, I don't like that. I would tell them to jump in the lake. I don't think it's necessary for me to take that kind of existence. I can get another type of position just as good, and if they don't like the way I would like to exist with them then I don't have to exist with them at all.

Even his house was unusual. It was at the top of a peninsula which jutted into one of Fairtown's largest lakes. As we talked we watched a pair of swans chase some mallards from their spot near Auslander's waterfront:

> Here I have roots. It's a place that's home. If I moved, even to a nice place, I wouldn't consider it home. It would be a place where my home is but it wouldn't be home. I don't want to take my roots away from here. This may be peculiar to you because most people when they transfer, transfer everything. I always come to a root. I like it here. I would like to have the last years of my life in this area. I consider this home and I don't want to lose it. I guess I put too much effort in here to start all over again. I like the neighbors. I like the setting.

Auslander was an engineer and had started his career with a large engineering firm. As is common with some engineering firms, their need for personnel was extremely variable, depending on contracts. This meant that Auslander, who was an executive there, frequently had to fire people:

> My first job was with a corporation where I was part of a nucleus. I was practically assured of going up fast and quick, but it was brutal, and I left that. I remember some of my bosses said I was stupid to do it—I was throwing away my future.
>
> It was a strong engineering company where we would hire and fire people like that. [He snapped his fingers.] There were only about thirty who were in the nucleus. Then we could

expand, like they did, to three or four thousand engineers and then just as fast we would get rid of them. I didn't like to see them go just like that. It was becoming a little too nasty— I didn't care for what I was doing. From an engineering point of view it was excellent; from a personal point of view it wasn't. That's why I decided to go to Global Products.

At Global Products he was out of the mainstream. An engineer in a merchandising firm, he was no longer in the running for the top corporate rewards:

My aggressiveness to reach a high position I discarded, and my aim was more toward doing a more competent job in my field. GPI was a smaller company at that time, not as cut-throat, and I knew they needed engineers for their growth. I know some of the people who stayed in the engineering company after I left. They made out financially very well. They've gone beyond the position I have. . . . When I decided to go to GPI, it was for a cut in salary. At a company like GPI an engineer is only a necessary evil—it's a marketing company. I knew it wouldn't treat engineers as well as they treat marketing people.

As a man who had relinquished any claim to the corporation's top executive positions, Auslander avoided the demands of initiations. He had transferred only once. It had been a difficult experience for his son and he decided never to transfer again. However, his function at the corporation, that of establishing new plants, required his presence in various parts of the country. Instead of transferring he would travel, leaving home Monday and not returning till Friday. He was, he said, away from home 75 percent of the time. When asked why he thought the corporation permitted and paid for his unusual arrangement, Auslander gave two probable reasons. On the one hand:

Many large companies have a lot of facts written down in

their books in which you are permitted to do things within their own regulations and laws. However, if you ask, not demand in too forceful a way, sometimes you get more than what's written. There are a lot of such things as unwritten laws. I'm not the only one, but it is unusual. Besides, between a transfer and this it's almost a washout for the corporation. It's not such a big thing, though they always present it to you as a big thing.

On the other hand:

Well, I'm considered an expert in my field; maybe that's the difference. No one is indispensable but I'm good in my field. I don't want to brag but sometimes they say, "If there's something impossible to do, get Auslander to do it."

He did not see the answer where it probably lay—in his abdication, in his willingness to give up the assurance that he would "go up fast and quick," and in his having given up his "aggressiveness to reach a high position."

For men like Auslander, men who have skills necessary to the corporation, men whose ambition is limited, there is room in the corporation. Their exchange with the corporation is more like the blue-collar exchange—mainly an economic one. They give their services to the corporation in return for a salary, usually a generous one—most of the men like Auslander were earning over $35,000—but they are not in line for those top executive positions where policy decisions are made.

Keeping the Pick of the Crop

If the staff of a giant corporation must, like the plantings of an exquisite garden, be kept well pruned, it must also be preserved and nurtured. Pruning is important, but it is not nearly so critical as the retention of prize specimens. Here the analogy between garden and corporation becomes strained.

Flowers are rooted, men are free-moving. A horticulturist need not worry that his favorites will, on their own, move off to greener locations.

A manager through training becomes increasingly valuable, not only to his own corporation but to himself and to other corporations as well. A fully initiated manager represents a sizable investment, an asset competing companies might like to possess, and in the process of forming their staffs giant corporations often develop executives for their entire industries. A manager explained the symbiosis between corporations that act as training institutes and smaller ones that receive the giants' discards:

> Small corporations don't hire on college campuses because they don't want to invest the money in training men and then having them leave. They'd rather let corporations like GPI invest that kind of money and then hire the guy away after he's matured.

The vice-president of a smaller corporation corroborated that relationship:

> As far as the management stratum is concerned, we don't take anybody out of college. Training can take a long time. When you're talking about, say, product managers or people like that, we'll get them from a competitor. We let the other guy do the training. It sounds crazy but it works.

It works for the smaller corporations and it works for GPI. According to the managers, GPI takes on the burden of training for the industry so it can have the first pickings of managerial talent. The GPI manager continued:

> At GPI there's very little hiring at the product manager or associate product manager level from outside—very little of that. They usually hire from colleges at the low levels and train their own. In a sense they're training for other corporations, but in another sense they're building their own organiza-

tion. They're building a more efficient organization—a better management team and all those kinds of things.

It's an investment, but because GPI is such a large organization it is not a big investment for the company; it can absorb that easily. A small organization might have a hard time paying a guy $12,000 to $14,000 a year when he's sitting there doing very little for the first year or two. But GPI can afford that. They feel that this way they can get the best people—the pick of the crop.

The price of the pick of the crop seems but a small fraction of GPI's budget—if the only expense considered is the salary of fledglings. But more—for instance, the time supervisors spend training their charges—should be taken into account. When Corelli described his advance through the ranks, he revealed the increasing proportion of time spent on the training, pruning, and nurturing of subordinates:

> When I became a sales supervisor my job was supervising salesmen, making sure they were trained properly to cover retail stores and get our products displayed. That's about the first level of management. Then when I went to the same job in Philadelphia I was doing the same thing, but there I headed people who had accounts reporting to me too. In some markets where you have salesmen and account managers you give your account managers the major customers and you give some of the smaller accounts to young salesmen who are being developed to become account managers and move up the ladder. I had about nine men and three of them had accounts, so I got involved in supervising accounts—supervising men who had accounts. . . .
>
> Finally I came to headquarters as region manager in the East. One of the main roles of the region manager is working with and giving directions to your district managers. Your responsibility as district manager is to develop your subordinates so that they are prepared for greater responsibility. In the time I was there I had three guys move out of the dis-

trict into headquarters and then later become district managers, which was very positive. It indicated there was proper training and development of the people and they got the proper exposures and we moved them around to different jobs so that they got exposure to everything that they needed so that they could eventually become district managers. When you're a region manager you kind of look at your district managers and make sure they're doing similar things—giving exposure to the people who can move up through the organization. You kind of ride with the starts to observe firsthand how they're doing and to kind of assess their long-term potential.

Assessing, exposing, overseeing, and moving men into strategic spaces is all part of a supervisor's job. It takes time. Corelli continued:

If a subordinate is having trouble, you sit down in his office and have a discussion, a nice heart-to-heart talk with him. Find out what's going on, what are the problems with this, what circumstances are causing that, and how we can alleviate the situation. Do it a little bit differently in order for the results to be a little bit different. I like to dig the facts out of him, and hopefully it will flow that he will see it himself, but I make suggestions too. That's part of my job, to make suggestions.

If nurturing fails, pruning is in order:

Then he's got to go out and execute it. If it doesn't work, we try to find out why not. If it wasn't realistic and there were external circumstances, we try to think of a different way of doing it. If the factor was his leadership or his ability to accomplish it, then he may have to be replaced.

The man who is replaced will probably go off to a smaller company, taking the corporate investment with him. That is no loss to the corporation; it's the price management pays to pick and choose. If, on the other hand, the men who go off are the ones supervisors judge to have high "long-term potential," then the corporation does suffer. The cost of initiating a manager was estimated by the fifty-year-old Jim VanDyke. After twenty years with GPI he had just gone off to be vice-president at Hill & Sons, a smaller corporation:

> Take a guy like me. Add up my salary and my transfer costs and the whole bit and that's cost GPI a million dollars. Then Hill comes along and for a pittance has bought a million dollars' worth of experience.

VanDyke emphasized the fact that "a million dollars' worth of experience" makes a difference in the way a manager handles his job:

> At Hill, when there's a decision to be made, I make it. But I never could have been in a position to make these kinds of decisions if I hadn't had all this experience with GPI. You are surrounded by very sophisticated management; your peers, your subordinates, your superiors—they're all quite sophisticated, and all the tools you have to work with are quite sophisticated.
>
> So when a guy goes to another company from GPI, generally a smaller company, he finds that he does things these people have never heard about, never thought about. They're not sophisticated and it's simply a matter of money. The small companies have simply never paid to develop this kind of talent. They haven't paid to do it on the inbreeding basis. They haven't paid to develop it; they're buying it.

However, they are buying it not from the training corporation but from the manager. He usually gets a substantial salary increase and lucrative perquisites when he switches to a smaller company. The corporation that trained him gets nothing. With "a million dollars' worth of experience" invested in each of its managers, a training corporation looks for ways to keep its best and brightest from being bought up "for a pittance." Corporations like GPI must somehow control their investment in spite of the fact that it is embodied in a legally free individual. Therefore, an important goal of initiations is the development of managers who are, in effect, as deeply rooted in their corporations as plants are in their soil.

CHAPTER 4

Exchange and Power
in Corporate Life

Sociologist Peter Blau has developed a model of power relationships that will help to show how corporations bind their managers. He lists four requirements for power and four parallel conditions necessary for independence. To be powerful, an individual must 1) "remain indifferent to the benefits others can offer him in exchange"; 2) "bar access to alternative suppliers of the resource"; 3) "prevent others from resorting to coercive force to effect their demands"; and 4) "sustain people's needs for the benefits he has to offer."

Conversely, individuals who would escape another's power can gain their independence by: 1) having a strategic resource to exchange through which they can create a reciprocal rather than a power relationship; 2) finding an alternative source; 3) acquiring the ability to use coercive force; or 4) being able to do without the resource. Throughout the initiation, in ways so subtle most managers never notice, they lose their independence and come increasingly under the power of their corporations.[1]

Strategic Resources

The most obvious strategic resource the corporation has is money. Most corporations in the center economy are rich and generous; they pay their managers far more than the managers could command for similar work in the peripheral economy.[2] Large salaries help keep men from going off to the peripheral economy, but they are not very effective within the center economy. Corporations, even the smaller ones, can afford to compete with each other for able managers, and they do. That is why money can be neither the only nor the most important resource in a corporation's hands. If it were, salary wars would be common and debilitating events, and the exchange between the manager and the corporation would be merely an economic one—so much money for so much time, a blue-collar type of arrangement. The manager gives more than the laborer and he gets more in return. Unlike most blue-collar jobs, managerial jobs carry intrinsic benefits: they can be satisfying, they can give a sense of self-worth, and they can confer status and identity.

Many managers genuinely enjoy their work. A plant manager's wife echoed many other wives when she told how her husband felt about his work:

> He loves it. Which is fantastic. It's so good to see someone get up in the morning and look forward to going to work.

A man can look forward to his work for several reasons. Some managers simply like the posh surroundings, which is one reason corporations invest heavily in office decor.[3] Others feel gratified when they find a solution to some technical problem, create a new product, or launch a successful advertising campaign. Usually, though, when the men discussed what they liked about their jobs, they talked about their role as supervisor. Auslander looked back on his work with GPI and said:

> I've enjoyed it. I've been known as being a teacher. Teaching people that have gone beyond me. I sort of enjoy saying, "Well, he was one of mine." Accomplishment is more important than getting ahead. Not only of doing things, but of doing well with people.

Corelli wanted to get ahead and he was not so altruistic, but he too enjoyed a situation that allowed him to help others by helping himself:

I guess a manager gets noticed by circulating the results of his people. So I guess I try to get recognition by publicizing their results. For instance, if somebody does something good, I'll let everybody know about it. I'll put something up on the wall or send a memo to everyone who has an interest in this success. I help that person and I help myself at the same time.

Of course, not everyone "loved" his work at GPI. The reorganization had cast a shadow over the corporate land-scape, and dissatisfaction had become a frequent topic in conversations among the men. Stew Green, a young accountant who had left GPI shortly before he was interviewed, commented on those discussions:

At work that's one thing we always talked about, and what I could never really understand is that if you don't enjoy your work, I don't see why you should be doing it. Get out of it. This is an argument we always had at work with guys on our level. They'd say if you don't enjoy it, no matter where you go you won't enjoy it.

Then he explained one of the reasons for his departure from GPI:

Down in the plant I enjoyed my work, I enjoyed getting up in the morning and going to work. But here at headquarters I got to the point where I just didn't enjoy it and I'd just as soon stay home—call them up and tell them I'm sick. I didn't, but I'd just as soon have. It got so I'd have to push myself. A lot of people said they had that problem, but they felt it was just to be expected. Maybe if I'd been there a long time I would have reconciled myself to it. But I don't know, I couldn't see how they could reconcile themselves to it.

One way men reconcile themselves to jobs they don't like is by not thinking about whether they are happy or not. Mrs. VanDyke described the change in her husband after he left GPI for Hill & Sons:

He comes home at night now with a smile on his face and he didn't before, although he was not unhappy. At least he didn't *think* he was.

Managers who are not enjoying their work often fail to face up to their unhappiness. Because joy is one of the benefits they are supposed to be receiving from their work, the admission that they are not happy would jeopardize their position. Either they are the kind of people who can never be satisfied with their work, as was argued by Stew Green's colleagues, or the corporation is not offering a situation conducive to enjoyable work. In the first case the manager would have to accept an image of himself as a malcontent. That would mean he's not a good prospect for promotion and he would have to consider his tenure uncertain. (Supervisors and other representatives of the corporation often encourage this interpretation by saying, "If you're not happy here maybe this isn't the place for you.") In the second case, the manager, recognizing the corporation's failure to live up to its part in their exchange, owes it to himself to seek employment elsewhere. In either case he and the corporation must separate.

In parting, the man stands to lose many corporate resources that came with the job. Also, he will lose justification for the years he has already spent with the corporation. As time passes and a man's life is increasingly invested in his company, leaving comes to seem like a repudiation of his past. Mrs. VanDyke explained why she thought her husband did not notice that he was unhappy at GPI until after he had left:

I think he just didn't want to feel that all those years were wrong. And they weren't, but there's always the fear that you've wasted all those years.

Such fears deepen with time, forming a noose that tightens as the men become more experienced and valuable. Pensions, health plans, and investment plans meanwhile increase in

value. GPI was especially generous on this score. VanDyke
tallied up what he lost and what he gained by leaving GPI.

> On every score I came off better, except for benefit plans.
> For benefit plans nobody can touch GPI—the medical plan,
> and the life insurance plan, retirement plan, things like that.
> You can't beat GPI.

On the surface it might seem ironical that industrialists,
who usually argue that welfare programs strip workers of incentive, should provide such complete benefits in their own
domain. There is, though, no great contradiction. Corporate
benefit plans are meant to thwart *self-serving* initiative. A
sales manager who had toyed briefly with the idea of leaving
GPI and buying a fast-food franchise explained why he finally
decided against it:

> You see, what happens when you've been with a company like
> GPI for ten years is you're security-bound, you've got all
> those benefits, income. That paycheck is nice—so you're
> security-bound.

Security, however, is not all that binds. Beyond the large
paychecks, the benefit plans, the justification of the past, and
the provision of a work place that is often enjoyable, the
corporation controls a trump—the manager's identity.

Paradoxically, managers must depend on the corporation
for their definitions of self precisely because they are moved
around so frequently in their jobs. Transfers create a need
for a ready identity—a label that requires no explaining. In
their transient world, where there is little time to develop a
reputation, managers lean on the reputations of their well-
known companies. The Al Corelli who just bought a house
in town might have to wait awhile to make friends and get
credit at local stores; the Al Corelli who is eastern sales manager of GPI is familiar enough to tradesmen and peers to
win easy acceptance, even respect.

Not always respect, though. Lately, because corporations are coming under increasing attack from ecology and consumer groups, there might be less honor attached to a man's association with a major corporation than there once was. However, such a change can make the corporation more, not less, necessary to the manager. By the time he has spent several years there, a manager is likely to have participated in the production and promotion of just those products or by-products conservationists and consumers find offensive. To them he is a collaborator, and the more hostile the outside world, the more each manager will need to cling to the rationalizations and supportive environment he finds at work. The corporation becomes a fortress.

Affirmation and support are precious in a plural and mobile world. They are generously supplied at giant corporations. The very fact that radical pruning is a constant process at the corporation enhances the self-esteem of those who stay. The belief that the pruning is done meritocratically, so the worthy are rewarded and the unfit discarded, provides a self-enhancing logic which proves to the managers that they are the best among the best. There was not one wife who did not make a point of describing her husband as exceptionally bright; and there was not one manager who didn't say something like this:

> When I talk about GPI people, I'm talking about a unique group of people. Probably the people you're talking to. Most GPI people are pretty sharp people after they've been around a period of time.

After they've been around a period of time and they've moved up, not out, managers develop a most positive sense of their personal worth. For a coal miner's or a farmer's son the upward mobility available at the corporation can be heady indeed. A manager whose father owned a small grocery store in a mining community told what it meant to him:

I got a job which I always thought was extremely high-level. I always thought that guy, the regional guy, was pretty great. When I was a salesman he came out in the field every once in a while and he was kind of the king of that area. So I'm now at that level where I thought back as a young guy, "That's a fantastic level."

Most managers' wives, living in a manner far better than that to which they had been accustomed, shared their husbands' pride in a great achievement. A woman who at the time of the interview was preparing to move into one of Fairtown's old summer mansions said:

I never thought that I would live the way I live now, never even entered my mind. The way we live is so different from the way we were both brought up. I never dreamed—and he's been out of college only twelve years—that we would be living in Fairtown, Connecticut, going to move into a house like we're going to move into. Sure, if you went for a ride on a Sunday afternoon and saw a pretty place and imagined what it would be like to live there, but I never could imagine living in such a house. So it never really was a desire. If you can't picture something then you don't really have a desire for it. We like to entertain and it's great to have friends come from Ohio and be able to see the house and appreciate it with us. Knowing where we started, because they can really appreciate it for what it is.

All that—pride, status, identity, large salary, generous benefits, security, justification of past and present, and an enjoyable work situation—flows from the corporation. But what, to return to Blau's schema, does the manager have that he can give or withhold in return?

For his part the manager has little to offer by which he might establish a reciprocal exchange and become independent. True, his training and experience represent a crucial resource without which the corporation would not exist; but the corporation, by creating a superfluity of managers, prevents any one of them from gaining countervailing power. As Blau explains:

> The large employer is not so much dependent on single employees as on a labor force . . . and his independence of any one employee sustains his power over all of them, unless it is reduced by their collective action.[4]

Managers are unlikely to join in collective action. First, because they would lose status if they approached the corporation as blue-collar workers do, but more important, because the competition among them is kept keen. Competition originates in oversupply and is sharpened by ambiguity and secrecy. In this, transfers have a useful function. As Wilbert E. Moore points out, they "create some uncertainty as to the pool of competitors for various positions."[5] Moreover, the unwritten (and in some corporations written) code of conduct that forbids discussion among the men about their particular arrangements with the corporation heightens uncertainty.[6] The value of all this to the corporation is suggested by J. M. and R. E. Pahl in *Managers and Their Wives.*

> . . . organizations prefer to have considerable ambiguity surrounding the whole question of salaries, appropriate career lines and so on. The greater the ambiguity or secrecy the less likely it is that men will know who their chief rivals in the organization are, how their salaries compare with those of colleagues and contemporaries and whether they would do better elsewhere.[7]

Though few of the men and women who were interviewed spoke about competition, both Mr. and Mrs. VanDyke did. Their words support the interpretations of Moore and the Pahls. Jim VanDyke:

> There's a big fear complex that operates within GPI because there are so many people who are, or will, or might be your

boss, or might be or do have an influence on you one way or the other. The fear syndrome keeps you from speaking up and it works in the compensation area as well. While you may know your salary, obviously more money is at the whimsical beck and call of your boss and his boss and a few other people perhaps.

Lisa VanDyke:

> The men, they just trap themselves—they made this trap themselves. It's the competition that's always there. That's probably the crux of it. Instead of just doing their jobs and getting the job done and enjoying it, they're always figuring out the angles of it. Who's going to think this, or who's going to do that, or who's going to get ahead of me.

Competition, some say, made America strong; but competition in fear and secrecy makes managers weak, especially when they must vie among themselves for tightly controlled resources.

Barring Access to Alternative Sources

With the corporation having so many ways of satisfying managers' needs, and the manager having no exclusive control of a resource necessary to the corporation, the second best protection a manager could have from the power of his corporation would be alternative job opportunities. Giant corporations are powerful, but they can seldom corner the job market. Instead, during the initiation, they implant mental inhibitions toward changing jobs, and these inhibitions combine with objective barriers to create a virtual corporate monopoly. Especially in the early years, there are several real restraints that narrow a manager's escape routes. Nonpirating agreements among major employers, frequent transfers, and training relevant to only one corporation or industry all serve to anchor young men. Later, inertia, fear, and the assumption that theirs is the optimal employer keep managers from exploring in an open job market.

Agreements among employers not to hire workers away from each other, though never written and always in violation of free trade laws, do exist, and GPI was a participant in at least one. A young manager compared his chances of finding work outside GPI when he was at headquarters with his chances in the field location he had just left:

> One thing about the East is there are a lot of job opportunities. In Kansas there was an agreement between the companies that you couldn't change from one to another without a year in between—a nonpirating agreement.

Nonpirating agreements cannot be effectively made in large metropolitan areas where most corporation headquarters are located, because too many firms would have to join in; usually, however, a manager doesn't get to headquarters until he's well initiated. In the field, where young managers get most of their training, the corporation is likely to be the only employer of persons with managerial and technical skills. Where it is not, potentially competing employers often make informal agreements that limit managers' job opportunities.

No doubt there are several reasons beyond the enjoyment of a monopoly on job opportunities for plants and branches to be located outside the largest metropolitan areas. The monopoly is a serendipity for the corporation. The same is true for the transfer. Though it is not instituted to cut managers off from outside job contacts, the transfer does serve to isolate them. By being separated from their hometowns and then moved frequently, they are seldom able to search out and develop the relationships that might make positions outside their corporation available.

The availability of other positions can also be lessened by a manager's training. In yet another of those ironies that pepper a manager's situation, it is often the case that the very experience that makes him a valuable asset also circumscribes his opportunities. The unformed college graduate who arrives at the corporation in his twenty-first or -second year has been taught general business principles and procedures. He can apply these almost anywhere in the business world. Later his knowledge becomes specific—to a single company or industry and to a specialized function. As he rises through the corporate hierarchy, a manager becomes both more experienced and less flexible. One regional sales manager, for example, though he would have liked to have some merchandising experience, found that it was not long before his direction was too set to change:

> I opted initially when I went with GPI to go into sales management. I felt I had an outgoing personality and I thought I would be more suited to sales than getting into the advertising, the creative, end of the business. I never thought I was overly creative, but I'm finding you don't have to be overly creative to be a product manager. So though I opted to go into sales, I tried to get into the product management area, but something always came up in the sales promotion area and I've taken it.
>
> GPI is a marketing company, not a sales company, and I think that you need to have that experience. I'm still trying to get over into product management, but once you get high in any given position or high in the organization it gets difficult to go back over to the other side because responsibilities at a parallel level are that much greater and you aren't really able to handle that capably. You don't have the right kind of experience at that level.

Specialization, monopoly, and isolation all curtail the availability of alternative employment. They are not, however, the primary means of keeping men with their training corporations. For that we must look to the subjective bonds developed during initiations. More than anything else, inertia coupled with fear and ignorance keeps men tied. Just as surely as the belief in a flat world kept sailors close to the shore for centuries, the belief in a barren job market now keeps managers close to their corporations.

Some societies send adolescents into the bush as part of their initiation rites. At least one function of the practice is to teach through loneliness and fear the desperate need individuals have for the group. Corporations don't send their managers out, they bring them in. When new recruits arrive at the corporation they usually come in from the insecurity of joblessness, confident that the offer they have just accepted is the best one available. From then on they seldom compare their position with others. If they do, it is usually with only a cursory glance that convinces them that there are dangers outside and they will be better off if they continue to stick with the employer they have.

Remarking on the prevailing fear of the world outside the corporation, Mrs. VanDyke talked about the comments other wives made when they heard of her husband's decision to leave GPI:

> When Jim left GPI, a number of friends, people within the company, could not believe that anyone with that much time behind him would ever leave. Up and down the block, they couldn't believe it. One girl said, "If George ever left, I'd be lost. I just don't know what I'd do."

Wives like that, who say they'd be lost without the corporation, can be a powerful influence on their husbands. In our society it is assumed that the husband's responsibility is to provide for his family. He cannot risk failure in his performance of that duty without his wife's approval. When "leavers" like Green asked unhappy "stayers" why they didn't quit, the answer was usually given in terms of family responsibilities:

They explained it with the natural argument that they had families and they needed the security to take care of the kids and they couldn't leave. Couldn't just get up and leave. They said it might be all right for my wife and me since we didn't have kids.

But Green thought there was more to it than that:

There always seemed to be some excuse, some reason why they have to be there. People are dependent upon the company.

His wife gave an example of that dependency:

A friend of ours thinks this, what we're going to do, is tremendous and terrific.

(The Greens had bought a resort that they planned to restore and run.)

So I said, "Come on up with us," and she said they're not ready for that move yet. They're not happy in their jobs and they don't have children or any other ties to hold them, but they won't go.

VanDyke, thinking about why it had taken him twenty years to leave GPI, shed some light on why others won't go:

My decision for years was that GPI was a big piece of my life. GPI was the great big father-confessor; tremendous security, great big corporation, lots of money and a good company. I think most people would say that.

And most people find a great big generous corporation hard to leave:

What happens, I think, is that a guy works his way up into what appears to be a lot of money and is doing a good job—and then he's afraid to run the risk of leaving.

What the man risks by leaving are those resources he has enjoyed. When, on the one hand, there is a "great big father-confessor" offering "tremendous security and lots of money," and on the other hand there is the possibility of something better but also the risk of losing it all, most men settle for what they know—especially if their wives are unwilling to share the risk. Because the risk is as much hers as his, the man who contemplates leaving generally discusses the matter with his wife, even if theirs is a relationship in which his work has seldom been a topic of conversation.

Yet even men who had their wives' support found it difficult to assume the risk of leaving the security of high salaries and generous benefits. Lisa VanDyke was more critical of the corporation than any other wife and she cheered Jim on as he departed GPI. Nonetheless, it was difficult for him to quit:

> I labored over this decision for three or four months—kept Hill on the string, and it all boiled down to this: All the financial factors were on Hill's side, but Big Brother was a very strong factor on GPI's side—and certainly no risk.

The assumption that there was "certainly no risk" at GPI was quite common. It was prevalent in spite of the fact that the corporation had just undergone a reorganization, a time when, as one wife put it:

> Everyone was just walking on eggs because they were consolidating, which meant a lot of people were going out the door.

It is not uncommon that when a depended-upon structure fails, the suddenly insecure people try to save themselves but do not reassess the institution that failed. Something like this happened at GPI. The men and women hoped to weather the storm. They hung on as they were shifted from job to job, sharing the faith of the wife who said:

> I have a lot of hope that GPI is going to give us what we want.

In the logic that helps maintain order, those who were still working for GPI when the reorganization was over had their faith renewed. Those who lost their jobs lost their faith as well, but they were no longer around to disturb the credulity of the others.

Belief in the benevolence of their own employer and ignorance of the world beyond their corporation are protected in many ways. First there is the quite natural reluctance of most persons to change their situation when they are not dissatisfied; second, when men announce their intention to leave they are usually urged to cease their search with promises of promotion; and finally, the prevalent attitude toward leavers is to discount their claims to having found greater satisfaction outside the corporation.

Most of the men were pleased with their positions. A typical appraisal:

> I've progressed at a pace overall that I've been desirous of. I have a good job right now. I'm enjoying my job.

Enjoying their jobs, most managers were not even answering the calls they were receiving from employment agencies, but some did acknowledge that there might come a time when they would listen. One of the regional sales managers observed:

> I've never put out my résumé. I don't especially want to be a region manager the rest of my life. But until I get to the point where I'm on the fringes of being dissatisfied, and feeling that GPI hasn't got what I want, I guess at that point I'll think about it.

He went on to describe the kind of situation that gets a person to think about it:

> Thinking of leaving depends on how hard the boss is coming down on you at any given time. Your degree of motivation at

any given time would have an impact on whatever grandiose thoughts you might have.

Leaving, to use his word, is "grandiose." Staying is ordinary. It takes a while for anybody to become dissatisfied enough to start looking. In the meantime, superiors who are aware of a manager's discontent and want to hold on to him can make an offer of promotion. When VanDyke told his boss he was leaving, he got "all the fancy promises for the future you can get." But he wanted something more specific and left when it was not forthcoming. Usually, though, the men are willing to wait and the new job does materialize. VanDyke explained why more men don't do what he did:

> A lot of exceptional people at GPI have opted to stay because they think maybe that next job is almost in hand and for the exceptional people it may be. I've got a couple of guys in mind where a promotion is immediately in hand—say within the next few months. They can see something happening, and it's easy to read, where they know they'll have a very good crack at this thing in a very short time. So they hang around for a little while longer.

Once in a new job, a manager usually settles down and entertains no grand thoughts for a year or two. He's got to "give the new job a chance." Almost all the men who were interviewed either had just taken a new job or thought an offer for a better position at GPI was just around the corner. They were not likely under those conditions to be listening to "headhunters" or to be learning in other ways what their choices might be outside the corporation.

Nor were they likely to learn much from their colleagues who had left. If the assumption is made that there are "a lot of exceptional people at GPI," and also that GPI rewards those whom it values, then it follows that those who left were not valued enough—they were perhaps not so exceptional.

So, most managers thought, if the ones who leave are not as good as the ones who stay, why listen to leavers? Lisa Van-Dyke put it this way:

> Guys frequently leave and say how great it is, and you never know whether to believe them or not, because they might be justifying what they've done.

By not listening, those who stay, according to Jim Van-Dyke, condemn themselves to lesser jobs than they might have won:

> I've gotten new perceptions from leaving. What has happened is that I've found that the perceptions from the last few years are valid. The people who have left GPI over the years have said to me, "I'll tell you, the grass is greener over on the other side. If you take what you know, you'll command top dollar, you'll enjoy life a whole lot more, you'll get your job satisfactions more so and faster, you'll stop beating your wife and children, and really start beginning to enjoy life." And I've listened to that for years and of course the higher up on the pole I go the higher up I listened to these things—from my peers, my friends. So I figured I'd try it for myself.
>
> What I found out in the last three months was that they are right. It's not like discovering something new, it's like finding it out for yourself. These other people who hear my story, I don't think they believed me, and they were in the same boat I was in—not sure whether to really believe this guy. Was he really getting that much more? Is he really that much happier? Does the future look that much better to him? Or has the whole thing really blown up on him and he's doing all this to save face? So you always whirl back into your little GPI hole where you're safe and comfortable and warm.

Safe—not only from the unknown world outside but from the painful knowledge that you might be doing much better if you only looked. VanDyke continued:

But the truth of the matter is that the guys who left are right; they aren't kidding you, it really is better. As a group of people they can probably go anywhere and do better. And they don't know that or they don't believe it. But there's more money outside of GPI for the people I know, the competent people, than they are presently getting or could even hope to get at GPI. The secret here is that they don't know that. They really don't know that. It doesn't even enter into their risk area. I know guys making $30,000, $35,000 over there that could easily get $50,000 and they don't know that yet because they haven't gone out and tested the job waters. Their names are not being thrown to the headhunters as being available or interested or wanting to leave or whatever and for the head-hunters a man making $35,000 is not much in demand. That's pretty low level stuff. So he'd have to make himself available generally at that salary level. When you start getting up around fifty grand you're bothered by headhunters.

Then, too, at GPI there's strong activity going on to let these people know for sure what kind of security they've got by working for GPI. There are a number of ways. They've got the internal house organs and it comes right down through the management organization from the very top.

The message is subtle and persistent. In one way or another —at the managers' annual evaluation sessions with their bosses, in discussions with each other, in the house organ— the men are reminded that GPI is a generous employer and a safe haven. Surely, they think, one must be at least as well off at GPI as at any other large corporation, and as they watch some of their fellows leave they notice that usually they go off to a smaller corporation. That, they figure, is less secure and not much more fulfilling than GPI. What they'd really like to do, many of them, is to go into a business of their own [8]— but that is a fantasy, not something they think seriously about. Instead, most managers exaggerate the risk and the cost.

The man who had thought of buying a fast-food franchise was one of those dreamers:

> Buying my own business is very appealing to me but it's not a real situation. My father has a small business back in West Virginia and I probably could go back and get involved in that. There's enough in this two-brother family so one of us could take it. But both of us couldn't take it and make enough money. It's enough for one but not enough for two, so it's not a real thing for me, and as I talk to my brother it's not a real thing for him, so probably my father will end up selling the thing.
>
> If you're down, if you feel your boss is too close to you— he's telling you how to run your operation, or he's just tough on you personally, then sure you're thinking about what can I do? How can I get out of here? But it may be just on the basis of going with a similar type company. That's much easier than going out and buying a Kentucky Fried Chicken place. Because you need $100,000, $150,000 for a chicken place and you can go next door to another company for $35,000 so the degree of risk is less.

VanDyke went next door for over $50,000, not $35,000, and he went to a smaller but similar type of company. When he talked about leaving the corporate world altogether, something he said he really wanted to do, he was as unrealistic as the rest:

> I'd like to teach at the college level, but I don't even want to get paid for it. The income doesn't interest me at all. Just to make things easier for everybody concerned, I don't want to have to depend on that for income. I don't want to count on that. If I could come up with half a million, I think that would see me through.

Whatever the real price of independence may be, clearly both of these men pulled a figure from the air that each knew he'd never have. Like all but one of the managers, these two had spent almost all of their high earnings and had made no plans to accumulate the wealth they thought might set them free.

Coercion

Blau's third requisite for power is the ability to prevent others from using coercive force to effect their demands. It seldom comes into play. There is no way a manager can coercively tap most of the resources he derives from corporate employment. Identity, status, an enjoyable setting, fulfilling work, and security can only be received as rewards for service.

The manager, on the other hand, can be coerced into selling his services to the corporation against his wishes. The former wife of a vice-president of a major corporation, not GPI, told a story of such coercion. It happened several years ago and is probably not at all common. As an extreme case, however, it does indicate the sort of measures a corporation can take if it is in danger of losing a particularly prized young man:

> The woman's husband was a young lawyer employed by a large multinational corporation. He had been educated first at a leading preparatory school, then at Yale, and finally he went to Harvard to take his law degree. In addition, he bore a name well known and respected in law. His grandfather was a distinguished jurist.
>
> Not only were this man's credentials exceptional, they were matched by outstanding personal characteristics. His quick intelligence, mature judgment, and quiet charm made him a perfect representative of his corporation, and he was rewarded with rapid advancement. Yet industry was not his first choice for a career: politics was. There he seemed to be a natural. His Lincolnesque bearing and approach made him the obvious choice as leader of a reform political organization.
>
> He was a paragon, but not flawless. In his early thirties he had some psychological difficulties which brought about a

strange episode. One day, without quite knowing how he got there, he found himself in the airport of a Southwestern city without money or credit cards. Because at the time he and his wife were estranged, he could not call her. He called his corporation. They wired him the money he needed and he returned home.

Six months later he was offered a job with the federal government—a position he had long wanted. When he went to his boss to announce his good fortune, he was not congratulated. Instead he was encouraged to stay with the corporation. He was offered a promotion and a raise to a salary far higher than any the government could match. When he said he wasn't interested, an even better position was offered him. He stood firm, explaining that he wanted a political, not a corporate, career. Finally his superior warned, "If you persist we will have to tell the government about that day in Albuquerque."

The man stayed on. His superiors did all they could to hide the trap and gently initiate him. He was invited to dinner parties in the homes of the president and the vice-presidents of the corporation, and he was given a tour of the corporate empire—being informed at each stop of the improvements the corporation was effecting for the people in each of the countries where it operated. They argued that his opportunity to make a good and important contribution was better with the corporation than it would have been with the government.

Effectively deprived of choice, he listened uncritically to these claims and was soon persuaded. He rose rapidly in the company and, by the time he celebrated his fortieth birthday, he was a vice-president.

Most managers are neither so valuable nor so vulnerable. Commonly, corporate coercion is limited to a manager's investment in retirement and bonus plans, most of which are set up so that the manager who quits will lose a portion. A young GPI manager explained why he would stay with the company until he had been there at least ten years:

The importance of being with the company for a number of

years is to maintain my vested interest in the company—in the retirement fund. Before ten years you can only keep in or take out your contribution, but after ten years you have the option of leaving the company contribution and yours too and tying up both.

But after ten years a man is likely to be well enough rooted in the corporation not to think of leaving. Moreover, leaving will still be expensive: VanDyke complained that he lost a big share of his bonus when he left:

Of course you hear terrible horror stories about what happens to guys who leave, so I figured I would get hurt by the bonus —and I was. I think I only got about half of what I would have gotten if I had stayed. I think I deserved all of it because the fiscal year ends the end of March and the bonus is based on that—I'd given them the whole fiscal year. If I had stayed with GPI until June, I would have gotten $10,000. I left in April and got $5,000.

Cutting bonuses and pensions discourages many; still, it is their deepening need for corporate resources that most emphatically keeps men from straying.

Maintaining the Need

Just as an addict's need for his drug increases with use, a manager's dependence on his corporation deepens with continued affiliation. With interests narrowed by the demands of his initiation, a manager's thirst for money especially, but for status and security too, grows until other needs are eclipsed.

In their one-sided chase after corporate benefits, GPI's managers were like the upper-middle-class respondents whose lives and values had been the subject of other studies of suburbanites. The people of "Crestwood Heights," "Park Forest," and "exurbia" [9] were all reported to be captivated by such a single-minded pursuit of status, money, and success that. like a magnificent obsession, it filled their lives and left little room for anything else. Paradoxically, as they quested after greater and greater success, they lost sight of the ends to which money and position were intended to be only a means. Most commentators expressed alarm at this substitution of means for ends. It seemed to them that affluence was turning out to be more a curse than a blessing; but they could not explain why this should be so.

One explanation is so basic that its key can be found in the scriptures: "Man shall not live by bread alone." But the exchange between the corporation and its managers leaves managers with more and more bread, and less and less of anything else. For them, needs usually fulfilled by human relationships become increasingly difficult to satisfy because almost all relationships outside their nuclear families are distant and fleeting. So like half-starved people who in the absence of proteins will fatten but not nourish themselves on starches, managers and their families hunger for goods money cannot buy, but reach for those it can. Each year salary increases put these within easier reach, and the manager's family finds that every purchase just whets the appetite for the next. This steady and hopeless pursuit of ersatz goods finally has the effect of smothering any desire for more genuine goods, i.e., for the kind that frequently are not for sale.

When asked what they wanted, what their plans or wishes were, hardly any of the men or women spoke in terms of what they would like to *do* or where they would like to *be*. They wanted "health"; they wanted "happiness," but they had no idea what might make, or keep, them happy. Even when the question turned to career aspirations they had only weak and imprecise hopes. One product manager expressed a common set of aspirations uncommonly:

I have no great visions of sugarplums and presidencies. I

have visions of moving ahead, of getting promoted, but no visions of grandeur. I simply want to do my job, do the best I can, and if progression comes, fine. I don't particularly aspire to be a president of a division or some level like that. I want to be recognized for the job I do and I want to attain more responsibility and I use these words strictly as generalizations, not in terms of specifics.

Generalizations, not specifics, are part of the corporate way. Faced with changing demands and recurrent reorganizations, corporations need to maintain flexibility and ambiguity in the career plans they offer to managers. Vagueness not only enhances competition, it is structurally necessary. Money, on the other hand, can be discussed in specifics, and it is a resource the corporation has in plentiful supply.

The managers were precise about money; at least they knew exactly the amount that would have satisfied them when they began their corporate careers. Almost to a man, they could remember the days when $10,000 would have been enough. Since all the men were now earning more than twice $10,000, they were asked if they weren't rather pleased with their salaries. The answers flowed in a pattern—a pattern of insatiability.

A district sales manager, salary $35,000:

My expectations were always more money-inclined as opposed to rank, title, what have you. They were just to get a fair degree of success and as I remember way back then, it was to make $10,000. That was a very appropriate figure. I must have started out at about $6,000 so I always thought, "Gee, $10,000, okay."

When it got to be $10,000, then I wanted $20,000, maybe $15,000. At each level there's always more. Next thing you know, you're close to $20,000 or you're making over $20,000 —it's not that big a deal, you've passed it. Or over $25,000 or $30,000. So what are you looking for? You're looking for making $40,000, you're looking for $50,000.

VanDyke, though he was able to leave GPI, was not able to explore the possibilities of the teaching career he thought he wanted most, because he could not imagine fulfilling his needs for money outside the corporate world. Those needs were even greater than the sales manager's:

> When I started twenty years ago I wanted to get ahead. In terms of money, that always changes with the times, and keeps getting bigger and bigger. At one point I can remember where $10,000 seemed like a lot of money, and then I guess it was $20,000 that looked good, and then $30,000, $40,000, $50,000, $60,000.

Another manager, with a salary of $30,000, showed more insight but the same hunger:

> I make a good salary, but I'd like to make more money. Everybody wants more money. You make more money and you end up spending more money and you never win in this game unless you stay in the hovel you were living in when you bought your first house ten years ago.

He knew he was in a game he could never win, but he played on. For him it was the only game in town. The translation of all their needs into the single resource, money, leaves managerial families with no alternate pursuit even if they recognize their no-win position. As long as the house they lived in ten years ago is remembered as a "hovel" and not as "that beautiful house we had in Atlanta that was so cheap" (as Lisa VanDyke recalled), the manager will never have enough.

Their need for money increases in proportion to their income, because they use money as a substitute for other satisfactions. But that is not the only cause of their frustration.

Inflation and the shock of arrival at headquarters play their part, too.

Although most of the couples began their careers in the Middle West, five started in the New York City area and had owned houses in Fairfield or Westchester counties. Of these, three reported that they were living in Fairtown only because they could no longer afford a house in the towns where they had once lived. Steep as their income increases had been, they had been overtaken by the inflation in housing.[10]

Such families were not the only ones who suffered a decline in their standard of living in the face of a rapidly rising salary. The move to headquarters invariably involved a loss of spending power and status. Whether the GPI couple began their career in the East or in another part of the country, they generally spent most of their initiation period in the Midwest and the South. When they were transferred to headquarters in the New York area, most reported status deprivation. From high man in the field, the manager became low man at headquarters. From living in one of the best homes in the finest neighborhood, their families had to settle for a middle-class suburb and an ordinary house—usually smaller and less attractive than the house they left.

A couple who had just come into headquarters from the field described what it felt like:

> *Husband*: If you would have talked to Beth and me nine months ago you would have found us walking on air. No question about that.
>
> *Wife*: Tom was totally fulfilled in his job. Constantly challenged, he thrived on challenge. The whole thing was very plus for him in Illinois. But he knew he had to get into headquarters and an opportunity came his way. It wasn't the greatest, but we had been there four years and you can't sit there and say, "No, I like it here, I'm going to stay." So he came.

> *Husband*: It's a traumatic move. I don't care who's involved in it. Anybody who comes in from the field, particularly when they come from a big plant, that moves into headquarters, feels it. When you're in the plant you're a big gun. You get into headquarters and you're almost undressed because there's a million of them just like you.

Many men suffer a crisis of identity when they come to headquarters and find "a million" others just like themselves. It is a time when quite a few men become disappointed enough to look around and quit. Others "adjust"; depending even more heavily on the one resource that is plentiful, they seek to salve their feelings of deprivation in more promotions and possessions.

Just as a child will sometimes cling desperately to a mother who withholds her affection,[11] a manager often becomes most dependent upon his corporation at exactly those moments when its resources are least satisfying. When money buys less and titles are without honor, managers hope most strongly that the corporation will take care of them—that the future will be better and, at the very least, secure. Their futures, then, are what managers ultimately relinquish to their corporations.

During the nineteen fifties and sixties, social researchers tried to solve the puzzle of some people's apparent failure to be upwardly mobile in our system of "open opportunity." One unhappy solution was the theory of a subculture of poverty. Simply stated, this theory suggested that the poor remain impoverished because they don't have middle-class characteristics. There were some disagreements about which characteristics were lacking, but a consensus did form around one: the ability to plan for the future. Probably the baldest statement of this theory is Edward C. Banfield's. In *The Unheavenly City*, he writes:

> The individual's orientation toward the future [is] regarded as a function of two factors: 1) the ability to imagine a future, and 2) ability to discipline oneself to sacrifice present for future satisfaction. The more distant the future the individual can imagine and can discipline himself to make sacrifices for, the "higher" his class. . . .
>
> At the present-oriented end of the scale, the lower class individual lives from moment to moment. If he has any awareness of a future, it is of something fixed, fated, beyond his control: things happen *to* him, he does not make them happen . . . he has no sense of the future. . . .[12]

Managers present a curious split. They are highly disciplined to "sacrifice present for future satisfaction," but they do as little imagining or planning for the future as any slum dweller. Corelli, though he didn't know it, was typical:

> I'm a unique guy. I usually take one step at a time. When I was an account manager I was very happy being account manager and I was usually very well motivated. I thought I'd like to be a supervisor someday but I didn't have any time to develop a plan and I guess I don't have one now.
>
> I've come to the conclusion that I'll plan six months in advance and to think beyond that just boggles my mind. I guess I was never a planner. I never really planned anything out. I do not have a goal in mind.

The men didn't plan. With their families they plotted the next purchase or the next vacation, but that was all. Even managers less than ten years from retirement had no ideas about what they would like to do. The wife of a vice-president who was indeed "a unique guy" in that he had mapped out his career, said:

> I've asked my husband where he would like to be buried but he's never answered. We've made out our will; the lawyer said a lot of people haven't even done that.

Oddly, the ghetto poor, if they plan for nothing else, insure their burials. Managers and their wives didn't even do that. Some explained the difficulty and frustration of planning when they lacked the ability to control events in their lives. A young salesman said:

> Sometimes I try to plan ahead on certain things, but what I plan is often the opposite of what I do. It's like right now, just for an example. There's a big shake-up in my particular district, guys are getting transferred all over the place and I'll probably be one of them. So odds are that six months from now I'm not going to be in Fairtown. But then again I might be. So right now, especially at this stage of the game, it's really hard for me to really plan ahead. It's not that *I* can't plan, it's that I can't plan because I really don't know what lies in store for me with the company.

Not planning for themselves, the managers never gain control of their lives. Lisa VanDyke complained:

> It's a marvelous way of always abdicating responsibilites for your own life because someone else is always directing it, which is much easier. It's much harder to take a hold of your own life and say, "Okay, this is what I want to accomplish and now I will go ahead and do it." It's much easier to let GPI take care of everything.

It might be easier, but sooner or later it is likely to be disappointing, because in truth the corporation isn't planning either. Jim VanDyke told what happened when he tried to find out what plans the corporation had made for him:

> I used to think someone at the national level had some kind of a long-range plan for old Jim. But I did not find out that that was not true until I came back here four years ago. There was no long-range plan for old Jim. They might have thought, "He's a good guy. He does a hell of a job and we ought to nurse him and cultivate him and keep him happy and when

he gets bored," which I do easily, "give him another job or send him off on a project someplace. That will keep him all mixed up and he'll find new things to do, new challenges." But as far as a long-range plan for Jim to have this job or that job, no.

I believed that there was such a plan until I got to headquarters and started to have a major impact on those transfer decisions. As I started to ask, "What do we do with this guy after we've moved him to Atlanta?" There was no thought whatsoever. And it's true corporate-wide, not just any division. We did not have a long-range plan for our people.

When I sat down and told GPI that I was leaving or that I was thinking of leaving, I asked for a long-range plan. And the answers came back: first of all, obviously there was no such plan; second, let's talk about the possibilities.

There are, as one manager said, "always possibilities for good people." And most managers were soothed by possibilities. They assumed that if they were "good" they would be rewarded; that is what had happened in the past, which proved both that they were worthy and that the corporation was reliable.

That belief in the efficacy of the meritocratic order ran deep at GPI. It came up in most of the interviews. A personnel manager, for instance, said:

Let me tell you about the Becks. He told the corporation in the recent reorganization that he did not want to move out of here. Therefore the corporation *valued him enough* that they gave him a job in this area.

If the corporation "valued you enough" it would give you what you wanted. That was the message. The other side of the coin is that failure is personal. If you are dissatisfied because you are not getting the rewards you desire, then it follows that the corporation does not value you enough—you are not good enough to deserve its rewards. Thus the price of dissatisfaction is the loss of a person's sense of worthiness.

A few years ago Richard Sennett and Jonathan Cobb held a series of conversations with working-class people living in Boston. Out of those talks came a sensitive understanding of "the hidden injuries of class." [13] In a social system like ours, which promises limitless mobility and which measures human worth by performance and reward, those at the bottom bear a double burden. Not only must they forgo the material goods enjoyed by members of higher classes, but they must accept the blame for their condition and endure the indignity of failure. If you do not rise in a meritocracy, the fault must be your own.

How much more punishing, then, is a system that purports to be meritocratic but in reality uses some other, some hidden criteria for advancement. Most of us, when we think of a large organization like a corporation, think of the term *bureaucracy*. In his listing of the characteristics of bureaucracies, Robert Merton includes:

> the assignment of roles on the basis of technical qualifications which are ascertained through formalized, impersonal procedures (e.g., examinations).[14]

But contrary to the way roles are assigned in true bureaucracies, such as the civil service, there are no examinations and there is no specified career path at the corporation. Advancement comes not always to those who do their jobs the best but to those who are, as one man put it, "people-oriented." When VanDyke asked what promotions were in store for him, his superior responded, "There are possibilities and a number of possibilities are political because appointments at higher levels in GPI are considered to be political appointments."

Political appointments depend not on merit but on favor. They are based not on technical qualifications but on subjective judgments by superiors. Where this is understood, an aspirant passed over for promotion can complain of unfairness and blame the whim of his judge; he need not turn inward for fault-finding. But where a political system masquerades as a meritocracy, a passed-over aspirant will work harder and harder in a misplaced effort to merit advancement, until his quest takes on that almost religious fervor that observers have noted in managers' approaches to their work. Recognizing his inability to control his future at GPI, VanDyke said, "Oh, yes, GPI is God, who can be good and also wrathful."

A god who can be good and also wrathful, who hides his capriciousness behind a façade of fairness, inspires constant efforts among the faithful—work performed blindly and goallessly. In a way, the corporation carries on the Protestant tradition, which taught that God calls men to their vocations. The distortion of that doctrine, which takes worldly possessions as a sign of God's approval, turns out to be the "Protestant Ethic," the ideology that helped bring us capitalism. It is a doctrine that sets men and women clamoring after material goods long after they have accumulated enough to satisfy their physical needs. When worthiness is measured by possessions, no one can own enough.

Thus the corporation, by controlling the manager's means to a positive sense of his own worth, also controls the manager.

CHAPTER 5

The Mind of
the Manager

When an institution develops an elaborate novitiate, complete with separation of neophytes from old associations, induced exhaustion, sheltering entrapments, and humiliating dismissals, we can be sure it is the kind of organization that cannot be adequately served by either casual relationships or ordinary persons. Managers are not ordinary. That became clearer as the interviews progressed, but even at first glance they were distinctive. They were neater, less obviously ethnic (even if thier names betrayed their origins), more affable, cooler—in short, more polished than most.

What was never apparent from the interviews was why GPI, or any other business corporation, might need to be served by men so different that they were identifiable without special garb (like, say, monks' vestments) and so enthralled by their employers that even without vows they stayed on until they were let go. The answer could come not from the managers and their training but from the corporation and its evolution.

Since its origin as the creation and medium of an entrepreneur's will and wealth, GPI (and corporations like it) carried within itself the seeds of its modern structure. Born of dash and drama, the modern corporation is now a thing of mass and routine; created by an adventurer, it now requires drones. The reversal should not be surprising: It is an example of what Max Weber called "the fate of charisma." "Charisma," as Weber noted, "is unstable":

> Whenever it comes into the permanent institutions of a community, [it] give[s] way to powers of tradition or of rational

> socialization. . . . In its pure form [charisma] . . . has a
> character specifically foreign to everyday routine structures
> . . . [and] may be said to exist only in the process of
> originating.[1]

It follows that an order begun by a charismatic individual, if it is to become permanent, must change radically.

It must be "routinized," and that involves several permutations. Authority no longer based on devotion to the charismatic individual must depend on some other, less emotional and more enduring base. Succession and recruitment, once the unquestioned prerogative of the leader, will have to rest on rules that will need to be developed and justified. And the organization itself, at first so flexible that its structure, methods, and even goals could change as the moment required, will need to become hardened and institutionalized.

The particular changes that came to American business as its activities became workaday caused it to need men quite different from the founders. The new men had to be less autonomous and more passive; less ambitious and more malleable; team players, not loners—in short, other-directed, not inner-directed. Behind this succession were several structural changes within corporations. Chief among these was the divorce of ownership from control within the corporation— a process first noted by economists Adolf A. Berle and Gardiner C. Means in 1932.[2]

When businesses were managed and controlled by their owners, the requirement was for men who dreamed of futures and fortunes, of cornered markets and daring deals. Now, since managers can benefit only indirectly from a corporate killing, ambitious men seek their fortunes elsewhere. The men who run corporations today are unaspiring; they seek safety, not success; security, not struggle. They have, as the manager said, "no dreams of sugarplums and presidencies."

Inventive persons, once the moving spirits behind business

enterprises, tend to avoid giant corporations when they can. Possessiveness is nearly always associated with inventiveness and there are not many innovators who can bear for long to have their corporation's name instead of their own stamped on their creations. Moreover, invention must generally be individual; inspiration tends to be smothered by committee meetings and the need for official approvals. Stultifying corporate hierarchies usually are attributed to modern technology, the argument being that so much diverse expertise is needed that many individuals must participate in new development. Yet it is not technology alone but also the separation of ownership from management that is to blame for the ever-lengthening lines of command at the corporation. Since managers are not owners, larger budgets and staffs, like little fiefdoms, are the primary rewards they can receive for their successes.

Technology, it is also argued, has restricted invention to universities and corporations by requiring sophisticated and expensive equipment. While it is true that during the twentieth century an increasingly great proportion of patents has been granted corporations over independent inventors, it is also true that of the patents granted each year about one third are still going to the independents,[3] in spite of corporate inducements to attract those graduates of engineering and scientific schools who seem to hold the most promise. So many inventions blossoming without the advantages of generous salaries and technologically exquisite laboratories might indicate a perpetual and dauntless superiority of unfettered minds over furnished matter.

However that may be, minds are a critical aspect of routinization. In its charismatic stage, a group depends for its legitimacy on the force and appeal of its leader and his message. Later, when it has outlived its beginnings, when its originators have died, and when it has taken on an independent and immortal life of its own, the organization needs a fabric of internal and external legitimizations—explanations and justifications of affairs as they are.

Berger and Luckmann explain the transition:

> Legitimization is not necessary in the first phase of institutionalization when the institution is simply a fact that requires no further support. . . . The problem of legitimization inevitably arises when the objectivations of the (now historic) institutional order are to be transmitted to a new generation.[4]

Problems arise, however, because the legitimations of the modern center firm are better suited to the workings of the more traditional peripheral economy. The center firm needs two sets of justifications, one to explain its position and activities in society and the other to explain its internal workings. As for the external justifications, they rest on a belief in the benefits of free enterprise, to wit: governed solely by market forces, the corporation will benefit society by producing the goods and services that society needs at the lowest possible cost. Internally, the corporation is presented to its managers as a perfect meritocracy that bestows its rewards upon those who are most talented and work the hardest.

Initiations are needed because these legitimations do not accurately or completely reflect reality. The center firm is a place of opportunity—possibly the most fertile field for upward social mobility in the whole society. But the old virtues of talent, initiative, risk-taking, and independence are not the ones it rewards. Acquiescence to the corporate values and social skills that obliterate whatever differences there might be between individuals are the new virtues, and the reward process, as already noted, is more political than it is meritocratic.[5]

Externally, the center firm can be credited with the production and distribution of necessary and beneficial goods and services. But because it is large and powerful, because it controls its markets as much as or more than it is controlled by them, the center firm does not distribute these goods and services at the lowest possible prices. Moreover, because they are powerful, center firms, when they threaten society, are difficult to control. From violation of antitrust statutes to price fixing, from environmental pollution to unsafe work places, from production of dangerous products to the creation of consumer demands rather than the satisfaction of consumer needs, center firms can be socially undesirable. Managers need initiations to blind them to the dangers their work sometimes poses to others, to render them sensitive to corporate interests and insensitive to other considerations, and to make them able to deny the problems caused by their corporations, especially when those problems seem obvious to virtually everyone but the managers.

Today social difficulties created by corporations so permeate our society that hardly a week goes by without some new report of corporate crime or depredation. Whether it be bribery committed by the executives of Lockheed and some 150 other, less well publicized firms; [6] or the suppression of research that proves the harmfulness of corporate products or production processes; [7] or the rigging of prices by dozens of packaging firms; [8] or the punishment of corporate "whistle-blowers," [9] there can be little doubt that the work managers do and the system that orders that work are a mixed social blessing. Social and moral problems surrounding the corporation are so pervasive that one knowledgeable reporter has noted: "Those of us who write daily newspaper stories about corporate corruption feel as if we are in a maze of muck." [10]

Chief corporate executives, if they notice that "maze of muck" at all, worry, not about the dangers their miscreant enterprises pose for the polity, but about the possibility that the public might not like it. Thus Fred T. Allen, the chairman and president of Pitney Bowes, announced at a recent meeting of executives that because of "the almost daily revelations of corporate bribes and payoffs in the U.S. and abroad," he was "a troubled man." What troubled him? Not the bribes and payoffs, but "the steep decline in the public's esteem for business and its practitioners." [11]

If a bad press was something for chief executives to fret about, even those worries were not seeping down to middle management levels, at least not at GPI. GPI's managers did not think that *they* were in a maze of muck. Quite the opposite. Although a few did complain about acts that the corporation made them commit, most viewed the environment in which they worked as a place of moral purity; any signs to the contrary were thought to be caused by deviants. A typical comment:

> I know Global Products is an outfit with great integrity. Great integrity, but I think, like in any other large body, there will be individuals within Global Products that don't feel that great sense of need for integrity and could cause some bad reflection on the company.

How is it that the reporter's impression of the corporate world was so different from the manager's? It could be that the reporter overemphasized the lack of integrity of the business world, or that GPI was a rare organization in an otherwise tarnished field, or that the manager was blind to moral problems that did exist. The last seems most likely.

GPI was not cited in the press for wrongdoing as often as many other center firms. Yet as it went about its business it encouraged its managers to behave in ways that might conceivably have raised ethical questions. Because GPI is a merchandising firm, much of its resources and its managers' energies were spent creating consumer demand rather than satisfying consumer need. That very activity bent traditional values. In addition, GPI had had several run-ins with federal agencies. And finally, in its handling of internal affairs GPI often appeared to promote unethical behavior. What was remarkable in all these instances was not that GPI and its managers sometimes transgressed, but that hardly any of the managers were able to comprehend a reason to doubt corporate perfection.

For example, according to the ideology current at GPI, "perfection" in the marketplace was free enterprise. But GPI was part of a merchandising oligopoly, and its behavior in the marketplace was not the same as it would have been under conditions of pure competition. Nonetheless, most managers believed that the economics of the corner grocery store were completely applicable to their giant corporation. A typical expression of that faith:

> I'm a believer in a free economy, unless it's a very obvious monopoly, and I haven't seen a very obvious monopoly other than the government-sponsored monopoly like the telephone company and the post office. Usually the big company puts out a product cheaper and better and more efficiently than the little company and if you just let them fight among themselves you're going to get a lower price.

It was, however, a curiosity of the interviews that GPI's products were seldom mentioned. When the subject did come up, it was usually summarily dismissed with some easy assurance like, "GPI doesn't make a bad product." Yet an examination of GPI's products revealed that for almost every one there was also available a better or cheaper competing product. Indeed, only a fraction of the entire industry's products seemed necessary to consumers.

And each year that fraction becomes smaller. If one looks at each of GPI's products and notes the year of its introduction, it often turns out that the more recent its inauguration, the less likely is its usefulness and the more questionable its safety. GPI, a merchandising corporation, probably leads other types of firms in the substitution of package for product and of fantasy for function, but the direction is general.

It is a trend that makes strange demands on all of us. Gerald Sykes, in *Foresights*, spells out those demands:

> In a society committed to turnover, to production and consumption in ever increasing amounts . . . merchandising is of greater value to the company than manufacturing, which can be handed over to robots, or semi-robots. . . . We have to become liars, and ingenious liars, capable of deceiving ourselves as well as others, if we are to do well in the new society. Hence the value of publicity. It backs us up in our deceptions, both public and private. The inner voice has become an anachronism and a nuisance.[12]

It is more of a nuisance to managers than to other Americans because theirs is the prototypical situation that demands dishonesty. It is not enough for them to learn the words that will back up deceptions both within the corporation and outside of it; they must actually invent the falsehoods.

Nor is it merely a question of merchandising empty boxes. That would be like a modern version of "The Emperor's New Clothes," with the corporation as tailor and the consumer as befuddled emperor. It has gone further than that. The parade is over and the little boy has pointed his finger. The emperor, he announces, has been fooled not just into nakedness but into sickness as well. When Ralph Nader and others point to the dangers inherent in many corporations' products, the manager is doubly threatened. If the products of his corporation are both worthless *and* harmful, then his inner voice is worse than a nuisance; it is a threat and it must be utterly stilled. Otherwise the manager might make that imaginative leap between product and consumer that would render him valueless, even dangerous, to his corporation.

GPI's managers made no such leaps. Sales managers and product managers performed the practical tasks of their work and mouthed the misleading words that went with those tasks with no apparent consciousness that any deception was afoot. Only one outside power, the government, occasionally threatened this euphoria. But even there the managers' certitudes about their corporation were equal to the challenge. Invariably they explained governmental regulations and court decisions against GPI as foolish acts of irrationality. Here is how one manager discussed an order from the Environmental Protection Agency:

> The corporation is pretty reasonable. They'll do things voluntarily. For instance, before the government ever told them, they went out and spent $5 million on antipollution controls in just one plant; and this wasn't noxious pollution, just carbon, no sulphur, nothing really harmful, just dirty, smoky, and it wasn't that bad. They had all kinds of antipollution stuff before, but in one year they put in $5 million and after that it gets to be extreme. Now they've cut down maybe 98 percent of all the carbon and the government wants it to go to 99. To get that 1 percent that's $10 million more. That GPI fights—they try to. So finally they lose and it costs over $10 million. The government is unreasonable in so many things it's unbelievable.

In another case, GPI had been ordered to divest itself of a recently acquired subsidiary because that purchase was judged to be in restraint of trade. The men argued that it was the court and not their corporation that had acted to diminish the market. Echoing the others, one manager said:

> I wonder sometimes whether the controls we have are absolutely needed. I think they can be depressant. I think GPI has taken some raps in recent years where the government acted too quickly.

These were the words they all used: "the government acted too quickly."

Indeed, managers were so incapable of recognizing the validity of governmental regulation that their most frequent complaint of GPI was against its too willing observance of the law.

> I think GPI is a very correct company, too correct. GPI will bend over backward to be correct in the eyes of the government. We just bend over backward trying to do what somebody in Washington says is right to do.

In the eyes of these men, "bending over backward" signified the spinelessness of top management, not its political wisdom. That was partly because politics was outside the ken of most managers. They denied the legitimacy of conflict and instead displayed that mode of thought Karl Mannheim has termed "bureaucratic conservatism."

> The fundamental tendency of all bureaucratic thought is to turn all problems of politics into the problems of administration. . . . The attempt to hide all problems of politics under the cover of administration may be explained by the fact that the sphere of activity of the official exists only within the limits of laws already formulated. Hence, the genesis or the development of law falls outside the scope of his activity. As a result of his socially limited horizon, the functionary fails to see that behind every law that has been made there lie the socially fashioned interests and the *Weltanschauungen* of a specific social group. He takes it for granted that the law is equivalent to order in general. He does not understand that every rationalized order is only one of many forms in which socially conflicting irrational forces are reconciled.[13]

GPI's managers were trained to see only one rational order—the corporation. It stood embattled in a world of irrational forces. Along with Charles E. Wilson they would maintain,

"What's good for the country is good for General Motors, and vice versa."

This fortress philosophy satisfactorily explained any conflict between GPI and the rest of society. However, within the corporation itself some occurrences did occasionally raise ethical doubts among a few managers. Most frequently these doubts arose when a manager as supervisor had to pass on bad news to subordinates. On such occasions language had to be devised that would preserve the corporate legitimacy in the face of disappointed expectations. To use Berger and Luckmann's words, ways had to be found to "justify the institutional order by giving a normative dignity to its practical imperatives."[14] The justification of the corporate order to its employees was nearly always its image as the perfect meritocracy; but when cutbacks were necessary, when "practical imperatives" conflicted with meritocratic processes, then supervisors had to translate corporate policy into terms that preserved the image. Often the quality of truth was strained in the translation.

A scientist described the situation that forced him to jump off the managerial main line and settle for a technical sideline:

> You see, one can be very competent technically, but there are other skills. After two promotions I found that you just come up to a harsher level of reality than just doing your research.
>
> The first time you're told to go tell a lie to a bunch of people, you make speeches to your boss about fairness and everything. I did that and he looked at me and said, "Frank, this is not the Supreme Court, and don't you tell me about fair and not fair. This is it and this is the story."
>
> What happened was this. We were making some new rules about raises which were screwing some people. I had to say that you couldn't get more than one raise a year. Since I had been involved in giving some people three raises in one year, some of the people would have known that I couldn't honestly

tell them that one raise was all you could get in a single year. At least I couldn't say that that was consistent with our past— the way things had always been done. So I was told to say that nobody was being hurt and that that was the way things had always been done. I said I couldn't and that we couldn't lie to our people since they'd know it and that would be like asking them to join your lie. You know, you say it and then you see who reacts and mostly people don't say anything because they don't want to get into trouble. Well, I wouldn't say it so my boss announced it. I was there though; I was listening and I didn't say anything.

This man was sensitive to the complicity involved in remaining silent when he knew his boss was lying to the staff. Most managers are not. Usually, by the time managers have been promoted to positions where they have to explain and justify the corporation to their subalterns, they have lost their capacity to make fine distinctions between truth and falsehood.

A more typical response to a similar situation was described by one of the GPI region managers. He was not without concern for others, but he had learned to bracket that concern and to respond humanely only when the corporate interests were not at stake. Talking about the emotional difficulties associated with transfers, he was mildly critical of his boss's ignorance and callousness:

I get a big kick out of my boss. He's never moved. (But he's gone all the time—he's never home.) I get a kick out of him saying to guys, "You'll move in the summer and it won't disrupt the kids' school" and all this stuff he's learned. "Move in the summer and you're ready to go in September. Don't upset the kids' school, let them get through the end of the year"— and that's terrific. But he's never moved; he doesn't know about some of the really painful things that go on in moves.

Then he told about some of the painful things that had occurred during his own transiency—the problems his son had making friends, his wife's loneliness, his own friendlessness. Yet, when a half hour later the discussion turned to his role as boss, the pains of transfers seemed as distant to this manager as they were to his boss:

> When I have to fill a position, I don't think beyond my nose in terms of what he might have to go through in terms of moving his family and what I have gone through. Like we're just moving someone from Florida to Milwaukee. We're looking for a supervisor. Our problem is finding someone who is qualified to be a supervisor there and not to worry about what his family will go through in a transfer.

Perhaps he was merely bragging about his toughness, but then he went on to rationalize his position:

> I wouldn't say it is not a concern. It's just something that does not enter your mind. It's not that you cannot allow it to enter your mind. Certainly you can allow it to enter your mind and you could have feeling for him and empathy for him, but it's something that does not come into your mind. There are so many other things that seem to overshadow that. It doesn't have any impact.

Finally, the fact that his own family suffered, rather than giving him empathy for others, gave him leave to expect them to go through the same trials. About a man who refused a transfer he commented:

> Probably I was more eager and more aggressive to get ahead than he is. I would say that to his face. He isn't willing to sacrifice to get ahead. Whereas I was willing to sacrifice.

And then the *coup de grâce*:

> Maybe his talents are in other areas.

And perhaps they were. Though it is not universally deemed a "talent," the ability to sacrifice to the corporation one's moral sensibilities as well as one's family and friends was a managerial requirement.

Only one group of managers expressed qualms over corporate requirements. These were the professionals. Accountants, engineers, and scientists, their disciplines provided them with a competing set of values, and thus they were sometimes moved by circumstances that meant nothing to their non-professional colleagues. A GPI accountant, for example, told of a superior whose orders clashed with the tenets of accounting:

> In accounting there's three ways to do something. Okay? The right way, the wrong way, and the way of whomever you're working for, his way. Sometimes you're given a professional set of guidelines to follow and you're trained to follow them, and all of a sudden someone who has not had this background but who wants to obtain perhaps a little bit different objective says, "No, you're not going to do it that way."
>
> It goes against everything you've been taught. And in some cases, it's just poor accounting. You know, people talk about creative accounting. Well, there is creative accounting but there's also creative accounting that is really falsified accounting and recording, and that's what I was being asked to do to make my boss's department look good.

More than the others, accountants felt morally put upon. Studies note the difficulty of specifying or evaluating the managerial task.[15] But accountants work in a world of absolutes. They believe they can measure programs and managers, and they often wonder why programs and persons that appear on the books to be obvious failures are promoted. Thus the accountants at GPI, all of those interviewed, doubted that meritocratic principles guided the reward system.

Moreover, numbers are not nearly as flexible as words. Subtle changes in verbal nuance can make right out of wrong, wrong out of right, or make a moral decision appear to be nothing more than a simple practical accommodation. Words bend particularly easily when they are spoken rather than written and, as we shall see, when they are put together by groups.[16] But numbers are different. Changing a number, or moving a number from one column to another, is not the sort of act that can be easily obfuscated or accomplished in groups. Thus accountants could not so readily hide from themselves their own transgressions, nor could others so easily hide from them.

Wilbert E. Moore has noted that "the appraisal of business results in financial terms can never be far separated from questions of the propriety of financial transaction." Because accountants have a "special function as agents of moral control," because they are "cast in the role of keepers of the corporate conscience, their jobs . . . do not yield an encouraging view of human nature"—or of their corporations, for that matter.[17]

Other managers did not view the corporate world so darkly. Although work at the corporation like work almost anywhere else involved managers in situations that would ordinarily require moral decisions, GPI's managers were blind to these choices. They seemed smitten by a moral numbness that could best be explained by the fact that during their initiations they were blinded to the moral implications of what they did and were freed from the cross-pressures and value conflicts most of us suffer.

The price of that freedom was a lack of affect. This was most noticeable in their speech patterns. Their speech lacked variety in tone and content. It was passionless. Neither anger nor joy ruffled their affability; no experience or issue seemed to touch their emotions. Especially when talking about corporate issues, what one manager said was nearly verbatim what all managers said, and their beliefs—about the corporation or anything else—were spoken without warmth. Such an apparent lack of deeply held beliefs is rare among the initiated of any organization, and it probably stems from a corporate trait rare among institutions that dominate lives. The corporation's legitimations are shallow; they do not give a meaning to life; they explain only one aspect of human existence—the material. Because the corporation competes with other social institutions that might fill in where it leaves off, the narrowness of its doctrine produces a corresponding narrowness in its managers.

However, that moral deadening, while it produces a cadre of unquestioning supporters, is at the same time the source of a major problem in the corporate world. Having imposed a moral somnolence on their managers, corporations then need to waken them to their daily tasks. In the terms of organizational psychologists, the problem becomes one of "motivation."

Difficulties in organizing work in large corporations so that workers are well motivated and satisfied have spawned hundreds of treatises and three major schools of organizational analysis. One school, the "cognitive-motivational," emphasizes the job itself and seeks ways to divide labor and assign tasks. At first this school suggested job simplification; more recently it has suggested job enlargement. A second school of thought looks to the social organization of the work place and recommends schemes for increasing the participation of workers in decision-making. The third school, made up chiefly of Marxist theorists, analyzes the organization of the workplace and the suggestions of the first two schools in order to show how each serves to strengthen capitalists and weaken workers.

Most recently Rosabeth Moss Kanter has criticized the first two for being too narrow and the third for failing to "offer much guidance to the development of alternative organizational arrangements." She observes that the key to alternative organizational arrangements lies in greater attention to the power and opportunity structures at the corporation.[18] I, in turn, would like to suggest that the key might well lie in a closer examination of the values and goals of the center economy and the ways in which those values contradict and impede realization of the goals of other institutions in society.

There can probably be little harm in increased fairness, in letting women, minorities, and other excluded groups onto the managerial hierarchy, as Kanter suggests; but that will not alter the deadening effects of initiations, nor the need for them. In fact, as Kanter recognizes, homogeneity is demanded at the corporation because managerial work calls for rapid communication in uncertain and unpredictable situations. Social homogeneity, Kanter says, lends itself to easy and comfortable communication, and that is why white Protestant males are usually chosen for managerial work. But because social homogeneity only lends a surface suggestion of internal homogeneity, even white Protestant males must be initiated. We can only guess how much more necessary initiations will become to ensure strict homogeneity of thought if managers do not even look alike.

To meet the problems of dissatisfaction among workers and managers that arise both from the structures of their jobs and from value conflicts that cannot be acknowledged but must be repressed, every giant corporation has a cadre of industrial psychologists. At GPI they make up an entire headquarters department, the Department of Management Development (DMD). A member of that department described his job:

> One of my tasks is to engage in "job enrichment," which is a term for redesigning the work to satisfy both the organization and the people. We end up redesigning the work and then we take some attitude surveys and usually afterward people are feeling much better about the kind of work they perform and they are much more productive.

Two of the changes the DMD suggested were a restructuring of jobs so that some managers' responsibilities were divided among many, and an increase in group decision-making. Both changes seemed to exacerbate discontent, not to ameliorate it. Concerning the first, a manager said:

> There's been a sales reorganization. . . . Before, you'd plan something, then you'd get involved in executing something and you realized the fruits of your total efforts. But now you become executors of plans someone else developed. You don't observe the fruits.

The complaint has a familiar ring in our industrialized world. It is the lament of alienated man, the cry of workers separated from the fruits of their labor. Once upon a time the worker in the factory, especially the person on the assembly line, was considered the most melancholy example of alienation. Now the manager is assuming that distinction. In the giant corporation he loses touch not with the things he makes but with the ideas he proposes. Not only the division of each task into its components, but also the greatly extended lines of authority lead to feelings of alienation. Two of the three men who quit GPI during the period of the study complained about just that. Green, the man who went off to operate a resort, said:

> Well, mainly my problem was when you have a corporation you have levels all the way up, and you're asked your opinion and you give reasons why you would make a decision and yet by the time it ever gets anywhere you never see any of your decisions implemented. They seem to get lost. A decision which seems like such a logical way gets lost and comes down to what seems to me like a wrong decision. You wonder why they made those decisions and it never comes out why they did.
>
> I had one idea where they could have saved money on transportation, labor, and packaging, but I don't know what

happened to it. I don't know why they didn't like the idea. They never did explain why they didn't go along with it.

I proposed it to the manager of cost accounting and he took it from there and proposed it to the marketing area. Then I don't know what happened. That's really my problem—I don't know what happened from then on.

Maybe it was something that I'm missing, like a potential customer problem. There may have been some reason that nobody explained to me. But I would have liked to have known the reason. Anybody would like to know.

Losing your work, not knowing what happened to it, is precisely what Bertell Ollmann emphasized to explain Karl Marx's approach to alienation:

The worker's . . . products are the property of another. Not only can he not use them, but he does not recognize them as his. It follows, of course, that he has no control over what becomes of his products, nor does he even know what becomes of them.[19]

It's a serious problem, of course; but like so much else that concerns persons, not profits, it is trivialized at the corporation. There alienation, the "intellectual construct in which Marx displays the devastating effect of capitalist production on human beings," [20] becomes just another case of psychological maladjustment to be dealt with in training seminars and management development sessions. Because basic issues cannot be raised, because homogeneity of values must be assumed, industrial psychologists must limit themselves to symptoms and settle for pain-killers, not cures. They thereby ensure in the manager a never-ending quest for job satisfaction—and a never-ending job market for industrial psychologists, as they try first one solution and then its opposite.

The other change DMD recommended to management, an increase in group decision-making, elicited the following explanation from a company psychologist:

The values of the American working person are different today than they were fifteen or twenty years ago—even five years ago. A person now wants more say in what he does and in the decisions that are made that concern him. People that came up in hard times, in the Depression, that were happy to have a job, tended to go along more with whatever kinds of decisions that were made and not feel that they had to be involved. In today's generation, people growing up in an affluent society feel that it's much more their right to be involved.

The way to get people to feel involved was to hold meetings where they could express their opinions and get some sense that they had participated.

But that method could backfire. VanDyke said it was in just such meetings that he lost his sense of involvement and his desire to work for GPI:

The biggest thing to me, going back to why I left GPI, was that the decision-making process at GPI just took forever—and it was going in the wrong direction. Instead of going to shorter communication lines and shorter decision-making processes, it was getting longer. The whole corporation was geared up for this team effort where you sit six, eight, or ten people around a room and there is no way to get a fast decision or a fast direction when eight or ten people sit in a room as a team. It just ran counter to the way I operated. I get unhappy sitting in meetings watching the wheels spin. When you spend five days out of the week wrapped up in going to meetings, it's boring. It was bloody murder.

It seems there was what the men in DMD would call a trade-off between involvement and boredom. Making the switch to more and longer meetings would hardly have been worthwhile unless it promised to bring greater benefits to the corporation than minor managerial satisfactions. As VanDyke discussed the meetings, the other value-related benefits became apparent. First of all, being included in countless discussions about some bit of business does not give people more control over the product. Quite the contrary; it intensifies alienation. VanDyke again:

> When you come here to headquarters you have nothing but meetings that generally end in a decision to have another meeting. You have a long progression of decision levels that have to be signed on the dotted line. It takes forever and it takes much higher up on the pole for a crummy little decision. Then at each approval level, each guy who signs, has got to justify his existence, which says he's got to make changes to whatever it is that you're proposing. Even a minor change, just so he's got his little pride of authorship in whatever it happens to be. So the decisions are lengthy, and by the time it gets all through, assuming it is accepted, you can hardly recognize it, or what it was originally. It really isn't your piece of work any longer.

What happens in those meetings is that each person's work becomes part of a corporate product. It isn't anyone's work any longer, yet everyone has had a part in it. The manager is thus at one and the same time deprived of pride in a *personal* product and made to participate in the *corporate* product. When the upshot is a decision that will affect the health and safety of the community, the full implications of group decision-making become apparent. VanDyke offered an example of one such decision, along with the reasons why he thought GPI had extended the lines of decision-making:

> That style of management, turning from the individual to the group, is the perfect way to hide responsibility. There isn't a better way in business to hide a personal opinion than to operate in a group, because the individual voice gets lost when you talk group decisions. Even if you take a vote, let's say, and you're outnumbered six to two—the two being on the right and the six being the ones that want to look right—

you've lost. But you've been part of that group that's decided to do something you think is wrong. Not necessarily something illegal. But something that may border on the immoral depending on your definition of immoral. For instance, if you want to continue to produce and push Scad, and they can't even produce it fast enough—it's moving off the shelves like there's no tomorrow. If you want to continue to make a profit for the stockholders, that's a great way to do it, but you know that it's no good for the people who use it. You know that. It's a fact. We don't advertise that it's bad. That gets stifled.

What gets stifled is the research that indicates that Scad has problems. We've got a lot of scientists over there that are just up in arms over a number of products that they make. But they're stifled.

So you can make a moral judgment and say we ought to do something about that. But there is no economic substitute for that ingredient that will continue to return to the company the same dollars. There are substitutes, but they cost more money. So you vote to spend more money to do away with that ingredient. But everybody else votes the other way. If I were making the decisions, I would have changed the formulation. So there's a way of stifling in a group decision. There are more yes men than there are— There's just a pack.

In "just a pack," individuals behave in ways they would not dare were they alone. And at meetings managers vote with the rest: naysayers are not welcome at the corporation. So managers become collaborators. At first they share in inconsequential decisions about tactical matters. Later, at headquarters, they help make policy. By that time, with their initiations virtually complete, most managers do not find it too difficult to vote with the rest. But some, like VanDyke, do —which is one reason there is such frequent fall-off at just that stage in a corporate career. It is a decisive moment. For those who stay, corporate policy becomes personal morality, and commitment to the corporation deepens.

Reports about the men who lead giant corporations suggest that for men in these positions the corporation becomes a strong alter ego, diminishing all other influences in their lives. If there is a need for such one-sided devotion, it might stem from value contradictions that managers still sense but must deny. Thus it is not the breadth of their work but its narrowness, not its complexities but its wasting simplicity, that causes so many captains of industry to submerge and exhaust themselves in the corporation. The hours they spend at their desks serve as protective blinders. But before a man dons those blinders he has had many opportunities to switch his course —to move on to a smaller corporation as VanDyke did, to try his own business as Green did, or to settle for the corporate backwaters as Auslander did.

It is impossible to know from this study what percentage of the young men who start with GPI choose those other routes, or what their reasons might be. Only the ones who were leaving, not those who had already left, could be included in the sample. What was clear, however, was that the managers and their wives hardly ever spoke of moral or social issues, and when they did, it was either to scoff or to recite the corporate formula.

PART 2

AT
HOME

CHAPTER 6

Marriage Corporate Style

Bridging Classes

One might think that the requirements of corporate employment would put a fatal strain on managers' marriages, but that was seldom the case. GPI's managers and their wives appeared to be enjoying surprisingly stable unions. No, corporations do not tear families asunder. On the contrary, by impeding the formation of deep or enduring relationships outside the nuclear unit they cause the members of managers' families to cling ever more closely to each other.[1]

As they move through life and from one community to another, these tight little families adjust to their corporate conditions. And because the families advise and copy one another, the solutions of each turn out to be like the solutions of all. After a while social patterns develop, and out of several million individual adjustments a subculture emerges.

It is an eclectic subculture—a mélange of patterns drawn from the poor and the rich, from laborers and from professionals—a subculture geared to the managers' mixed circumstances. They own their homes yet they live like tenants, careful lest they make a mark that some potential buyer might not fancy. Their houses are in middle-class suburbs, but their neighborhoods are so transient that they remind one of those early industrial slums whose unskilled inhabitants shifted from city to city in search of work. Amid such shuffle managers try to establish self-enhancing identities by surrounding themselves with material signs of success. In so doing they display not the thrift of the middle class, but the instantaneous-spending characteristics of the poor. Managers enjoy large incomes but small wealth.

Richard C. Gerstenberg, former chairman of General Motors, reflecting a widely held sentiment, has remarked, "If you want to get anywhere in this life, get away from where you were born and brought up." [2] GPI got its managers away from the mining towns, farms, and urban ghettos where they were born and raised, but it is hard to say where that has gotten them. There can be little doubt that they have been released from that stultifying narrowness some sociologists identify with small towns; but they have not been set free.[3]

Their days are as circumscribed as were those of the first factory workers who, without the protection of labor laws, toiled from dawn past dusk. Although managers are salaried executives, professionals, members of the upper middle class, they lack the autonomy and independence usually associated with that class. They age, but they do not become mature and responsible. There is about the patterns they have evolved a lingering on of childhood, with its dependencies, its serial progression through grades, its seasonal order, and its evaluations from on high. In short, the managers and their wives have left the working class and arrived, not at the middle class, but at a curious combination of it and the lowest class, the one Marx termed the *lumpenproletariat*.

Members of that class

> form a mass sharply differentiated from the industrial proletariat, a recruiting ground for thieves and criminals of all kinds, living on the crumbs of society, people without a definite trade, vagabonds, people without tie or home. . . . at the youthful age . . . [they are] thoroughly malleable, as capable of the most heroic deeds and the most exalted sacrifices as of the basest banditry and the foulest corruption.[4]

That harsh description cannot, of course, be applied, *mutatis mutandis*, to the managers. Yet, though the managers are not exactly a *lumpenproletariat*, they are not entirely different from that class either.

On the one hand, managers are educated; they live off the fat of the land, not off the crumbs of society. Except for the corporate crimes some are occasionally led to commit, it is not from among them that thieves and criminals are recruited; they are generally of good or conforming character, by no means the dregs of society. On the other hand, they have characteristics in common with those dregs. Because they have broken away from the proletariat from which they sprang, managers are without seminal attachments. That is why they so readily fasten themselves to their corporation and make its interests their own. At the youthful age at which they are recruited they are both malleable and capable of great personal sacrifice in the service of their corporations.

The magnitude of that sacrifice is most apparent in their homes, since the managers' greatest self-denial is familial, not personal. In the service of the corporation, managerial families give up claims to husband and father; they allow themselves to become like vagabonds, with their homes periodically uprooted and transplanted; and they then put the blame for any human disorders that may result among members of the family not on the corporation but upon the ailing family members themselves.

All the while there is little sense of sacrifice and none of disorder. Instead, an aura of rightness prevails as men and women play out their family roles in a corporation-serving way. The man proves himself to be a good provider by giving himself over to his work, and the woman proves herself to be a good wife and mother by doing all she can to aid her husband. In this way the competition between family and industry, which came with the industrial revolution, seems to have been capped by a symbiosis in which family needs are satisfied through unstinting devotion to the corporation.

The "Stage 4" Family

It has been an unexpected development. Most commentators on the family have thought that as our political system moved toward greater equality among classes, and as technological advances spread affluence into lower and lower strata, sex-linked differentiation of roles within the family would give way to an increasing parity between men and women. Michael Young and Peter Willmott, for instance, have identified three distinct stages in the development of the family from its pre-industrial to its current form. In the first, the preindustrial stage, the family was unified around production. On farms and in handicrafts husbands, wives, and children worked to-gether—under the direction of the husband. Then, when mechanical power displaced human power, family members were drawn out of the home and into the factory as wage laborers. The old economic partnership was supplanted by an estrangement in which men, women, and children had competing rather than complementary interests. Later, in the third stage, rising incomes and the technology that made possible small personal machinery, such as cars and television sets, reunified the family around its functions as the unit of consumption, not of production.

The stage 3 family is "symmetrical." It approaches, more than the first two types, an equality between the sexes and it has been generated as much by feminism as by affluence and modern technology. In their study of family patterns in the London area, Young and Willmott found this type in as-cendancy among working-class families.[5] Its patterns remind one of the slogan with which *McCall's* magazine promoted itself and saluted a middle-class family ideal in the nineteen fifties—*togetherness.*

It is quite in keeping with Young and Willmott's "principle of stratified diffusion" that a middle-class ideal of the fifties has worked its way down the social hierarchy to become a working-class reality in the seventies. According to that prin-ciple, family patterns are introduced in the upper classes and, over time, work their way down through the social classes.

At any one time all styles would be observable in different segments of the society.[6]

Now, even while the "symmetrical" family is proliferating in the working class, Young and Willmott have detected a new family stage at the top of the social ladder. In a sub-sample of managing directors (chief officers of major corporations), they found that these powerful men were more like the stage 2 than the stage 3 husbands. They were

> less home-centered and their marriages seemed to be less symmetrical. . . . Their wives belonged to a minority who were prepared to settle for a different sort of compromise in an asymmetrical family, married to a dominant man with whose successes they could to some extent identify, very well off in material terms, home-centered because their husbands were so much the opposite.[7]

The men from GPI were like the managing directors from the London area—with one overwhelming difference. They were not nearly so wealthy nor so powerful as those directors, and they were not likely ever to be so, coming as most of them did from the working class.[8] Nevertheless, as part of their initiations, and in order to preserve the myth of the meritocracy, they had to appear to be able to take over from the managing directors and therefore to be as much like them as possible. They had to be just as work-centered and they had to establish within their marriages the same relationships managing directors did in theirs. Their lack of money and power simply forced greater sacrifices from managers' families and a more extreme asymmetry.

Transfers provide an example of the difference. Both the wives of the GPI managers and the wives of the managing directors Young and Willmott studied had to reconcile themselves to the fact that their husbands were preoccupied with work and would therefore be available to them far less than most other husbands were available to their wives. The directors' wives, however, could fill out their own lives and complement their husband's position by building interesting and powerful careers of their own in community organizations.[9] GPI wives could not. Because the husband was neither powerful nor rich, the wife was unable to trade off his prestige or use his wealth to make noticeable donations. She could not even stay long enough in a community to build a reputation of her own. Instead her life was a succession of settlings-in and movings-out. That was because her husband, far from being the one who determined the location of plants and offices, was not even powerful enough to decide on the location of his own dwelling. As his job was shifted from one corporate branch to another, he was forced to disrupt his home and family.

We have seen that a transfer almost always has a promotion attached to it. For the man it is a reward. For the woman and the children it is a penalty. As the corporation gives to the husband, it takes from his wife and children. He gets higher status; they lose home and community. True, the house is generally replaced by a bigger and better one made possible by the manager's greater income, and that goes far to compensate the family for its loss. But that is no cure for the injuries suffered during transplantation. And there *are* injuries, especially if transfers continue beyond the earliest years of a marriage.

Hiding the Injuries of Mobility

Though many were reluctant to talk about it, most couples were aware that family members had been hurt by many transfers. One woman, who had been transferred eight times in her husband's fifteen years with GPI, discussed the problems her children were having at school:

> Switching schools was rough on the children. Like when we

came here Dick was in fourth grade in his fifth school and it was telling on him. Whether he just didn't care about learning anymore or what, but his grades were going down and he just didn't like school—period! And of course, not being in a school system very long, he was more or less a loner.

And we had conduct problems with our girl. . . . Janice is an excellent student and she, I think, for the most part, was bored. She just caused trouble. She just plain didn't do her work because to her it was too easy. She pestered the other kids and wouldn't let them do their work. I mean that kind of thing. And I'm sure it had to be because they were moved around a lot.

Sometimes the men were more ready than their wives to talk about the problems transfers caused. Then it almost sounded as if they were bragging, as if they hoped to get credit for the sacrifices their families had made. For instance, the manager who reprimanded a subordinate who had refused to transfer for not being "eager and aggressive" enough, spoke of the toll transfers had taken on his own family:

There are some hard things which go on in moves, which people who don't move don't understand. The emotional problems which kids go through, which you may see and you may not see. And the fact that they suddenly have no friends and have to start all over again.

One of the problems is that David doesn't have any kids his age right around the house to play with. So it requires me to go out and play basketball with him—but he's more of a loner anyway.

Most families had at least one child whom the parents called a loner. Such labeling of the family member whose behavior was adversely affected by transfers was an example of the pattern common among corporate families of blaming the victim. When asked, most parents could remember a time when their "loner" had many friends. As in the case of David, that time usually corresponded with the family's unusually long residence in one place:

> David did have some friends in Chicago that he really liked and he used to go over to their house for visits all the time. He hasn't visited a house for years. But in Chicago he had some friends in the next street and he would go over and play with them. We were in Chicago two years, which is the longest we were any place.

Children are not the only ones who become loners when they have no time to develop friendships, but adults, unlike small children, can communicate with friends in distant places and they are less likely to glibly pass themselves off as loners. The same man described his own and his wife's loneliness:

> It's easier for adults. But even Janet, the wife, she has to start all over again. Whereas she may have developed a good friendship with some other woman over a period of two years' time, you no longer have that person you can talk to—which is obviously very important for a woman to have—someone to talk to during the day. The man has the business and the business people he's working with, so he's got someone to be with all the time and his mind is occupied. The woman doesn't have that.
>
> But even for myself, while the business end of it is really no problem—business is business whether you're in Chicago or New York and the business people are primarily business people; they're not social people. But when I come to a new place it's different. I'd like someone to play golf with.
>
> I'm an outgoing person, but I'm not that full a person. I need the other person to initiate something with me. When you move from one area to another, it's just the complete cutting of the umbilical cord or whatever you want to call it. Everything changes. There's no gray. It's black and white. It's a whole new ball game. You're starting straight from scratch in identifying yourself to other people and developing the image they have of you.

Charles Horton Cooley was one of the first to point out that our sense of self is developed, in part, by what we imagine others may think of us.[10] The managers were especially sensitive to this "looking-glass self." Though never directly asked, almost every GPI manager offered two descriptions of himself: the first as he saw himself and the second as he thought others saw him. In the case of one manager the characterizations he offered didn't seem to fit the man being interviewed. That man seemed relaxed; though his small, dark eyes were ever so slightly more intense than some of the other men's, he did not seem any less cool or genial. He spoke in well modulated tones and, on the whole, seemed more on the quiet side than otherwise. It was strange therefore to hear him describe himself:

> I'm the type of person that people don't get a good first image from. I talk in a high-pitched voice. At times when I get going and I get excited, my voice rises and I talk quickly. I exude in my mannerisms a great deal of confidence in myself and whatever. And some people resent that. Many people resent that—they identify it as coming on too strong. I don't think of myself that way, but that is the way people look at me. It takes people a while to warm up to me. I don't think it takes me time to warm up to them.

It was as if, failing to get more than a surface reflection from his brief relationships with others, this man's view of himself had become shallow and stereotyped. There were two Jewish men in the sample; he was one of them.[11] With such a burden, the problems of establishing new friendships were exacerbated for him:

> When you do realize that people don't warm up to me right away, and then you have to start all over again, it really is a pain in the rear end. You may not do the right things in the right way with some local neighbors, and that's all you need.

You move in and that's the place you're going to be for a long time and not hit it off right—which you certainly don't want to do. Sometimes you call that a shooting match. You just might do the wrong thing or say the wrong thing or whatever and then you're wiped out.

This manager's problems, though they were enlarged by his ethnicity, were typical. Children who once had friends saved themselves from grief by becoming loners. Wives, heavily burdened by the problems of breaking up old homes and friendships and starting out anew, became exhausted, unable to do anything but their housework. Men who because of their work could not retreat into aloneness worried about their "image." [12] But of all the difficulties suffered, none seemed so overwhelming as the trials of one young woman who was unlucky enough to be twice in the last weeks of pregnancy at just the moment her husband was asked to transfer. As she told her tale, her sculptured face and large, doelike eyes remained expressionless—cold as marble:

I was due to deliver our first child when he was transferred to New York, to headquarters. They let him wait around a few days hoping that I'd hurry up and have the baby before he left; but I didn't. Finally, I talked the doctor into inducing labor and I did have the baby; but my husband didn't stay long enough to bring us home. I had to get the next-door neighbor to help and we had to stay there two weeks without him. . . .

When it was time to deliver the second baby he was transferred to Atlanta. He was working in Atlanta for a couple of weeks before I delivered. He would come home on weekends and he hoped that I'd have the baby on the weekend; but I didn't. When I went to the hospital to deliver, the neighbor people came in. On the fifth day after the baby was born he came to the hospital and took us to a Howard Johnson's motel. Then in two hours he left for Atlanta, but in the meantime he brought the first child over from the person who was keeping her.

So I was in this room five days after delivering, with a new infant and a seventeen-month-old child; depressed. I had to call the person who kept the first child and ask her if she'd please come back. I just couldn't do it.

Like that lost soul Blanche in *A Streetcar Named Desire*, this woman had to depend on the kindness of strangers. Yet she saw no irony in the fact that the job which should have provided her with a home left her alone and homeless at just those moments when her needs for comfort and support were greatest. It was only when she was asked if she thought the corporation ought to have postponed the transfer until the baby was a few months old that she became at all critical:

I think so. I don't think it would have made one bit of difference to them. Somewhere back in those stages my husband was also traveling a great deal and when he wasn't traveling they'd have some kind of a, I call it rest and recreation—fishing, playing golf—and anyway I felt rather resentful. I just think I could say they took the man as an individual and completely ignored the fact that a family or wife existed.

Then, as if the word "wife" reminded her of something, she stopped and, in a manner typical of GPI wives, turned the criticism on herself:

But he was trying to get somewhere with his company. Whenever he was transferred it was usually a promotion or a raise. I could have been more encouraging and more congratulatory at those times but instead I was "Oh, poor me." I've calmed down since then—more mature, I suppose.

"Mature" wives minimize problems and turn complaints inward. Just as their husbands, believing the corporation to be a meritocracy, blame any failure to receive rewards on themselves, so the wives, enjoying the material fruits of their husbands' hard work, feel that their dissatisfactions must stem from personal failings. Therefore they repress feelings of discontent and caution their children to do the same. It is taken for granted that managers' wives must subordinate their interests and those of their children to corporate demands on their husbands.[13]

When it comes to transfers, this means she must go about the business of moving cheerfully and efficiently and discipline herself to think mostly about the happy aspects of moving. The woman who described the troubles her children were having in school added:

> But I think probably the advantages outweighed the disadvantages. I think it's been exciting to live in all the different parts of the country, and I have always decided I was going to like the new place, or at least try to.

The Parable of the Bad Wife

To show what could happen if a wife didn't try to like the new place, she recounted the story of a wife who faltered:

> We have known a lot of people where the wife has been absolutely miserable because she just would not make any effort to like the place. One couple we know, he quit his job with GPI and they moved back to where they came from. I didn't know them that well, but we had met them a few times. She was so discouraged because they were moving to a different place; especially since they were coming from a place they really liked. She just started eating and eating and eating and gaining weight and just refused to get out and do anything about getting acquainted. Never even got up in the morning to get her little girl off to school—that type of thing. She was just so miserable. And that's not good for the rest of the family either.

Mrs. Corelli gave her account of the same woman:

> I have one friend that was very miserable living where she
> was living and she made it miserable for herself because she
> wouldn't go out of her way. She just hated it where she was.
> This was a friend that lived in Connecticut and is now in
> California. She is happy now that she's in California, but
> when she lived here—I have never seen such a difference in
> a person. Her husband was very worried about her. He
> thought she was going to have a mental breakdown. And this
> was her home, New York, where she was from. But she was
> close to home and she hated it and she made no bones about
> it and I think she made life miserable for everybody.

Since GPI's men and women tended to be without opinions on most matters, the condemnation of this woman was
all the more striking. Both of the wives who used her as an
example of what might happen if a wife played her part badly
thought that the woman suffered willfully. Both had sympathy
only for the husband.

The first wife, Mrs. Cobb:

> That had to be hard on *him*. I mean knowing that that was
> going on, and here his job was, and how can you do your best
> when that's going on at home? I don't think that's good.

Mrs. Corelli:

> He was really forced to go back to California because of her,
> and I don't think he really wanted to leave GPI, because he
> had a good future there.

Mrs. Corelli, who was herself unhappy about her most recent
transfer from California and wanted to return, was certain
that the woman could have pulled herself out of her misery—
and that she should have:

> I think she should have adjusted. I don't think she should

have put that much of a strain on her husband. I thought she handled the whole thing poorly.

Mrs. Cobb, on the other hand, allowed that the woman might not have succeeded had she tried, but she didn't give her very high marks for trying:

> I think the wife should adjust to the new place—make an effort. Maybe some of them can't. I have known of people who just absolutely cannot adjust to certain situations, but I think the effort should be there if that's what the husband wants.

As for the husband, Mrs. Corelli didn't think very highly of the way he had behaved, either:

> I've never met a man quite like him, because he will do anything his wife wants him to and I don't know if I like that feature in a man. I think he could have been stronger with her.

Mrs. Cobb, after some reflection, decided that in this case it was probably best that the family returned to California:

> Maybe in that case it was best to leave and go back.

The Bargain Struck

As she thought out the problem, Mrs. Cobb inadvertently expressed the ideology that enforces and rationalizes the asymmetry of corporate marriages:

> I think your family is important, too. I mean if they're un-happy, I don't think you can do your best in your job. I would have to say that between the family and the job it's sort of fifty-fifty. I think the family is very important and I don't think his job should be his whole life. But I think the rest of the family has to make sacrifices for the husband's career. Not to the point where they're miserable or anything like that, I don't mean that. But I do think the husband's career is im-

portant, because unless he's happy the rest of the family isn't going to be happy either.

It seems to be a perfect circle: between the family and the job it's fifty-fifty. The job is important because it makes the man happy—if he's doing well at it. But it can't be everything because he can't do well at work unless he's free of worries at home. He can't be free of those worries unless the family is happy. And, to complete the circle, they can't be happy unless he's happy. It goes round and round, all intertwined with happiness. It's the mystique of corporate marriages.

That mystique, when unraveled, urges a ratio between work and family that is far from fifty-fifty. Family members can be controlled, the corporation cannot be. Unhappy wives and children can be exhorted to give the appearance of happiness, whatever they may actually feel, by pressing the belief that if they disturb the man with their troubles he won't do his best at work, and if he doesn't do his best they will all be cut off from corporate sustenance. During the manager's initiation the dependency bred in him at the corporation spreads to the family until its members begin to reinforce each other in the belief that survival without the corporation may be impossible and must certainly be far less comfortable. Their tie to the corporation is at once so crucial and so tenuous that few men risk talk about familial hardships (except to point out their devotion to the corporation) and fewer still request corporate concessions for fear their boss might find them not "eager and aggressive" enough. Instead, the family must learn to accept major dislocations so that the corporation need not be asked to make minor adjustments. Only in extreme cases is the corporation petitioned to yield, and then only when the family member who has caused the request for corporate deference to be made can clearly be labeled a deviant.

To indicate the benevolence of the corporation, many men and women told of managers whose family problems had been taken into account by the corporation. The case Mrs. Corelli reported was of a sales manager who for the unusually long period of four years had moved neither up nor out:

> There is one fellow that they keep wanting to promote and he keeps turning down jobs because he has a wife with a mental problem and he wants to stay in this one area that's their home. He doesn't feel she can take the pressure of moving and making friends. She's had two mental breakdowns and he just feels he can't do this, and I think eventually he'll get a good job down there. They'll work it around for him to have a region manager's job, which is what they want him to be.

Of course, there is more leeway even than that. If the family is at a stage when a transfer would be overwhelmingly disruptive, the manager *can* pass up a promotion and still be offered others. The young woman who had to take her newborns from the hospital to a motel was probably married to an exceptionally ambitious, fearful, or insensitive man.[14] Other arrangements could have been made. Many women reported being pregnant at the time of a transfer. A vice-president's wife said she had had to be treated by three different obstetricians in three different locations before her third baby was born; and her husband was never in town for a birth until their fifth child arrived. Yet even she always went home, not to a motel, when she left the hospital— albeit on two occasions the home was her mother's, not her own. And Mrs. Corelli, though she wasn't sure she liked the kind of man who would do "anything his wife wants him to," was, in fact, married to one of the most considerate of corporate husbands. Maybe he felt more secure than other husbands in his position at GPI, or maybe he wasn't in such a hurry to get ahead, but he alone among the sales managers was able to forgo two transfers in order to make conditions at home easier. His wife told of the incidents:

> He has turned down two transfers. One move was when I was pregnant and not feeling well. He felt he couldn't leave me at the time and he told them so, but they came back and gave him another promotion about a year later. And in California he turned down one promotion because it would involve extensive traveling, and although he does some traveling he doesn't like extensive traveling, and they came back later with another promotion and we ended up back here.

So it is possible for a man to give some thought to his family without ruining his career. It is not customary for men to do that. They are usually far too deeply absorbed in their careers to notice any but the most extreme symptoms of distress at home; and at work, where they spend all but a few of their waking hours, they are submerged in the ideology that affirms the asymmetry of their marriages.

The message is transmitted in many ways. For instance, Melba Cobb and Betty Corelli were affirming the imbalance of their own marriages as they were criticizing the woman who forced her husband back to California. A woman interviewed during the first phase of the study told of a meeting of wives called shortly before her husband's graduation from the Harvard Business School:

> They got all the women together at the end and they made a little speech saying that they wanted everyone to know that their husband's career was the most important thing and they should not rock the boat and do anything to upset their husband's careers. If their husband was going to be transferred, they should go happily. It means more money and it means a better career for him, and, of course, they didn't say this, but it means more money donated to the Harvard Business

School. They were sort of saying, "Forget what you might want to do in this world, your husband's career is the only thing that's important."

Lisa VanDyke heard it from a less lofty source:

> Many years ago when we were moving into Atlanta, the guy whose job my husband was taking—his wife called me up to find out if there was anything she could do to help me get settled. And I said no. They were moving to Kansas City and she said she hoped I'd be very happy in Atlanta. She just loved it there. And I asked if she was sad about moving, and she said, "Yes, very much so. But," she said, "if Joe's happy, I'm happy." That was her stock phrase. This was one of those things I've long remembered.

But rather than confirm that view, Lisa VanDyke found fault with it:

> It was long before Betty Friedan or any of those guys, but what a position to put yourself into. Why can't Jane be as happy as Joe? We just accepted for years that Joe had to be happy before we could be happy. What a hell of a way to live. I think that's horrendous.

Horrendous as she thought it was, all the wives, including Lisa VanDyke, accepted it. Why?

The answer is complex. In part the reasons are historical. The corporate marriage and its mystique is a special case of the longstanding patterns of inequality between the sexes that Betty Friedan wrote about.[15] These patterns peaked during the nineteen fifties—just the time most of the GPI wives were coming of age. They were, therefore, primed to accept an asymmetrical marriage.

It would, however, be incorrect to brush the corporate marriage off as merely a passing phenomenon likely to wane as feminism waxes. Marital ideals are changing under the influence of feminism, but it is hard to imagine how that fragile force could eliminate the need giant corporations have for transfers and initiations. It was, after all, during their husbands' initiations at work that the wives experienced at home the complementary processes that led to their subordination. The corporation dominated the wife by dominating her husband, and for both it was a gradual process.

It began even before they were married, when they were graduating from high school and the idea of being upwardly mobile was being promoted. One of them told why he went to college:

> I hadn't planned to go to college up until my senior year of high school, when two of the teachers that had taught me said that I really should go to school because it would be a waste and that I'd be sorry if I didn't. I was just headed toward a high school diploma and that was it. So they said, "Why don't you take some tests?" And I did very well in them so I headed off to college. But did I have any real idea of where I wanted to be? No, I didn't. It all happened in my senior year of high school.

In many ways their upward mobility cost the managers their independence. Except for those very few whose parents were middle class, the decision to go to college, to be, indeed, the first in their families to go to college, loosed these men and women from a world they knew and set them adrift. One manager, the son of a Bronx, New York, policeman, told what it meant for him to go to college:

> I didn't have any expectations coming from there—it was a ghetto. There were policemen and firemen and Con Ed people. You just felt that you went to school and you went to high school and you got toward the end of high school and it just seemed that you'd fall into something. I think most of the kids then that went to college from high school really weren't sure what they wanted to do except that the passport

for that group was college. It was the passport of not being a letter carrier, of not being a Con Ed employee, of not being a policeman. The passport to what, I don't know, but it had to be better, you see. It was an opportunity your father didn't have. You take the opportunity and what you do with it you don't know.

It had to be better; they accepted that on faith, it was the prevailing ethos. Whether they came from urban ghettos or rural villages, whether their parents were ambitious for them or some teacher singled them out and pointed them toward college, they were sure they were going toward a better life.

Once they got to college there was nothing in their backgrounds on which they could base the choices they had to make. A young GPI salesman explained how he picked his major:

You're not going to decide what you're going to do the rest of your life when you're eighteen or nineteen years old. I couldn't do it, that's for sure. I was a political science major. I guess it's what most sophomores do when they decide on a major. The line is less on this side, so I'll just register on this side. And that's what a lot of them do, I think. A lot of them throw their hands up, look back and see where they got their best grades in the first two years and choose that.

One district sales manager, like so many men who went to college in the fifties, wanted to major in engineering, and like so many of the men who ended up in sales or merchandising at GPI, he had to choose something else because his talents didn't run in that direction:

I never knew what I wanted to be when I grew up, and probably never will. That's been my life's dilemma. Mother said when you got out of high school you went to college. So I went to college. I majored in history because it's probably the easiest thing to major in that you could have majored in. I was interested in it and I was no good at physics or any of those type of things. I was interested in engineering, so before I went into college I took some aptitude tests and found out that I had no spatial, so that knocked me out of engineering; and history was liberal arts and I liked it so I went into history.

Such uncertainty is not peculiar to managers. Making lifetime decisions without the necessary experience is difficult for all adolescents. It engenders in youths a period of change and anxiety that Erik Erikson has termed an "identity crisis." [16] No longer children, they are not yet adults. Out of their childhood experiences, out of what they observed in the adults around them, and out of their cultural and social environment they had to fashion the adults they would be. It is a hard and sometimes frightening task, and for the managers from the working class especially it was a trying time, because they had left the world they knew and stepped into a strange environment where the experiences of their childhoods could not be drawn upon to imagine their futures. Never having seen adults play the roles they were about to adopt, they didn't have the examples with which to think about them; so they were without plans or dreams.[17] One of the women put it succinctly:

> Who knows what your life is going to be like? No one really thinks about it. You just have all those years stretching out in front of you and we didn't plan it much.

But if you don't actively plan, if you don't actively find out what is available and make choices based on *your* preferences, you will be carried along like so much flotsam, obeying the choices of others. That is what happened to the managers. From their choices of a major through their entire careers, the managers were passive. They went on the shortest lines and accepted what opportunities were offered, never venturing to see what else there might be, never trying to make opportunities emerge. In this they were very much like the British managers the Pahls studied:

> Many of the couples seemed to agree that a new job is not something to be actively planned for, sought out, and discussed at length; their attitude is more passive, a job presents itself, or is offered, and the decision is about whether to accept that particular job.[18]

So when the job with GPI presented itself, it was as happy a day for the rest of the couples as it was for the Corellis:

> We were very young when we got married, and when he got this job he was thrilled to death.

GPI was large, it offered security, it offered opportunity, and it offered the wherewithal for these couples to fashion that part of their existence over which they did have a bit of choice—their material possessions and family lives. This was yet another similarity between them and their English counterparts:

> It is in decisions about where and how they shall live, where they should go for the holidays, and above all about the children, that a more positive attitude is seen. . . . It may be that it is because the couples feel that they have most autonomy in the private, domestic sphere that this is the sphere they stress. The decisions made in this sphere are the ones in which they have more power. The decision to move a factory, to open up a new market, or simply to offer a man a better job is made by others.[19]

Managers had more power over the private sphere, in part because they had experience there. Though they knew nothing of colleges, giant corporations or the life of a manager, they did know something about marriages and families.

For the most part, GPI managers and their wives were raised in stage 2 families that were trying desperately to become stage 3 families. As children they had endured few privations, but they had enjoyed even fewer luxuries. Their parents had to struggle to provide them with the necessities. Many came from families that were already upwardly mobile —fathers who had started as miners or laborers later became small proprietors. Often their mothers worked, not because they wanted to but because they had to. The managerial couples wanted something better—more security, bigger houses, wives who didn't have to work, and all the accouterments of a stage 3 marriage—those things that would enable them to enjoy in private and at home the satisfaction of those needs and desires that in earlier times and poorer families were met in public places. For, as Willmott and Young maintained, an important aspect of the stage 3 marriage is the privateness that was made possible by the technology of small personal machinery. As the car replaced public transportation, as television took the place of the movie theater and music hall, and as small appliances replaced commercial services, family members were able to join each other to share leisure and consumption in their homes.

The job at GPI provided the means toward that connubial consumption, and it was not long before it seemed to many of these couples that they had happened upon an industrial goose with golden eggs. With the corporation's up-or-out policy, the longer they stayed, the higher they rose and the more they earned. Moreover, once the young manager was identified by his boss as a man with a future, his initiation began and psychic benefits were added to the emoluments he already enjoyed. A belief system and a self-enhancing identity were there to fill the vacuum left when these couples rejected the cultures of their youth.

The importance of an ideological structure to adolescents has been emphasized by Erikson:

> It is in adolescence that the ideological structure of the environment becomes essential for the ego, because without an ideological simplification of the universe the adolescent ego cannot organize according to its specific capacities and its expanding involvement.[20]

The corporation provided both a world and a world order, and it was therefore usually without much question that when the first transfer came as part of the package of advancement the young couple packed up and went to the new location. The mystique of the corporate marriage was beginning to take hold. The men felt their prospects justified the uprooting of their families and the women felt it would be wrong to hold their husbands back.

Moreover, the corporate ideology established the corporation as the workplace of the future, the managers as the men of the future, and transience as the way of the future.[21] Mrs. Corelli voiced that notion as she explained why her many moves were as inevitable as they were unexpected:

> I guess he realized it at first, but I didn't know that we would do as much moving as we have. Neither did our families. They think we're gypsies . . . But moving is becoming a way of life. It seems in the last few years in the United States if you're with a big company . . . I would like to settle down, but it just doesn't seem possible anymore in this day and age.

Even if the wife didn't so easily accept the idea that careers came first and transiency was unavoidable, the authority and the pervasiveness of the message usually overwhelmed her. The wife of the Harvard Business School graduate described her feelings at that pregraduation meeting where she was first told what her place would be:

> I was appalled. I was even mad. But at the time I went along with it because this sort of seemed the thing to do. They told

me that I should, and he was convinced that this was true. Gordon was sure that his career was very important.

The husbands, reinforcing each other at work in the belief that their careers were of utmost importance, were able to argue with great authority at home that whatever hardships the family might suffer had to be borne. Even Jim VanDyke, the only man to meet strong opposition at home, felt certain he was in the right:

> I did it all those years because it seemed to be the thing to do to get ahead. Very simple. When you work for a major corporation that's far-flung, like GPI is, all over the damn place, that is the way to do it. We thought over the years that it was an appropriate way to do it. I did think so. Lisa never did agree.

Whether she agreed or not, Lisa went along. All the wives did —or their husbands left GPI.

Actually, not being aware of what was in store for her, Lisa VanDyke took to the first few moves as most wives did: with great spirit:

> On my part there was a sense of going out to the next adventure, so I went along fairly easily early on. And we did live in a lot of interesting places, I must say. All the places we lived in were interesting places to live in. And we took advantage of that. We had to adapt to all kinds of people and I think that in many ways this was very good for the children because it gave them a picture of other people.

Mrs. Corelli wasn't so adventurous at first, but she too caught the spirit:

> We had lived all our lives in Cleveland and I think the first move was the hardest. But after that I really got to enjoy it— meeting people and seeing the country and traveling around. . . . It is a strain to move but then it becomes enjoyable.

It's just emotion, you hate to leave, but then it's exciting to go to a new place and meet new people. I think it's been a good education for all of us.

I have friends I went to high school with in Cleveland and they still live there all their lives and I don't know if I'd like to live like that, all your married life in one place. I think it tends to stunt your growth a little bit.

Then, to give an example of the broadening effect a transfer had had on her husband, she told of an experience in California:

We had a black couple who lived next door to us. He was with the Oakland Raiders, a football player, and that was a nice experience for us. People were kind of panicky on the block when they heard they were moving in; my husband was. It didn't bother me too much. They were a nice couple and we got to know them and invited them to our house. Though we had one friend who would not come to our house after that because we had invited them. Which was fine if that's what they wanted to do. We still wanted to invite them because we liked them very much. They had us in their home, and it was a nice experience to have them living next door.

But I know in Cleveland, even my family is very prejudiced, and if a colored family moved next door to either one of our families, they would just think that it was a fate worse than death. When I told them a colored family was living next door they thought it was terrible, but then I told them it wasn't. I'm just trying not to be a prejudiced person. I guess everybody has a little bit of prejudice in them but it just upsets me when people talk like that. They know it, so they don't bring it up in front of me, but I know how they feel because I was brought up in that atmosphere.

It didn't bother me at all when that family moved in. It really didn't. And it surprised my husband because it really bothered him. I guess the difference was that he's never really been in contact with them too much, but when I was working after high school I got to know some of them and they're very nice. They're just a different color.

But I think my husband learned from that experience, because actually he got to know them and he really enjoyed talking to them and it's made a better person of him. Because it didn't bother him after a while, it really didn't.

So there were lessons to be learned and experiences to be had that enhanced understanding and expanded tolerance.

But there was another side to the managers' wives' tale. After a while, with transfers coming rapidly, one upon the other, each year began to take on familiar and habitual patterns. As in their school days the patterns were seasonal. During midwinter, sometime between late December and March, decisions about who would be promoted and who would wait another year were being made at the corporation. By March the family usually knew if they would have to transfer. If they did, the husband would move off to the new job in April. It was a season of separation, as one of the wives described it:

Of course when you move the husband has to go off to the job and the wife is left behind to sell the house and get the children through school. Usually they transfer in March or April and we stay till school closes. When we moved here from California, he went to work the first of April and we moved here, I think it was July fourth. And he came back to visit once or twice. So we were separated and I was by myself for months and months. It was just like not being married at all.

During those spring months each has a separate task. The wife must show the old house to potential buyers and the husband must get adjusted to his new job and find a new house. Usually he scouts the area and finds a dozen or so houses to show his wife on the one or two trips the company will pay for. Another wife explained how that works:

He canvasses first all the areas that people tell him to look at homes in and then when he has at least ten homes I can look at, he has me come out. The company pays for that—three or four days. We make a fast decision usually. One time I was pregnant at the time when we were moving to New Jersey and we couldn't find a house and he bought one without me seeing it. That's the first time that's ever been done. We liked the house. It was very nice. He saw this house and he knows what I like and he said, "I think you'll like it," and he was right. Poor thing, it's hard for him though, going into a new job and having to look at houses, too.

The summer and early fall is for moving in. First they get to know the new area. Mrs. Corelli:

I'm very good at getting around in new places. I get a map and I go. *We* go. Sunday is always a good day for sightseeing, and we always look a place over thoroughly and find out all the things we can about it. I never did like traveling but since we've been married I've had no choice and I find myself wanting to see more and more things that never were important to me before.

Back together again, looking around, and being the only people they know, the family strengthens its ties. Lisa Van-Dyke:

I think that in many ways the moving made for a closer family. We kind of all had to band together.

But family is not enough. There are no peers in a family and after a while it's time to make friends. A manager-father:

In terms of transferring, I worry about the kids finding kids to play with. Is everybody going to be able to get back into the swing of things? Not crying because they haven't got any friends and stuff like that.

Usually after a month or so at school, children begin finding new friends. A mother described her family's recent move:

> We moved right after the school year was out and the whole summer they really didn't meet any children around here, before they went to school. But once they got into school, they made friends.

By Christmas-time the family is usually well settled in. But then, after New Year's, the round begins once more.

After five or ten years like that the excitement fades and new places pall. At first most young managers and their brides are adventurers together, welcoming each transfer with its raise and promotion as a joint triumph, but by the fifth or sixth move they travel different paths. The corporation nurtures the man—it gives him a sense of self-worth and identity, a sense of progress and achievement—a community. The wife has none of that; for her there is no community, she has experienced movement but no progress, and she suffers a declining sense of personal worth. Lisa VanDyke complained about the difference:

> Moving is so hard that I can't believe people get through it so easily. I just can't believe it. To me it is so difficult and I don't mean the physical aspect of it although it's very wearing. All the physical aspects of it, practically all of which the wife does, just because they're there and somebody has to do it. But it's not only that. He's got all his friends wherever he's going. He's still got the company, which is the mother-father figure, and the wife has nothing.

It is because of their aloneness and because of their lack of ideological or institutional support that corporate wives who might have wished to change the family's course were seldom able to do so. Moreover, they were usually at their weakest moment at just the time when protest might have been effective. The transfers that came one upon another usually coincided with the arrival of the couple's children—a time when even nontransient mothers tend to be so exhausted by the twenty-four-hours-a-day care of their infants and toddlers that they often end up in doctors' offices.

Once in those early years Lisa VanDyke broke a finger:

> I went to the doctor to have it set and I had this terrible rash all over my hands and the doctor said, "Never mind the broken finger. What on earth is wrong with you? You are a complete nervous wreck. What you need are tranquilizers." So I told him what my life was like for the last ten years. It was just absolutely incredible. And I never complained. I don't know why I never complained.

Another wife told of her visit to the doctor for her yearly checkup:

> The kids were all tiny. Eric was five months old, Tracy was two, and Sharon was four and so I was really tied down. I went to the doctor for my checkup and said I thought I needed some iron pills, I was really tired. He asked me how old the kids were and I told him and he said, "Honey, if I had a nickel for every young mother that came in here and said, 'Oh doctor, I'm so tired,' I'd be a millionaire and wouldn't have to practice anymore. What you need is a maid and to get out of the house once a week." And I said, "A maid! You've got to be kidding, I can't afford a maid." He said that it was cheaper than iron pills. So he really encouraged me to look into it, and I did. And for five dollars a day you can get someone to come in and clean and watch the children. I had a lady who came at eight-thirty and left at four. In the morning she cleaned the house and in the afternoon she ironed and watched these three little kids and when she cleaned she even polished the sides of the furniture. My furniture hasn't had it so good since.

It's a familiar syndrome of early motherhood, and doctors have their standard prescriptions: cheap black maids in the South and tranquilizers in the North. For the most part the

GPI wives with a bit of help from their doctors did so well that their husbands enjoyed the soothing impression that everything was fine at home. One incident from those days stuck in Lisa VanDyke's mind:

> I remember one day in California. We had horses and we always took them with us and you can't imagine, it was all my responsibility. One day we had the horses in the corral and this guy came over to look at our place, he was a friend of my husband's. And he said, "Gee, how do you do all this?" and Jim said, "Oh, Lisa does it all, it's easy." I think that was the point at which I thought, "You know, it's not easy. I do do it all, but it's not easy and I don't do it with ease." There is a point at which you just can't do all those things.

Dick Watson, the husband of the woman whose doctor prescribed a maid, remembered a moment from a few years earlier when he and Ellen had discussed the competing demands of family and career:

> So then I traveled, traveled all the time. I was home maybe six weekends during that whole period of time. My wife was pregnant and had a baby then. Her sister was living with us. That was a tough time for us and we had to decide, "Hey, is all this worth it?" We decided it was, because my wife and I have a relationship which has always been, ah, she's the kind of gal who wants to do everything I want to do.

Ellen didn't really *want* to do everything Dick wanted to do, but like the wife of the Harvard Business School graduate she went along and said nothing to disabuse her husband. In the context of a discussion of GPI's reorganization, Ellen Watson said:

> I felt that he would come out of it okay. Which he did. He got a bigger area, more responsibility, rah! rah! and I guess if he hadn't I wouldn't have really cared. . . . He probably wouldn't like it if I said it so I probably shouldn't say it, but

> I really, personally, wouldn't mind going to Maine and cutting
> bait. But he would be very unhappy if he did not have a
> challenge.

The notion that their husbands' manhood called for the corporate challenge was another plank in the ideology that
kept women who might have wanted to "cut bait" from mentioning their own reluctance to keep up the corporate pace.
they feared their husbands' frustrated energies would over-
whelm the family should they ever cut away from the corporation. Fear of the loss of material well-being turned out
to be a much weaker goad to wifely reticence. Lisa VanDyke
put the matter into perspective:

> We've always been well off. We're always saying we're broke
> but we're not. People in these companies, we all have plenty
> of money. We don't think we do, but we really do. That's not
> really a problem. The only thing you're moving for is your
> husband's promotion. But a family can't go on just catering
> to this one person, to the goals of one person.

Because they had catered to the goals of their husbands,
most wives unwittingly put a subtle pressure upon their husbands. The better they played their parts—the less they complained and the more they acquiesced to the demands made
upon them—the more their husbands owed them in return.
The husbands saw their debt to their wives in terms of an
ever-increasing income. The income, of course, came from
the corporation. For the husband to be able to reward his
wife *he* had to be obedient to corporate demands, which again
forced him to make demands on his wife. Thus a spiral developed in which husbands and wives pressured each other to
accept the domination of the corporation.

The picture is clearest in the case of the two couples who
broke the cycle. Barbara Green and Lisa VanDyke were unusual among the corporation wives. They encouraged their

husbands to quit the corporation. Lisa tried for many years to get Jim to quit because she found the transfers exceedingly disruptive. For a long time she had to contend with Jim's resistance:

> One of the big arguments for slogging along, I know, is "We have this large family which we have to take care of and we can't afford to lose the job," which I always thought was perfectly silly.

She tried to convince Jim that that argument was silly:

> We went around the maypole on this so many times, and I'd say, "If we'd only stayed in Atlanta, we had that beautiful house and it was so cheap and we could have it all paid for," and my husband would say, "Well, I wouldn't have had a job either." And I just could never believe that two people, college graduates, fairly bright, who have a fair amount of ability between them, cannot live the way they want and raise this family without going to the poorhouse.

But she never was able to win Jim over, and without his concurrence there was nothing she felt she could do:

> I felt very strongly that the two of us, if we wanted to live a certain way and raise our family, that we could have made it.
> But I knew that if he didn't believe it there was no way we could make it. I always believed in him but if he didn't believe it, that was an unknown area that I couldn't predict. If he had to quit the company because I wanted him to, then I don't think we'd have made it. It also had to be his choice, but I never could convince him.

She complained that Jim consulted her about switching jobs but never about transferring:

> There were other opportunities. These guys are always getting offered other jobs, but somehow he was always very wedded to the idea of slogging onward in his company. When

he did leave, when he was thinking about it, he asked for my opinion. I said, "Well, it's entirely your choice," and then he said for the first time in twenty years, "Oh, no, I think you should help make the decision." Whereas if he had just asked me once along the way I would have been glad to make that decision. Now we knew it didn't count because we knew we weren't going to move anyway; it was just a matter of switching jobs.

It might not have counted to Lisa because this change wasn't going to upset *her* life, but Jim insisted that she share in the decision. His was a traditional notion of the implied if not spoken bargain struck in most marriages. He felt compelled to support the family to the best of his ability but he expected Lisa on her part to do all she could to help him, including following wherever his opportunities took him. By complaining about the transfers, Lisa was trying to change the terms of the bargain. She wished to set other goals besides highest possible income from Jim's job, and in return she was willing to share risks:

So when he told me that my opinion would make a difference, I said that it didn't make any difference at all, do what you want. And he said, "What if it doesn't work out?" So we made the decision—at least that was my part of the decision —that if it didn't work out, so what? We'd do something else.

That relaxed wifely attitude toward the possibility of failure seems to be a prerequisite to independence. Mrs. Green responded the same way to the question of failure:

We feel that if we fail (and we won't) we're only thirty-five years old and if we built up enough cash once in eight years to do this, we can do it again.

Few wives feel that self-sufficient. Restricted to their homes, without a vocation of their own, wives tend to become more dependent than their husbands. Jim VanDyke thought his situation was unusual:

> Lisa is different, but I suspect that most of these wives would resist their husband's leaving GPI. I really think they would. Because they've reached the level (most of the GPI people in Fairtown are at that level) where the security aspects of the thing are very deep.
>
> And you'd be amazed at how many people convert this to money. Let's say the guy's making thirty thousand a year and the wife considers it to be one of the top jobs and she gets that from her husband, who can't say otherwise to her—that he is doing real well and it is a lot of money and they've worked hard to get where they are and so on.
>
> So it's the security. People who started out making five thousand and are now making thirty-five thousand consider themselves to be doing pretty well, and GPI is treating them pretty good and they don't want to risk that.

The difference between the VanDykes and the other GPI families was not so much what they did all those years (for twenty years they averaged a move every other year) as it was the tensions under which they did it. While other women were accepting their roles and exchanging parables of bad wives, Lisa VanDyke was resisting. Her lack of effectiveness and the stress she placed on her marriage was probably a warning to the wives who knew her. Her story indicates why other women did not openly rebel but instead repressed whatever dissatisfactions they may have felt.

The Trivialization and Isolation of Opposition

Like most of the other corporate families, the VanDykes had been moved all over the country:

> We started out in Virginia when my husband was in the Marine Corps. Then we lived in Pennsylvania for almost five

years. Then we moved up here to New York for a while, then
we moved to Delaware, and from there we moved to Dallas
and then to Wisconsin. Then we moved to Atlanta and then
to California, then to Denver and then back to California and
then we came here.

Unlike the other wives, when the moves started bothering her,
Lisa was outspoken—even at company functions where other
wives would have noticed how she was being treated:

After a while, if you're a thinking person at all, it does pile
up on you. You just feel like a piece of baggage. And for a
while I got very vocal about it. I always said what I felt in
front of the boss, anybody.

There's one old man who always said, "Now, Lisa, you
don't still feel that way." And I'd say, "Oh, yes I do, stronger
than ever." And he'd say, "You'll realize that it was right and
it was not all that bad."

No one ever took me seriously. In fact, my whole complaint all those years was just put aside as silly female complaining. I'm sure people that know me at GPI think of me as
a complete nut.

Even her husband, though he didn't think of her as a "complete nut," could not understand why she didn't "go along"
as the other wives did:

Lisa started after we first moved to express her dissatisfaction
with this nomadic way of life. But I ignored her—as much as
you can ignore anybody like that. I ignored her because I
thought I knew all the answers. This was the right way to go
and she didn't know what she was talking about. That kind
of thing. This goes back a long time. I thought, "All the other
wives move, why don't you?" But I knew that that was her.
She's always been a little different. You cannot call her an
organization wife at all.

Comparing herself to those other wives, Lisa, too, wondered
how they managed, and why she couldn't do as well:

No one seemed to feel the way I did and I thought, "My God, these women must be nuts, what's wrong with them?" Then I got to the point where I thought, "Well it's me, it must be me." And I think my husband just saw me as a complainer. And I was, for years and years.

Her complaints fell on insensitive ears. Hers was a solitary voice. There was no one with whom she could share or even test her feelings.

Other corporation wives seemed not to be having the same problems:

I've never met anybody at all those company functions who thought even remotely the way I did. There really wasn't anybody that I got to know. I have one friend in Darien and I'm just crazy about her. They're with GPI and we've known each other a long time; our little girls were friends in Denver and we've lived in several parts of the country together. She's a wonderful person and every time she moves, and she's moved often, she just never complains. I am waiting for her to go through the roof one of these days. But I've never talked to her about moving. She's very hard to get really close to although we've been friends a long time.

Or, if there was another wife who felt as she did, Lisa sensed a danger in discussing such feelings with her:

My husband and Ellen Watson have talked about this at a party. She said the same thing. She really gave him an earful about her experiences with the company. And he said, "She feels the same way about it that you do, you and Ellen should get together," although we never did. It just didn't seem wise for two wives to get together and talk like that.

Friends outside GPI could be sympathetic, but, not having shared the same experiences, they did not really understand:

I did have one close friend in Denver and we used to talk about this quite a bit, but they had always lived there and

they just weren't aware of my problems. If it hadn't been for
Shirley and Ben I just don't think I could have ever gotten
out of Denver.

It was not until situations such as hers became the subject of
books and articles that Lisa VanDyke found the support she
needed:

When Betty Friedan's book came out we were living in Atlanta, I remember that very well. I remember reading the
book and thinking, "Gee, I'm not crazy." It was a real reve-
lation. I'd look at it every once in a while; I was thinking, "I
really am not nuts and isn't that a wonderful feeling."

Even then she still had to think of herself as being different
from the rest:

When Vance Packard's book came out he made a point that
I thought was very valid. It was only a paragraph in a chapter on what kinds of people don't move well. I know that I'm
very flexible so it's not that. But he listed other types, and
one was people that have such specialized interests that they
cannot find anyone else to identify with or that they have to
start all over each time they move—which was me exactly.
I showed it to my husband and said, "See, I'm not crazy after
all." He agreed with me. By that time he was coming around
to my way of thinking.

The specialized interest that kept Lisa VanDyke from
traveling well was her art. Though it gave her the strength to
resist the subordinate status to which she was being relegated,
a strength similar to the moral strength some men derived
from their professional training, she was able to pursue it
only at great personal cost:

I escaped from the whole thing by constantly going to school.
I entered about fourteen universities. I have a fantastic tran-
script. And that's the way I solved it because I knew I wasn't
going to be happy with the church work and the usual, so I

just, as soon as we moved, I got myself into school. My husband always said, "Settle in, we will never move again," and I don't know why I believed him all those years, but that never happened, so each time that I started over I truly did believe that I was going to finish. I had my bachelor's degree from Northwestern so I was always going for a master of fine arts or whatever was offered in my field. I never did get it.

But that did isolate me in a neighborhood where everybody else was doing something else. I remember I used to tell people, like when we lived in Dallas the company had a bowling team that met the night I was going to school, so I had to make something up as to why I couldn't bowl, because in those days ten, twelve years ago, no self-respecting company wife went to school at night. Heavens, that just wasn't done. Of course, now, everyone thinks it's great, but then everyone thought that it was a little weird and I just didn't want to explain it. I'd just get tired of explaining it.

Of course, there never was very much opportunity to get much of my own creative work done, and also the peace of mind to settle down and know what I was going to do. When you're in your early thirties and most artists are settling into what they want to do, there I was still working around, getting the furniture put in place every year, this kind of thing. So it really was difficult.

I think until the book came out and told me it was all okay, I was waiting for some kind of approval, and my husband certainly never said no, you can't do that or you can't go to school. I have friends whose husbands still tell them that they can't work or go to school but I never had that problem. I always went everywhere on my own, traveled everywhere. And he encouraged me, very much so. He would say, "Stop complaining and go back to school." But what he didn't provide was the practical means for me to do this. The maid, or whatever it was. So I was doing everything. It was almost like doing penance, although I'm sure he didn't look at it that way. He didn't realize what was involved. Since I was

> going to school or whatever it was and also raising the chil-
> dren and taking care of the house, it was almost like my
> punishment for doing my own thing after all this other work
> was done. I was always exhausted.

Since she had so much to do and had stretched her time
and energy so thin to do it all, Lisa was particularly sensitive
to corporate incursions upon her time:

> And there were many other problems. Things that you just
> can't believe. My husband's boss (this is really not funny)
> had a mentally retarded son. His wife was dead and he used
> to bring the boy out to us to see the horses every weekend
> that we were there. That's all you need. I was very sym-
> pathetic and it was a terribly painful situation, but it just
> became unbearable. It was there again, a connection with the
> company. We couldn't be nasty to the boss. You really
> couldn't. But we were being used. I know we were, but my
> husband was very kind and felt this was a very sad situation
> and they needed help. Didn't see it really for years.

It was only when the reward system failed that Lisa found
the argument which led Jim to begin to question the wisdom
of following the corporate way:

> We'd really enjoyed Atlanta, very easy living down there.
> We had this marvelous, very contemporary house. I was ex-
> cited about going to California. But California is very differ-
> ent from Georgia and the cost of living was so high. We paid
> twice as much for a house that could have been a guesthouse
> to our place in Atlanta, and here I was sitting in this dumb
> place and we got this big promotion and more money and
> here we are with half as much. And I think that's when it
> began to not make any sense even to Jim.

That was when Lisa gave full vent to her unhappiness. But
her haranguing almost destroyed her marriage:

> That's when I began to blow. I really had almost had it. And

it really almost did all blow up. When we moved here it was chaotic, absolutely chaotic. Because by that time I had built up ten, twelve years of this resentment and I must admit that I really was a bitch. I know I was. But I was trying to tell somebody that there was trouble, let's get help.

You know, these things build up and you think, "Why don't I get off that track, now why did I say that?" But I just don't think people are made that way. Ultimately you have to get it out.

Finally, to save her marriage, Lisa began to redirect her tirade:

I had thought about staying behind in California. I decided that I would stay there and slug it out, but I guess I didn't have the courage to do that. I could tell you all sorts of high-flown things but I felt that basically it wasn't my husband's fault. I felt that he was as much a victim of the system as I was. I think that that was really what it was more than anything. I felt as sorry for him as I felt for myself. And he didn't even know it, poor slob. He didn't know he was a victim. I told him. We had terrible arguments over it for years. Because that's where it all blows up, when you're feeling something that your husband isn't aware of.

Then I used to get so mad at the company; I couldn't get mad at my husband. I knew that I shouldn't, so I'd get furious with the company. I wouldn't buy the products and I'd complain about the products just to get even with them, because I felt I had no recourse. I mean my only recourse would have been to leave him; to break up my home.

To avoid that she raged against GPI. Even she had to laugh at her own impotence:

I think I may get over my mad at the corporation at some future date, although I rather doubt it. But it was really like bearing resentment against a living thing, which is really silly.

But she never stopped wondering how the other women managed:

> I think we overcame a lot of our problems but I just can't believe people can stay married on this trip. I think it may be possible where the wife doesn't have too many plans for her own life. And a lot of people with the company that I like very much would fall into that category. I know one gal who just doesn't mind moving and moving and moving, and finally one day I decided this kid is really crazy because she never wants to settle down to commit herself to anything. . . . I just don't see how that's possible.

More than being just possible, it was common for corporation wives to be without the training or temperament to have interests of their own.

While she was being interviewed, Lisa was preparing some work for an art show. She talked about a book she had been commissioned to write and a course she would be giving the following semester at the Brooklyn Museum Art School. She acknowledged the fact that she drew strength from her professional success and that without it she would not have been able to discuss the problems of being a GPI wife:

> Now that I've found my own level, I can talk about it. A couple of years ago I could not have talked about it.

Most of the other wives had no such serious professional interest. One was a trained nurse but had given that up when her first child was born. Another had worked for a while with the Fairtown police force, but stopped when she became pregnant again. Yet another had played the organ for her church in the Midwest, but the church of her denomination in Fairtown had no need for her services, so she was hoping something else would come up but it hadn't yet; she had moved to Fairtown eight months before the interview.

Two wives were involved in the community life of Fairtown: one was on the board of directors of the League of

Women Voters, the other was active in the local Women's Political Caucus. Even for these women, as for all the GPI wives except Lisa VanDyke, feminism was a threat, not a support. There was one question in the interviews with the wives that invariably boomeranged. When asked what they thought of the women's liberation movement, the women would answer with the question, "What do *you* think of it?"

A few words about equal pay for equal work would settle things, and the discussion could turn to other matters such as the ways in which corporate families coped with their problems. That was a subject the women could warm to.

Patterns

If they could do nothing to prevent repeated disruptions of their homes, there was much wives could do to minimize the attendant hardships. These expedients formed the patterns of corporate lives. To ease the way to new friendships for children and adults, they chose neighborhoods where others were likely to be similar to themselves; to ease the problems of buying and selling, they chose houses without distinction; to ease the sense of rootlessness they made believe and tried to live in every community "as if" they were to be there a long time, or they continued even after a decade or more of marriage to call their parents' place "home"; and when problems became too pressing for denial but still not within their control, they trivialized them.

It was with their children that the tendency to deny or trivialize problems was most apparent. Only Frank Auslander took the problems a child had with transfers seriously enough to let it guide his actions. After a transfer that had caused his son unhappiness he decided never again to force the boy to move. Instead he spent weekends with his family and weekdays at the distant job site. "I'll take the extra traveling," he said, "mostly because I don't want to disrupt the children." Then he thought awhile and added, "Everybody says children adjust quickly. That's true. Also they never adjust."

Children find new friends, though many become loners. They get through their days at school, albeit less successfully than nontransient children with similar capacity and background.[22] And whatever psychic wounds they bear are usually hidden. A woman of forty, whose engineer father was one of the earliest transient managers, told of a recurrent dream she was still having:

> We moved almost every year and I remember that we would move in the summer. They sent me to my aunt's house for the summer and when I came back home it was always to a new home which I had to get used to. I don't think it was all bad because we have a very close family but I still occasionally have this awful nightmare: I'm walking down a street trying to find my house because I want my mother for something, and I open the door to this house which I think is mine but it turns out that it's not mine, my mother isn't there; and I keep going from house to house but I can't find my place.

When the tears over lost friends stopped, most mothers and fathers assumed the adjustment was complete. It was part of the corporate ideology that until they were of high school age children could not be harmed by repeated partings from their friends. Betty Corelli, who could not have been speaking from experience because her elder daughter was not yet in high school, mouthed the company line:

> As they get older I think it's harder for them. When they're younger they make friends easily. They run up to anybody and say "Hi" and play with them. But as they get older they choose their friends and it takes a little while. That's why I want to settle now, because my daughter's going into high school and once they get into the upper grades I think they find it hard to move.

A young woman who was about to move reflected the same opinion when she discussed the effect she thought the change would have on her four-year-old son:

> He has a few playmates here; he has a kid next door and there's a little girl up the street that he's played with. I think he'll miss them, in fact I know he will because when we moved from Portchester there was a little boy down the hall that he played with and he still talks about. He'll miss them, but as long as there are other children to play with he won't be heartbroken.

To prevent broken hearts and to be sure there will be other children around to play with, managers have devised several techniques for choosing neighborhoods. One woman explained how she and her husband did it:

> Usually when we choose a house we think of the kids and try to go into an area where we know there'll be a bunch of kids the age group of our kids. We ride around about three o'clock and see where the kids get off the school bus. If there's a bunch of kids in the area where you're looking at getting off the bus, then you have a pretty good idea that there are a bunch of kids there. I guess on occasion we've gone off to a neighbor's house and asked them.

By making sure there would be youngsters for their children to play with, transient couples were also guaranteeing companionship for themselves. The woman continued:

> Once we moved into an area that was not our age group. Right in our immediate area there weren't enough kids and we were just learning to move at that time. Now we know when we move, first of all to make sure you move into a community where people will have similar likes and be in a similar experience as you. Usually if you're in the same age group as the other people you'll have similar experiences, or likes and dislikes as far as experiences, so you try to move

into an area where if you have a couple of kids three years old that there's people of a similar age group around there. Usually it happens that you find people that you enjoy being with just because you have that common age.

One peculiarity of the managers and their wives was the ease with which they could tick off the exact ages of their friends and neighbors. The man who said he had no close or semiclose friends in the neighborhood explained that they were all older than he was:

I guess Jack is in his early forties, and Dave's in his late thirties and Malcolm must be in his late thirties and the people next door, Stuart's in his late forties. I'm thirty-five. The man to the left of me is in his mid-forties. The guy across the street is in his late fifties. So it's a much older profile than we've ever been used to. I think I'm the youngest just in this general local area. I was one of the older ones in Chicago. We were in the upper tenth percentile in the age range there. In Charlotte we were about the same. The reason being the house in Charlotte took the same amount of money as the one in Chicago. So when we moved from Chicago we did not upgrade. Even though we were getting more money we didn't think it was necessary. And it worked well. We could have afforded more but it would have put us with people a little bit older.

Men like this one, who rise rapidly at the corporation, have a problem. If they buy the most expensive house they can afford, they will find themselves in a neighborhood where others are at their income level but are older. With only a few months in which to make friends, it is important for them to move to a place where there will be as few differences as possible between themselves and others. On the other hand, if they buy a less expensive house, their families might complain, since it is only through a rising standard of living, expressed most significantly in the houses they buy, that a family can share in the managers' rewards. Jim VanDyke explained why each new house had to be better than the last one:

> You know, if I'd tried to buy a fifty-thousand-dollar house in Fairtown I wouldn't have gotten very much. I would have gotten a hell of a lot less than I'd had already. That would have seemed like a step backward. The path of least resistance is that you spend a lot more so that doesn't happen. The kids are gonna say, "Jesus, this big promotion looks like it set us back, Daddy." You don't want to hear that. You hear enough of that from Lisa.

So the house has to be bigger and better, even if that means that the other people in the neighborhood might be somewhat older or in a later stage of family development. The houses they choose must also be easily salable and in transient communities. There are, in suburban communities all over the United States, two sorts of neighborhoods: one for transient corporation managers and one for the more permanent residents who work in the peripheral economy.

The two exist side by side but there is little interchange between them. Because they and their places are new and flashy, the managers seem to be taking over; but those managers who landed unwittingly in an established neighborhood know that the other economy with its sort of people is still very much alive. One of the managers analyzed the situation:

> I would say that if you went to every individual part of the country, every metropolitan area, that you could find in every individual section two types of community. You're going to run into the situation where you have a couple of streets where people are very friendly and outgoing and you can develop a good relationship. And you'll find in another area of that same town a neighborhood where the people are maybe more local and they have their own local friends and there aren't as many transients and a new person moves into the area and they don't warm up to them and don't want to

get to know them as well. I think you can find that anywhere. So the communities themselves that we've lived in were very transient where people were continuously moving in and out. And they don't change much. Those communities are similar from one part of the country to another.

But if the communities they seek are similar from one part of the country to another, what happens to the adventure, to the excitement, and, most important, to the personal growth that might have come from their movement and turned the managers and their wives into intellectually alert cosmopolitans? [23] The answer is that it is lost. Robert Park made a distinction between human movement that is occasional and movement that is habitual. The first awakens sensibilities made somnolent by repetition and ordinariness. It pits one culture against another, enriching both. The second does nothing of the sort. It is, culturally, no different from sedentariness:

> Migration is not . . . to be identified with mere movement. . . . The movements of gypsies and other pariah peoples, because they bring about no important changes in cultural life, are to be regarded rather as geographical fact than social phenomenon. Nomadic life is stabilized on the basis of movement.[24]

Managerial families whose lives are stabilized on the basis of movement and on the basis of patterns that seal them off from other peoples and other cultures are in many ways more isolated than they would have been in the city ghettos or small towns they left. At least in those places they would have had the opportunity to come close to others older or younger than themselves. In their age-graded, income-graded subdivisions, the members of managers' families are cut off from the experiences of life. Never seeing others pass through the stages of life that they are approaching, their future is always as it was in their adolescence—fearsome and unpredictable. They are, as Richard Sennett has observed of suburbanites,[25] locked into an eternal adolescence. That adolescence is, however, caused neither by a willful refusal to grow nor by a craven fencing out of others, but by the managers' need to structure that part of their world which they can control so that they are not utterly cut off from others. What appears to be a closing in is, in fact, a reaching out.

Nonetheless, when initiations lead not to responsibility but to servitude, then men and women are turned into "specialists without vision" and "sensualists without heart"—a warning uttered half a century ago by Max Weber, who saw large impersonal organizations taking over the work and order of modern communities.[26]

PART 3

IN THE COMMUNITY

CHAPTER 7

Two Worlds

Corporation managers are popularly called nomads and gypsies. Those labels are misleading, for managers, unlike nomads and gypsies, do not take their whole social world with them when they move. A more apt analogy would be with soldiers or priests—persons who work for centrally headquartered but geographically dispersed organizations. But here again there is a crucial difference. The army and the Catholic Church are total institutions: they provide a complete social environment for their personnel. Except in rare cases, usually on compounds in foreign countries, corporations do not do that.

Thus the corporation does not provide a civic life for its managers and their families. Nor does it permit one. Because managerial families must move frequently, and because managers must devote virtually all their time and energies to the corporation even when they are geographically stable, their reachings out beyond the spheres of work and family are weak and stunted. They have to depend on ongoing communities where others maintain the social structures. Managers live in communities but seldom become part of them.

Being in, but not of, community is a difficult distinction, one that can best be made by drawing comparisons. Shortly after completing the interviews with the GPIers, I had the opportunity to interview and observe another group of Fairtowners, one different from the managers, especially in the ways they related to the Fairtown community. These were the members of the Republican and Democratic Town Committees, the persons who managed the local political parties. There happened to be an almost equal number of Town Committee (TC) members—thirty-six—as there were GPI families. Five of them, one a GPIer, worked for "*Fortune* 100" corporations, and those five were similar to the GPI group in so many ways that they will not be included in the following comparisons. The others were local merchants, contractors, schoolteachers, housewives, independent professionals, and managers or technicians for firms too small to have more than a branch or two. Almost all had lived in Fairtown for more than six years (four had grown up in town), and none was considering leaving town in the near future.

The average income of the two groups was also about the same, but the range was far greater among the TC members. There were a couple of millionaires among them and a few with family incomes in the midteens. It was neither the range nor the amount, however, but the source of their incomes that made a difference. TC members worked in the peripheral economy while GPIers worked in the center economy. Virtually all the social differences between these two groups were related to differences in their spheres of work.

Persons attached to the center economy, such as GPI's managers, need a world that is easily understood, a world where creature comforts are provided without social complications and where identity and status are quickly read. Those in the peripheral economy, persons such as the TC members, lead stable lives and build over the years complicated relationships and idiosyncratic communities. In Fairtown, the GPIers' sort of world was being superimposed upon the TC members' sort of world, the latter serving as a base for the former.

GPIers and TC members were a part of each other's environment. Yet, though they may have passed on the street or in the shops or sat next to each other at school functions, few from one group had ever been introduced to any from the other. Members of the town groups led different kinds of lives. TC members were geographically stable, GPIers were transient; TC members had risen slightly or not at all above the economic and social status of their parents, GPIers were extremely upwardly mobile; TC members were deeply involved in town affairs, GPIers had virtually no interest in local matters. They shopped in different kinds of stores, approached political life differently, and enjoyed different kinds of friendship with different sorts of people. In short, they lived in sharply contrasting social worlds.

Gemeinschaft and Gesellschaft

Some say sociology was born of the need to understand and describe those two kinds of social worlds; or, more precisely, to explain the social order that came with the industrial revolution. As people moved from small, self-enclosed feudal estates, where everyone knew those they might see in a day or a year, to large industrial cities, where most encounters were with strangers, and as the few statuses of feudal times expanded into the many interrelated, specialized roles and ranks of modern times, social life changed drastically. The less there was of a stable, lucid social order, the more there was a need to discover the underlying patterns that would explain the surface confusion and make social life predictable once again.

The most influential concept developed to explain the differences between industrial societies and the social order from which they sprang was Ferdinand Toennies' *Gemeinschaft* and *Gesellschaft*.[1] Scholars who attempted to find English words for those two German terms usually settled for "community" and "society," which wasn't quite what Toennies had in mind; so today most sociologists rely on explanations, not translations.

Gemeinschaft societies are small and relatively unchanging. They are based on intimate, face-to-face, rounded associations —primary relationships that emerge from proximity and a sharing of fates and understandings. Gesellschaft is the opposite. It signifies a social order based on instrumental, rational (not emotional), limited relationships. These come about through contracts, actual or implied, and do not, as in gemeinschaft relationships, necessarily emerge from social and physical proximity.

It would be a gross oversimplification to say that the Fairtown of the TC members was a gemeinschaft or that the Fairtown of the GPIers was a gesellschaft, but if one thinks of these two types as polar points on a continuum, then it seems fair to say that virtually all of Fairtown's social life pointed toward the gesellschaft side; but most of what was gemeinschaftlike about Fairtown was made that way by the social and civic activities of the TC members and others like them, and most of what was gesellschaftlike had come with the arrival of the GPIers and others like them. Not that the GPIers were willfully turning the town into a gesellschaft. Quite the contrary. Most GPIers chose Fairtown for its gemeinschaft qualities. But then, once having come to town, they were put off by the insularity of the older residents and did not attempt to break down their barriers; instead they sought substitutes for or shortcuts to a gemeinschaft social life.

To show these differences and to bring out the dynamics of the two worlds, we will start at the most obvious point by describing the physical settings TC members and GPIers inhabited; these physical settings are the outward reflections of the different sorts of social interactions they sheltered. From there we shall move on to the neighborhoods. For though the esthetic sensibilities of TC members and GPIers were much the same—even if they caused dissimilar physical structures to be built—what each group wanted from its neighborhood was markedly different. GPIers looked to the neighborhood as the source of any relationships they might have outside the family or work, but the sort of quick-turnover neighborhood that could provide such speedy sociability was precisely the sort

TC members disparaged. Neighborhoods that met the needs of one group caused problems for the other. More important even than the difference in what they wanted was the difference between the two groups in how they went about getting it. TC members did what they could to *create* a social environment that was to their liking; GPIers looked for one that was *ready-made*. The first were world-makers, the second were world-users—a difference arising mainly from a sense shared by TC members that they could form their world and from a sense shared by GPIers that they could not.

After examining these issues, we shall turn in the next chapter to the subject of friendships, and conclude this section with some observations on the TC members' and the GPIers' contrasting influence on local politics.

Social Relationships Reflected in Physical Settings

Fairtown's center, about three blocks long and in the middle of town, has been the place to shop and meet for more than ten generations of Fairtowners. Town Hall, an old gray stone building approached by four deep steps on which people often stop to chat, stands at one corner. The police station is just behind it and the firehouse, served by volunteer firemen and a small paid staff, is down the block. Across the street from Town Hall is Brown's, an even better place to stop and chat as evidenced by the small clusters of people who are there on most fair days. Brown's is a stationery store where, if Mr. Brown knows you, you can drop off small packages or messages for friends to pick up later.

With its small shops and village ambiance, the center is one of Fairtown's major attractions. Some GPIers said it reminded them of their hometowns:

> I think the reason that we really chose Fairtown was that it felt more like a town to us. On the day that we were house-hunting, we went into that little restaurant and sat at the

counter because we were in a hurry and were just going to have a sandwich. Every time the door opened we looked up. After about the third time, Ted asked me why I kept looking up every time the door opened, and I said that I had the feeling that I was going to know somebody who walked in. And he had the same feeling. I think we just felt comfortable.

GPIers were attracted by the sense of gemeinschaft that permeates the town center, but few of them ever became a part of the social relationships that created it. As the population of Fairtown doubled between 1960 and 1970, those who were part of the community at the beginning of the expansion continued in their small-town ways almost untouched by the newcomers. Few of the newcomers, and none who did not stay in town at least two years, were able to find their way into that longstanding Fairtown community. Instead, some built separate institutions such as the Newcomers' Club, which organized entertainments at which new arrivals could meet and whose only requirement for membership was that one's residence in Fairtown did not exceed two years.

The new physical structures in Fairtown reflected the new social structures. Because of the large and rapid influx, the area that had never been home to more than four thousand until the end of World War II had to serve more than eighteen thousand by 1970, and that required much rapid building. First, lots behind the main-street stores were cleared for parking and more stores. Then, by 1970, something larger was called for. So, about two miles north of the old center, a new shopping center was built. With its vast parking field surrounded by glass and aluminum storefronts, it had the standardized look of shopping centers from coast to coast.

When the shopping center was proposed, the Planning and Zoning commissioners tried hard to keep it from altering the appearance of Fairtown. They restricted the height of buildings and the size and color of signs. McDonald's applied for a sign permit but was told that its yellow double arches were not acceptable. If Fairtown didn't want the double arches, McDonald's decided it didn't want Fairtown—a decision most GPIers, and even a couple of the TC members who had small children, resented and blamed on the backwardness of the Planning and Zoning Commission. A GPI mother remarked:

> Some of their building codes are quite outdated. I'd love to see a McDonald's come to town. My children love McDonald's.

Why would the Planning and Zoning Commission want to keep out a McDonald's while some citizens would welcome it? Probably because a McDonald's exemplified for the commissioners the erosion of gemeinschaft.

The surface sameness of all McDonald's promises a corresponding social sameness. Not only are the buildings and signs all alike, but the workers as well are made to look and act as if they were products of cloning. At every outlet, employees are required to don the same uniform and trained to treat each customer in a prescribed manner. It is not so much McDonald's efficient service that makes it appealing to children; luncheonettes can serve up food in as little time. What is fast about McDonald's "fast food" is its uniformity, as in a fast dye. Shoppers who have no time to become familiar with local peculiarities prefer national franchises.

Luncheonettes are different—one from another, as well as from McDonald's. They are usually run by their owners, and customers can seldom predict what they will get in the way of food or mood unless they've been patronizing the place for a while. Most of those who eat at the luncheonette in Fairtown *have* been going there for years.

I ate at the Fairtown luncheonette twice—once when I was interviewing the GPIers and a year later, after I had met the TC members. The first time, I noticed the lunchers chatted amiably from table to table. When the door opened they all looked up; usually they recognized the new arrival. There was banter and exchange of opinions and news. I didn't know whom or what they were talking about, and unlike the GPI couple I felt a bit uncomfortable—left out. The second time, I did know some of the people there, and I knew what they were talking about. They were members of the Republican Town Committee. By that time I had learned that the luncheonette was a place some Republican TC members frequented and that a liquor store down the block, owned by a Democratic TC member, was where some Democratic TC members often gathered.

The luncheonette in Fairtown's center, or the liquor store, or any of the shops where some of the same persons came each day for camaraderie and necessities; where the business of the town was decided over a purchase; where, in other words, several activities were mixed—these were gemeinschaftlike. McDonald's and supermarkets in shopping centers are gesellschaftlike. The first form settings for community; the second do not.

Philip Slater has observed that "community life exists when one can go daily to a given location at a given time and count on seeing most of the people one wants to see." [2] That overstates the case for most TC members, but there are some for whom it is an apt description. One such is the Republican vice-chairperson, a woman who celebrated her eightieth birthday in 1974, having spent fifty of those years in Fairtown. Every day she picked up her newspaper at Brown's, then strolled over to Town Hall to visit with a couple of relatives and some friends who worked there, then on to the luncheonette. She spread the local news of the day as she made her rounds. If she didn't appear and had made no explanations, people at Brown's, at the Town Hall, and at the luncheonette would ask each other if she had been seen that day. If not, someone would try to find out what had happened to her.

It was that kind of caring that attracted W. H. Auden back to Oxford after he had lived for two decades in New York City. "I'm getting rather old to live alone in winter and I'd rather live in community," he said. "At Oxford," he explained, "I should be missed if I failed to turn up for meals." [3]

Slater and Auden seem to be in substantial agreement about the meaning of community. It's a place where people expect to see each other each day without making special plans. The same, of course, can be said about homes and workplaces. However, a defining characteristic of community is that the people who meet each day are usually not members of the same family, nor do they work together; yet without the force of life-sustaining functions that bring families and work groups together, persons in communities become part of the daily routine of each other's lives. Family and work are necessary, community in the modern world is voluntary. Whatever life-sustaining qualities it might have are emotional, not physical.

Most TC members did not go down to the center each day, but they went there often, and when they did they could be pretty sure of meeting someone they knew. GPIers stayed away. For them the center was only for shopping, not for socializing; and as a place to shop they found it wanting. The stores in the center "are overpriced," they said; "too small"; "not enough variety"; "some of them look like they're falling apart." The woman whose comfortable meal at the luncheonette convinced her that Fairtown was the place for her didn't eat there or shop anyplace else in the center once she moved in. "The shopkeepers down there are rude," she complained. "They act as though they're doing you a favor even to acknowledge that you're there."

Actually, the local shopkeepers, most of them, are not rude, but they have only recently had to deal with strangers, and many have not yet learned that graceful, surface warmth that managerial families, who except for each other hardly communicate with any but strangers, have mastered so well. Most often anyone entering a center shop will find the salespersons chatting with each other or with a customer or two. A familiar can join the conversation, but a stranger must interrupt or wait patiently. GPIers feel roughly treated when their business is conducted with few pleasantries and much dispatch, after they've been standing around hardly being noticed while the merchant and the other shoppers converse.

It takes a special kind of circumstance for persons new to town to be noticed by the more permanent community. A week after one GPI couple moved in, their son was in an automobile accident. He suffered no permanent injury, but the accident was serious enough to be written up in the local weekly. That unveiled for the family an aspect of Fairtown that other GPIers never saw. The boy's mother told what happened:

> This is one thing that we have noticed here, people that we come into contact with, they are just all so nice. A perfect example was when we had that accident. There were so many people we did not know who phoned and said, "Can I do something for you?" or brought food here. A barber called after we were home and said, "I know your son was hurt badly and I wondered if I could be of some help to you by coming to your home and cutting his hair." Just things like this that we were just overwhelmed by the concern of people that we did not even know.

The concern of people they do not know is something not likely to be experienced by TC members. The strangers who offered their assistance to this family knew from the news story that they were new to town and would not have friends and family around to help. That's why they called. In similar circumstances a TC member could depend upon friends and acquaintances.

A case in point was the experience of a TC member whose son had recently died. When I interviewed her, she spoke freely and critically about the other politicos. But about some her opinions were tempered. Though they were her political foes, they had come to her side at her son's death and then she learned of a generosity and kindness that political competition and her own sharp tongue had kept hidden. She still condemned their political views, but she added that although they were politically misguided, they were "good people."

One difference, then, between the world of the GPIers and the world of the TC members is that in the former a personal tragedy brings out the kindness of strangers, who after the incident remain strangers, while in the latter it brings out hidden facets of both friends and foes. Community exists when there are many connections between individuals so that every interaction builds upon those that went before and also prepares for the next. Over time the social roots of those who belong to a community become intertwined, and a labyrinthine pattern of relationships develops.

Houses and Neighborhoods
Just as the GPIers were first attracted by the glow of Fairtown's gemeinschaftlike commercial center but could find no way to tap its core and then became angered and turned away to more gesellschaftlike establishments, so they were first attracted by the residential settings TC members inhabited, but finding no way to become part of them, turned to settlements of their own that were more quickly accepting and more gesellschaftlike.

Except for the center and the commercial strip along the state highway north of the center, Fairtown is almost entirely residential. There are areas where houses have been added one at a time over more than two centuries, and new developments where scores of houses were built at once. Visitors and house hunters coming to Fairtown are likely to get their impression of the town from its older residential areas, not from the new developments. The latter have roads that lead nowhere but to the houses in the developments. Older houses stand along the state or town roads, the ones used to get around town. So when one drives through town it seems to be untouched by the developer's hand. And that is what GPIers liked. A woman who had recently moved from Indianapolis gave a typical explanation of why her family had chosen Fairtown:

> When we lived in New Jersey, my husband worked with a gentleman who lived in Fairtown (they no longer do) and we came over here on a Sunday to visit and just fell in love with the town. So when the transfer from Indianapolis came about, there really was not much question in our minds about where we were going to live.
>
> We just thought it was the quaintest little town and oh, the ponds and the hills. And all the trees which we did not have in New Jersey and we did not have in Indianapolis. I don't know, it's more rural, more country; we just thought it was a lovely town.

But the house she bought was not in the kind of setting she described. It was on land smoothed by a bulldozer and left treeless by a chain saw. All over Fairtown there were places where builders had turned the landscape from woods and winding country roads to treeless expanses with horseshoe-shaped drives lined by large, regularly spaced, identically designed houses. One contractor had built more and larger developments than any other. His name was Bonate, and "Bonate" was a catchword for all that TC members and other long-term residents found distasteful about the new developments where managers lived. The accepted TC wisdom was that Bonate houses, though spacious, were overpriced and poorly built, tending to fall apart even as they were being put together, and that their inhabitants were an impecunious lot who had been able to purchase the houses only because Bonate, unlike more responsible builders, offered second mortgages and low down payments. Even so, it was said, new owners of Bonate houses had used up their small savings at the closing and so had nothing left for furnishings. Their dwellings were bare.

Two GPI families (no TC members) lived in Bonate developments and, as if purposely to fit the stereotype, their living rooms held but two or three pieces of furniture. But the rooms were deeply carpeted. In fact, there seemed to be an inverse relationship between the height of a manager's position at GPI and the depth of his carpet at home. But that was only an impression.

Another impression, more dependable because the ten GPI homes that did not fit the pattern stood out in sharp contrast, was that GPI's families lived in environments that resembled chain motels. All the comforts that could be desired were provided, but there was nothing unique inside or outside.

Most GPIers did try to put some individual mark on their house. Over the fireplace in a few homes there hung large photographic or painted portraits of the children of the household. Or, more commonly, wedding pictures or photographs of the couple's parents would stand on a side table. In the interviews many of the women made a point of mentioning some object they owned—a large grandfather clock, an oversize breakfront—which meant that real estate agents would have to show them something special; just any house wouldn't do.

Nonetheless, there was a sameness from one house to another almost as predictable as the sameness from one McDonald's to another. One woman who was especially sensitive to the prosaic quality of her home explained why, even if the house didn't suit her family's taste, it was nonetheless the sort of place she had to live in:

> I have one friend, she's very insulting. She looked at my house and she said, "Are you really happy living in an ordinary house?" I should have slugged her. Yes, she lives in

an unusual house. But not everybody can have a very special house. We bought this house with the idea that it would be a very easy house to sell in case GPI decided to transfer us. It's a house most people would find no objections to. The house that she bought was on the market for two years before someone bought it. . . . A house has to meet your basic needs but it can't be something oddball where only one in ten million people would like it. Especially if you have to get rid of it fast when a company says they're going to transfer you. You have to be able to move within a couple of months at least.

Many GPI managers and their wives said they enjoyed fixing up their homes, but most chose only projects that would enhance the house's market value. Once a transfer was in sight, they stopped doing anything at all. The woman just transferred from Indianapolis explained why she would rather not know of an impending transfer too far in advance:

In Indianapolis, I knew a year before we left that we were going to be transferred and I don't like that because there were so many things that I wanted to do to the house like change the wallpaper here, change the carpeting there, do all those things. But whenever you know that you're going to leave it and you also know that you're not going to get any more money for the house, then it just takes all the incentive out of it. So we did absolutely nothing except keep the yard up and that sort of thing.

A few GPI families grew so involved in the chance for financial gain provided by a move that their residence became more a business than a home. One man who had been transferred eight times in ten years insisted that he and his wife had had enough, and no matter what offers he had to turn down, he would not leave Fairtown. But after four years in one house they moved to another, and they planned to move again as soon as they had made their present house more salable:

> We'd move within this town. We just did three weeks ago. We did this as an investment and someday we'll sell this house. I probably wouldn't be doing that if we hadn't been transferred. I got a taste for it after I bought a couple of houses and found out what you could do with it if you worked hard on the house. You fix it up, put the gingerbread on it, and make a nice profit. See, I made forty thousand dollars on the house I just sold. . . .
>
> You've got to watch what you put into a house to get the money out. Don't put in swimming pools; that will detract from the sale of the house. In some cases, people don't want a pool; you can't get any more. . . . Things that you'll get your money back on are additions to the home: recreation rooms are a big factor if you can fix up a basement or do something to that effect. You can't get carpet back. All it does is enhance your home, makes it salable.

There's a vacant look to houses whose owners reside there with an eye to the market, houses that are kept up or altered so as to appeal to the largest possible number of buyers. It's a look TC members disparaged. One told a story about a couple who had been transferred so often that they had grown to like the barrenness of new developments. Nonetheless, they bought an older home that was surrounded by established lilac bushes. The couple cut the lilacs down. "The house looked newer without them," they said.

The story is probably apocryphal, telling us more about the way Fairtown's stable population regards its more transient half than about the transients' taste. Still, there was an obvious difference between the homes of GPIers and TC members. TC members' homes were not so neat; such things as magazines lying around, music stacked on pianos, plants grown lush with attention and age, or the corner of a couch scratched ragged by the family cat—all this attested to the care and carelessness of families whose homes were for living, not for selling.

Almost all the TC members lived in the same Fairtown house they had bought years earlier. If their incomes or family needs had increased to a point where they wanted a bigger house, they made improvements on the one they had. They stayed in one place so that their social surroundings would not change. That was odd, because the TC members did not depend, as the GPIers did, upon the neighborhood as a source of friends.

Good Places and Bad Places: GPIers

GPIers all said that the most difficult aspect of transfers was leaving friends. Yet almost all were willing to leave anytime a good opportunity presented itself, claiming as one woman did: "We find we can make friends anywhere." They argued that their feelings for the friends they had left were not diminished by infrequency of contact: if it was really a good friendship they could pick up right where they left off whenever they got together again. But distant friends could not have satisfied the need for nearby friends, for almost all GPIers judged the places they had lived in by the speed with which they had made new friends. They preferred "fast-friends" neighborhoods.

There were two characteristics common to all places where neighbors were friendly and easily met. First, they were homogeneous; all the neighbors were at about the same age, income, and stage in family development. Second, none of the neighbors had lived there very long. The woman from Indianapolis explained why that was the best place she had ever moved to:

> We were amazed. We were in our house for about ten days and one of the couples that lived in our neighborhood was

going and our neighbors had sort of decided they would have a little farewell party for them; very simple spur-of-the-moment sort of thing. . . . So they called and asked us if we'd come down. Now there were about twenty-eight people there and out of those twenty-eight there was only one couple that were natives of Indianapolis. Everybody else had been transferred there. Our house was four years old and there were some there that were like six years old when we bought ours and there had already been quite a bit of turnover from what we heard.

Then she described the worst place:

Once when we first moved to New Jersey we rented a house for a year and it was a brand-new house but it was in a much much older neighborhood and that was the only place that I was ever miserable. Not that I have anything against older people, don't misunderstand me now, I have absolutely nothing against older people, but they had been born and raised there and these were people like sixty years old and at that time we were much younger and the children were just little things, so we really had absolutely nothing in common, and neither did the children because there were no little children there.

New Jersey also received bad marks from another woman whose first transfer had brought her there:

When we went to New Jersey that was really my awakening. Good Lord, I hated it with a passion. Everybody was so cold. We lived in a two-family house and we lived there a year and a half and it's the only place we've lived that we don't have a single person we send a Christmas card to. The houses on the street, there were several two-family houses that were quite new, but I guess the rest of the street was eight, nine, or ten years old, I don't know. It wasn't a development or anything. But I didn't even get to know my neighbors.

Cindy was about fifteen months old and I was just pregnant

with Jamie and my husband was traveling a great deal. They went out on Saturday and they'd stay for two weeks and then they'd come back, and there were a whole bunch of fellows who were doing the same thing, so the only companionship I had were the other GPI wives.

Well, I was working in the kitchen one day and we lived on a hill that went up quite steeply and there were other houses in the back but you couldn't walk in the back unless you were a mountain goat. I saw a playpen on a porch up there, and I thought, "Ha, there's somebody with a child." So after I got my dishes done, I dressed Cindy and went up and knocked on the door. And I had some stupid excuse like what store do you recommend for so and so, I'm Carol Wells, and I just moved here and I wonder if you could tell me. I thought it up as I went along. The door opened and she looked at me for a moment and then she said to come in and she gave me a cup of coffee. We chatted for a few minutes and she seemed like a real nice girl, which she was. I went on my merry way. The next day the phone rang and she invited us up for dinner. I had just gotten back from church, and when I got up there she said, "You know, Carol, I was so shocked when you came to the door yesterday, that I didn't even think about asking you if you would like to come up and have dinner with us. It's a good thing you came to my house and not anybody else's on the street because you probably would have gotten the door slammed in your face."

And it's true. Nobody there wanted anything to do with you. She was just a nice person and she had little kids, so we had something in common that way. But even with that, we never became really good friends. I liked her and I think she liked me and we were both the same age but they had lots of family in the area and lots of longtime established friends and she just didn't need anybody.

Most managers learned to avoid long-established neighbor-hoods and find the more transient ones where they would be needed as much as they needed others. But some were not so careful when they came to Fairtown, and for them it was as difficult a place to find friends in as New Jersey had been for the other two women. One woman who had not chosen her neighborhood carefully enough gave her assessment of Fairtown:

> I can't really say the people in this area are very friendly. Unless you get into Newcomers' Club you really don't get to meet any of your neighbors. You have to go out and make an effort to meet people. . . . I've gradually met my neighbors but it's been through the children or walking around canvassing for United Fund or something like that. But other than that, except for the couple next door, I really don't know my neighbors very well at all.

Some, however, knew a different Fairtown. They had moved into a larger development where recreational facilities and neighborhood associations encouraged meetings between neighbors. A woman with teenage children felt grateful she had happened upon one such neighborhood:

> Lakeside Acres is our saving grace because this is an association of a hundred families here on the hill, and we have that beach down at the bottom. About everybody here has moved from someplace else and it is great. The second day we moved in teenagers were coming up to say, "We hear you have teenagers in your family," and invited them to go down to the beach and to do this and that.

The Bonate developments, for all their reputed short-comings, have pools and tennis courts and community associations. The two GPI couples living in them did not complain of the coldness of Fairtown's people. Indeed, one of the men was president of his community association. But for the rest, for those living in established areas or in developments too small to have formal organizations, getting to know the neighbors was difficult. Some never did.

One summer's day, driving to an interview, I was stopped by a moving van pulling out. A woman standing by the curb was watching it. She waved to me. I waved back.

"We're moving to Florida," she called.

"Oh," I said, "is it a transfer?"

"Yes. I hate to leave."

"It's not bad down there," I said.

"I really liked living here."

"How long have you been here?" I asked.

"Eighteen months."

Her husband called to her.

"Well, good-bye," she said. "It was good getting to know you."

Perhaps I looked like one of her neighbors. Or maybe her need to say goodbye was so great it didn't matter that we had never met. I asked the woman down the street, the one I had come to interview, if she knew the family that had just left. She didn't. "We haven't gotten to know a lot of people, we haven't been here long enough" (six months), she said. "We know across the street and next door and that's all in Fairtown that we know."

The only persons most GPIers knew in Fairtown were their nearest neighbors and other GPIers. Although when they spoke of a place where they had lived, GPIers invariably named either the city or the state—California, Atlanta, Indianapolis, New Jersey—they were, in fact, only speaking of the street on which they happened to buy a house. Their knowledge and opinions about any place were limited to immediate environs. Thus it was that Fairtown was judged mostly by what a GPI family could see from its front door. Most "loved" the appearance, and "hated" the weather; the social climate received mixed reviews.

Good Places and Bad Places: TC Members

TC members had a broader outlook. When they spoke of Fairtown they were referring to all of it—the schools, the services, the political structure, the complex mix of persons that made up its citizenry, the changes that had come over the years, and finally the opportunities it offered and the limitations it imposed upon chances for personal expression and growth. No TC member ever said, as the woman whose son was in the automobile accident did, that the people in Fairtown were "all so nice," nor would one say that "the people in this area are not very friendly." Instead, they spoke of individuals and groups. "Friendliness" or "niceness" was not an issue; political perspectives and tactics, and their presumed effects on Fairtown, were.

Though most of the TC members' friends were Fairtowners, few were neighbors. TC members made a distinction between friends and neighbors. Neighbors would be considered "good" if they shared such tasks as snow shoveling and care of children, or helped out when someone was ill, but geniality and sharing did not constitute friendship. Nor was a "bad" neighbor someone who simply kept to herself. That was nothing a TC member would complain of. A "bad" neighbor was someone who invaded the TC member's territory with roaming dogs, excessive noise, intolerable messes, or with complaints about such nuisances if the TC member was the offending party. The children of TC members often made friends with neighborhood children, but the parents did not expect neighborliness to develop into friendship.

Yet the TC members made every effort to stay in one house, and they could not understand why corporation managers did not do the same. One young woman who lived in a newer neighborhood because she had only recently bought her first house in Fairtown expressed that wonder at the managers, and some anger as well:

> Since I'm not involved in it, when I think of how the corporate way of life affects me, I always think in terms of my kids. My next-door neighbor is a corporate family. They've been living in Fairtown, I guess, four years, and though he's not thinking of being transferred, he's at the point where they're looking for a bigger house.
>
> He said they wanted to live in a bigger house because he's making so much money now. On the other hand, they love this neighborhood and they like their house. They like their neighbors. They're very friendly with their neighbors. Still, they're going to move to wherever they can find a bigger house. It doesn't matter to them much that their kids will change schools and lose their friends. I suppose it doesn't do any terrific psychological damage, but on the other hand, it's very nice for kids to grow up with the same kids around. I don't see why they leave when it isn't necessary. I just don't understand it. Their house is like mine, but they want a grander house, and to me that typifies the corporate way of life. . . .
>
> It affects me in small ways. It affects me that my kids are going to lose their two best friends, and that this happens all the time. The people in that house just moved to buy a bigger and better house. We remain and everyone around us moves, and I'm sad to see that happening. There's no such thing as a stable neighborhood, and I find that sad. . . . Even as we remain, they're making transients of us.

In many ways transiency seemed to affect those who stayed behind as much as it affected the movers. Even GPIers who had come to a point in their careers when transfers occurred less frequently or had stopped altogether found to their surprise that others could make a transient of one even if one did not move. And they could be even more sorely distressed when a neighbor moved out than was the TC member. The following are comments by two women who, for the first time since their husbands joined GPI, had lived in one palce for more than two years:

> People around here have been moving in and out at a tremendous rate. Now that we know we're going to be here, we rather resent that. I try not to let it bother me but when my friend Sally was transferred, I was as unhappy as if I were going. I really did resent it at the time, which is probably silly. It's very hard on the children too. They have to cope with their friends leaving as well as leaving themselves.

> It was funny; the neighbors over here moved a year ago and it was the first time a next-door neighbor of ours had ever moved, because we were always the ones that moved. It was a funny feeling, it really was, to see somebody else moving out. And they were great people. I really hated to see them go, so that was even doubly hard. But it was an odd feeling and I had never thought of that before. You see, we had always done the moving and nobody else in our neighborhood had ever moved while we were there. That didn't mean that those people never moved, but they never moved while we were there. It was just like you lost part of something—I don't know how to put it in words. But from the time they told us, I felt, well, that just can't be, nobody moves. Because we knew them better than we knew any other neighbors before. You see, we had been here three years when they moved and we had never lived anyplace that long before.

When it came down to a decision of whether to stay in a neighborhood and pass up a chance for career advancement or to leave and pass up an opportunity for stable human relationships, it was a rare family that considered the effect of its decision upon neighbors. But TC members were more likely than GPIers to realize that they were making that choice; and they often chose stability over advancement.

Inevitable, or a Matter of Choice?

Popular and scholarly wisdom assumes a Gresham's law of social development. Just as bad money drives out good, gesellschaft chases away gemeinschaft. The complex division of labor necessary to an industrial society brings about a change from "mechanical" to "organic solidarity," as Emile Durkheim put it, a change from a society held together by the similarities among individuals and what they do, to one held together by their differences and interdependencies.[4] Interdependency in turn calls for greater numbers of people, each adding a necessary speciality to the whole. As societies become larger, settlements become denser and human relationships become "impersonal, superficial, transitory and segmental."[5] It all seems so logical, so inevitable, so beyond the control of human will.

Viewed from this perspective, the competition in Fairtown between the TC members' way of life and the GPIers' way of life can have but one outcome: TC members are anachronistic; their world must give way to the GPIers' world. As a microcosm in which the inescapable transition is being played out, Fairtown will soon lose all those small-town, gemeinschaft qualities that make it so attractive to GPIers and TC members alike.

Surely there are signs that this is happening. Young people who grew up in Fairtown and wish to spend their adult lives there, and older persons who would like to stay after retirement, find that they cannot compete in a real estate market where values have been grossly inflated by the influx of managerial families. So the native children and the old-timers leave, and with them go the gradually and continually maturing social relationships on which the Fairtown community is built. Woods are cut down to make room for shopping centers, and the old town-meeting form of government is periodically threatened by charter-revision commissions searching for a more efficient way to run a growing town most of whose citizens have neither the time nor the interest to help govern.

Yet there are signs in Fairtown and elsewhere that notions of the inevitable demise of gemeinschaft may be based on false assumptions.[6] For example, one underlying premise is that there is a limit to human social energies. Relationships can be few in number but deep, or great in number but superficial and fragmented. The more there are of the latter, the fewer there can be of the former.[7] But that was not the case with the TC members. They had their full complement of gesellschaft relationships—brief contacts with persons playing narrow roles to match the narrow roles TC members sometimes played, the sort we all have with telephone operators, IRS agents, airline pilots, and the like. But those exchanges, precisely because they were fragmented and took little time or emotional energy, did not diminish the possibilities for gemeinschaft relationships. If the GPIers, on the other hand, had fewer gemeinschaft relationships, it was not because their gesellschaft relationships had squeezed out the possibilities for gemeinschaft, but because the broad range of community associations—with shopkeepers, teachers, town officials, even with friends—that were gemeinschaftlike for the TC members were gesellschaftlike for the GPIers.

Superficially, that difference appeared to be based on the length of time each group had been in town or planned to stay. More fundamentally, the difference was that TC members were making conscious choices and taking responsibility for precisely those aspects of life where GPIers believed no choice could be made. When it came to the town, TC members saw themselves as creators; by their very activities on their town committees they were using their energies to shape the town. Even staying in one place long enough to develop deep relationships was a choice many TC members made—sometimes at the cost of lower incomes. GPIers, on the other hand, took their transiency as a given, something they could not control, and they took the town as a given, something they could praise or complain about but could not alter. They failed to see that their very attitude and the ways they used the town were changing it in directions they would not like.

A few years ago the Irish Catholic priest-sociologist Andrew Greeley wrote an acerbic complaint against his fellow intellectuals, who, he argued, shared none of the "primordial values" so important to people of his ethnic neighborhood. He was comparing ethnics and intellectuals, but what he said might as tellingly be applied to TC members and GPI managers, to those who work in the peripheral economy and those who work in the center economy. In the ethnic neighborhood, Greeley wrote:

> Friends do move, poker clubs do break up. . . . But there is a thrust toward permanency in the assumption shared by all concerned that the longer the group survives the better. In the neighborhood one does not lightly break up one's network of friends to set out to some strange place (perhaps only a neighborhood or two away) where one will have to break into new networks of friends.[8]

Reflecting the view that gesellschaft must eventually wipe out gemeinschaft, most GPIers felt there was nothing they could do to keep family or friendship groups together. One woman, who said she would like to stop moving and who visited with some of her high school friends whenever she went back to her hometown to see her family, predicted:

Even if we do settle down, our children will always go out from the area and I doubt very much that they would live in the same town. It's hard to put down roots . . . you just can't.

TC members saw things differently. They valued permanency and knew there was something *they* could do to achieve it; they chose to work in the peripheral economy. One woman explained how she and her husband had based their choice of the company he would work for on the kind of life they wished to live:

When we married back in the fifties, if you were an engineer you didn't need a job offer. You offered your services and they hugged you to their bosom. But even at that time he avoided the companies that have a lot of branches and transfer. We looked at IBM and I think he had an offer from GE, but we knew that they were out.

We always knew what we wanted. IBM and GE always did transfer their personnel and it was a well-known fact. I can remember *Fortune* doing an analysis of the companies about the time Bob graduated. We read some of that material at the time Bob was getting ready to look at jobs. We knew they transferred and we said "no way." We ruled that out right from the start.

Most TC members, when they compared their lives with what they knew of a corporate career, could not understand why anyone would choose the latter. A man with a master's degree who had grown up in Fairtown said:

I work for a corporation, but in its research facility, and that's a low-key operation. There's only two positions higher than the one I have and I know I'm not going to get them because they're going to go to Ph.D. mathematicians and physicists. But I've known that for a long time and I'm satisfied. What people give up in the corporate rat race is a great deal of stability. The most they're going to get is fifty to sixty thousand dollars and that's absolute tops, and I don't know if it's worth the aggravation. They're very conscious of their image. But say if the place I'm working for closed down or moved and said you're forty-five years old, if you want to work, you have to move, I'm not sure what I would do. I've never seriously considered moving. In fact, I don't see how these people put up with a thing like that.

It could be argued that the TC members were in a better position to choose. The two quoted above had technical degrees to trade upon, not just the bachelor's degrees most GPIers had. Moreover, they were more likely than GPIers to come from middle- rather than working-class families. They did not have to climb socially and economically as most GPIers did to enjoy the comforts of a suburb like Fairtown. They had experienced the life-style they wanted and they had the credentials they needed to set their own terms. TC members' backgrounds were more like that of Frank Auslander, the GPIer who refused to be transferred.

Indeed, in spite of the dependency inculcated during corporate initiations, the fact that managers were simultaneously rising socially sometimes triggered an uncharacteristic independence. One GPIer felt that after years of transferring and working himself into better positions at the corporation he had gained the means to demand stability:

My wife and I consider our transient period to be over. We would not consider another move; we would not move out of Fairtown. We've made that decision. I've had offers and I won't go—better jobs, higher-paying jobs, out of GPI. I absolutely won't consider it. We'll stay here and educate our children in this town. I've turned down VP jobs in other corporations that meant a relocation to California, a relocation in Georgia, and a relocation in Michigan. But I won't take it. If GPI wanted to relocate me I would quit, and they know that. Under absolutely no circumstances would I move.

He had risen rapidly through the ranks and felt he had earned the right to stay in town:

> We've moved a little faster than some of the other GPI people that you've met in this town, in terms of moving up in the organization. I hit the region job at thirty years old and nobody's ever done that. It makes a difference. If you move fast and you put up with the grief that we had to put up with, and I mean it was real sacrifice—we bought one house, lived in it a month and were transferred again, and we gladly picked up our bags and left. And we did that eight times for GPI. And many times a week I've put in eighteen, nineteen hours a day doing my job so I could get on with what I wanted to get on with; and that's got to say something. Now I feel they owe me something. They know that and they accept that. They were moving all the region managers out into the field into their various locations and I was Southern regional manager. They knew I wouldn't move to Atlanta so they put me in the East. I like to think it's because they thought I could handle the job. [This was the man about whom another manager had said, "They valued him enough so they found another job for him."] But under no circumstances would we move.

Nonetheless, this was the same man who after four years in Fairtown had moved into a second house, was going to fix it up and then move on to a third in order to reap a profit. So at precisely the moment when he was taking a stand for stability he was planning to move. That was typical of GPIers. In spite of their greater dependence upon the neighborhood for friends, almost all the GPIers who had lived in Fairtown longer than three years had changed houses at least once.

The longer a GPI family had been in Fairtown, the more local friends they were likely to have and the more they talked about the pain of leaving; but only a few felt as deeply attached to Fairtown as most TC members did. The difference could have had nothing to do with the size, density, or heterogeneity of Fairtown, those characteristics usually associated with gesellschaft, for they were the same for both groups. It did have to do with their different experiences and the way those experiences had shaped their values. TC members had lived in Fairtown for many years and intended to stay; GPIers had moved from community to community, and while almost all said they would like to stop moving, hardly any intended to do anything that would win them residential permanence. Perhaps GPIers had less opportunity to choose; certainly they expressed a weaker sense of autonomy and a stronger sense of fatalism. And, perhaps as rationalization, they belittled the importance of community and long-term friendships.

CHAPTER 8

Fast Friends

The subject of friendship has not been extensively studied by social scientists. Writing about trust, a state akin to friendship, Andrew Greeley has caustically commented: "One of the reasons why there is so little study of trust by sociologists is that there is so little trust among sociologists." He then describes what happened when he tried to talk about emotional matters with some colleagues:

> I remember raising with a group of social scientists the question of tenderness, of "taking care," and of encouragement in intimate relationships. It was almost as though I had said something obscene. Very quickly the "proper" words were supplied to cover up my indiscretion. "You mean, I was told, 'nutrience,' or 'mothering,' or 'stroking,' or 'meeting emotional needs,' or 'level of emotional satisfaction,' or 'division of socioemotional labor.' " [1]

Those social scientists might have added "reciprocity," "bonding," "play groups," "primary relationships," "mutual aid," and "mutual regard."

In the forty-three years that the American Sociological Association has published its journal, *The American Sociological Review*, "friendship" has appeared in the title of an article only twice. In part this is because the word itself is so ill defined that we almost always use a modifier. We speak of "best friends," "close friends," "friends of the family," "mutual friends," "good friends." Then, too, friendship, the prototypical free relationship, stands outside the formal social structures that have generally commanded the attention of sociologists.

Nonetheless, we shall have to confront this subject, for it is central to the difference between GPIers and TC members as citizens. Specifically, I intend to compare the different kinds of friendship experienced by the TC members and the GPIers, and then, in the next chapter, to link friendship to the different ways in which members of the two groups approached their roles as citizens. Although friendship does not often find its way into political theory, friendship patterns within a community are closely tied to patterns of participation in self-government. For democratic political systems are based in community, and community, in turn, is held together by friendships.

Toward a Definition of Friendship

Georg Simmel, a contemporary of Toennies, was one of the few major sociologists to write directly about friendship. He distinguished between the idea or ideal of friendship as it comes to us from antiquity, and its modern reality. Ideally, friendship is a complete relationship; it "does not center around clearly circumscribed interests that must be fixed objectively," but instead is built "upon the person in its totality. . . . It aims at an absolute psychological intimacy that connects a whole person with another whole person in its entirety." But as societies changed, so did the possibilities for all-embracing friendships. By the end of the nineteenth century, Simmel thought, the ideal was no longer possible— friendships had to be differentiated. They "cover only one side of the personality without playing into other aspects of it." However, he argued, "friendships which connect us with one individual in terms of affection, with another in terms of common intellectual aspects, with a third in terms of religious experiences" may nonetheless "stem from the center of the total personality. It may yet be reached by the sap of the ultimate roots of the personality, even though it feeds only part of the person's periphery." [2]

Simmel, it seems, was describing gesellschaft friendship,

an apparent contradiction in terms. Yet it is a concept that many today embrace. In industrial societies where the roles we play are separated by space (we go one place to work, another to sleep, another to vote, and yet another to play) and separated socially (all our roles are played with different groups), friendships *must* be differentiated, each one joining a different aspect of our personality with another. And, as Simmel argues, there is no reason to suppose that the quality of a segregated or specialized friendship need be any different from the quality of a friendship that is whole.

Extending the idea of segmentation, there are those who also argue that physical proximity is not a necessary part of friendship: the written and telephonic word can serve as well as face-to-face conversations for communication, and any insistence that space must be shared in order for ideas, affection, and community also to be shared is narrow and unrealistic. "People can have all sorts of experiences of community which do not depend on living near to one another." [3] Indeed, it is argued by idealists and transcendentalists that the experiences people have of each other in their minds is prior to and of greater reality than their actual physical experiences of each other. The early-twentieth-century American sociologist Charles Horton Cooley went so far as to claim that "there is no separation between real and imaginary persons; indeed, to be imagined is to become real," for society "in its immediate aspect is a relation among personal ideas whose only possible locus is the personal ideas in the mind." [4]

Using the contrasting experiences of the GPIers and the TC members, I shall attempt to make a very different case—namely, that friendships with persons seldom or never seen; friendships that tap only a small fragment of the personality; friendships that have no grounding in a living community and are divorced from place, though they may call forth strong feelings, are markedly different from the long-term ongoing relationships that emerge when the same group of persons shares the same space and some of the same fates.[5] Place matters. And it matters, if for no other reason, because a people, to be self-governing, must have relationships rooted in a geographical locus. That is because governments are place-bound; their tasks are, as Scott Greer has noted, "all generated by the condition of their defining area." [6] Friendships generated by this condition differ in quality from friendships not tied to locale. Proof for this is to be found in the contrast in friendships and civic lives between the GPIers and the TC members.

Most of the TC members' friends were within easy visiting or inexpensive phoning range; most of the GPIers' friends lived far away. GPIers seldom saw their friends, depending almost entirely upon the mail and the telephone for communications. GPIer friendships tended to be with former neighbors, other GPIers, and former schoolmates; TC members had some friends from the neighborhood, school, or work, but most derived from a variety of other community social settings. For this reason, TC members enjoyed a broader range of types of friendships and a wider range of expression among friends. GPIers avoided controversial subjects; TC members welcomed issue-oriented discussion. GPIers generalized their friends, seeing one as not much different from another; TC members differentiated and individualized: each person was special, each relationship unique. GPIers' friendships were either frozen in time or new; TC members' friendships were fluid, always moving through deeper or shallower reaches of intimacy. Members of both groups valued what they had. GPIers, especially the younger ones, enjoyed making new contacts; TC members enjoyed exploring new avenues among old connections: their friendships were ongoing and dynamic. GPIers desired instant intimacy, and most of their relationships were narrowly segmented; TC members moved slowly in and sometimes out of intimacy, and their relationships were many-faceted. The friends of TC members knew each other and some were friends of each other; GPIers' relationships were almost all limited to two persons or couples. Thus there was for the GPIers no unbroken line through friendships to all parts of the community, as there was for the TC members. GPI friendships had nothing to do with the life of the community; TC members' friendships were imbedded in the community, and herein lay the significance of friendship for the political life of the community. For TC members shared with many of their friends a day-to-day concern for community, and from time to time they worked together for political purposes. GPIers' friendship activities were limited to forms of entertainment and had nothing to do with the collective life of community.

All of these differences arose because of demands made by the corporation upon the managers. Its effect on their friendships was most sharply noticed by those GPIers who had leaped from gemeinschaftlike farming communities straight into the corporate world-without-community. They had no inkling of a social setting halfway between gemeinschaft and gesellschaft, like the one TC members inhabited. But they were keenly aware of the difference between friendships in the social settings of their childhoods and those of settings they inhabited as adults. One woman explained the difference by comparing her own and her husband's friendships with those enjoyed by his parents:

> We've been here less than a year and I think we have almost as many friends as we had in Youngstown. Now I don't think they'll ever get as close here. But in Youngstown even, you only had three or four couples that were really what you'd call close. You had a lot of acquaintances, but not real close friends. Like Gene's parents have lived in the same very small farm community for fifty years. His dad has only had

one job in his entire life. We will never have friends like they have. Because you can't grow that rapport unless you've been with people year after year like they have. It takes a lot of years.

Now we have some very close friends from service; and we lived in Muncie and we have some very close friends from Muncie as well as from Youngstown. Because of the communication and keeping up with correspondence I think maybe over the years we'll have about a dozen, but nothing like Gene's folks because they've never been moved around. They know people so well because they've known them all their lives. They know all about them. They're very casual. They would feel free to come into their homes at any time without an invitation. Or if there was sickness they'd just drop everything and go. I feel here and in Youngstown, most of your friends are still on an invitation basis. You might have a woman friend who would drop in for coffee or something, but out there it's very much the whole community. It's close; it always has been; it always will be. They go through every single thing together. It's a very close wonderful relationship. We will never have it because we move. I don't think any of our generation will. Maybe, I don't know; Gene's brother is still there, but very few of our friends that we graduated from high school with are still there.

Another GPI wife who had grown up in a small town described that sort of life and explained why she would not like to return to it:

No, I don't want to go back to a very small community again. We liked it. It was great. But everybody did know each other and it's nice for Bill to be working in one place and living in another. He lives his life-style up here and nobody knows what he's doing in his place of work. My parents, literally, their lives are an open book in their town. There is concern for them, which is the other side of the coin. If my mother's not in church on Sunday there are many people that are concerned she is ill. Or if she's not seen on the street for a week, many, many people, maybe one hundred people, would check and see if she's all right. Which is a tremendous sensation of being needed and wanted and loved and all that. That's great. But you don't have any privacy. Everybody knows what you're doing. This is all very ambiguous because on the one hand you want one thing and on the other hand you want the other.

The TC members' Fairtown was not the same as the communities these GPIers had left. It was too large for everyone to know everyone else, and privacy was possible. Most TC members, like the GPIers, worked out of town. True, their community work was an open book—that was the public part of their lives—but they had private lives, too. Their friendships, especially those with others active in the community, straddled the intersection of their private and public lives. It was just that sort of friendship—part public, part private—that GPIers lacked; and that was largely because most of their friends were not Fairtowners.

When asked about their friends, most GPIers, especially the women, reeled off the places they had lived and the number of friends they still "kept up with":

> I have friends in Cleveland from high school that I still keep in contact with, and a couple of people in Detroit that I still write to. California, I have several friends there I keep in contact with. Memphis, I really no longer keep in contact with the people because we weren't there that long and really didn't make any real close attachments in the short time we were there. All over I have a couple of people I keep in touch with.

Keeping in touch usually involved just a letter once a year. Another woman:

> I still have a lot of friends from college and we have friends

from all the places that we've lived. Even though we've only been there a short time we still keep in touch with maybe one or two couples in all the places that we've ever lived. A lot of it is mainly at Christmas time, but we still keep in touch—not only with a Christmas card, but I mean a long letter letting them know. Some of it is oftener, but I would say for the most part it's once a year. Everybody's scattered all over the country, so unless we happen to be in an area we don't make a point of visiting with them.

Even "close" friends did not have much more contact than that. One woman had not seen her "best friend" in ten years. They spoke on the phone twice a year. Another said she kept in "frequent contact" with her friends, and added:

When I say frequently, I mean twice-a-year contact with people we haven't seen for ten years. We have some very good friends in Wisconsin and she sends things to my daughter at Christmas, and two or three times a year I talk to her on the phone.

Friends from high school were seen more often than other friends, because couples went back to their hometowns to visit with family on vacations, and that gave them an opportunity to see old high school chums:

In Cleveland where we grew up and our families still live we call or try to see our friends when we go in. We have two very good friends there that we keep in close contact with. We went to high school with them both.

But the one couple that did not go back home each year (of their parents, only his mother was still alive) saw the most of their out-of-town friends. They used vacation time to go camping with them:

We still keep very close contact with our friends in Maryland and go back and forth a lot. We lived there almost two years and it's not that far from here—just a five-hour drive. We spent our vacation with them last year, camping, and a couple of years before that we went to Maine with them, camping. And there's a couple in Memphis. They're great people and we've camped with them a couple of times, too.

Some women have developed a tradition of birthday calls:

My friend out in California, it's difficult to keep up. I call maybe once a year on her birthday. We haven't been back to California since we moved here but we still feel close. I made a very good friend out there and I think she'll always be my good friend.

The men have a certain advantage. They can combine visits and calls to friends with business trips. The husband of the woman just quoted explained:

I'll occasionally pick up the phone, but I don't write. Now on my new job I travel nationwide and I'm going out to California in August and I'll see these friends then. That's one of the benefits of the job.

That, in essence, is what GPI friendships amounted to. GPIers had many people all over the country whom they thought of as friends, but, with few exceptions, those friends were seldom seen. The few who had been in Fairtown for more than two years had developed local friendships, but even though those local friends could be seen fairly often, there were a number of GPIers who seemed to be groping toward an intimacy not found in any of their relationships.

Instant Intimacy

Most GPIers argued that they felt as close to faraway friends as they did to nearby ones. A manager said:

We seem to have a lot of good, close friends who are people that we've met in other places, and some good, close friends here; but in many ways the ones here are not closer, and in some ways they're not as close as those friends we have in other places, because we still see those friends—we visit them, or they visit us; Joan writes.

His wife, Joan, cited more evidence:

If you've made a good friend and had something to talk about in the first place, you're generally going to have something to talk about ten years later, if you were talking about something that was other than what was happening at the moment.

There were people we saw in December that we hadn't seen in six years, and we walked into their house and started talking and didn't quit till we walked out the door. I think this is why it doesn't bother me to think about moving and trying to make new friends.

Indeed, what bothered Joan was staying. They had not moved in four years, and a transfer was not in the offing. That was a problem:

If we stay in the same area I'm going to have to find ways to meet new people. Fred has more contact at work with different kinds of people than I do so I have to find a way for myself to meet people that I don't know any other way.

She thought she had found a way:

I don't know how long it's going to last, but I found it in a consciousness-raising group. I want some people I can talk to deeply but not have to entertain. That's something new for me. I never felt that way before. But I'm meeting new people and since pretty obviously we're going to be here for a while and we've got a big enough group of friends that we can hardly keep up with entertaining or being entertained now, I don't want to get into any more of that. So I've got to find a way to get into somebody and know about all that they're thinking without having to entertain them.

The consciousness-raising group Joan had joined was

formed by some Democratic TC women along with others from the local chapter of the Women's Political Caucus. Joan's link there was another GPI wife, one who had not been transferred. She was an active member of the Women's Political Caucus and therefore had something in common with both groups. Her fellow GPIer, Joan, as it turned out, was an alien in the TC members' world. The founders' goal was to lend support to each other so that more women would be able to break down barriers they felt were keeping them in traditional roles and barring them from important political positions in town. Their probing had a purpose: social change through personal change.

Joan was not a feminist, nor was she interested in Fairtown's political life. The other women had joined in order collectively to reform aspects of their community. Joan was using the structure others had created for different, instrumental, ends. She wanted instant intimacy with no encumbrances; they wanted long-range social and personal development. The form they chose, however, was similar to forms more commonly associated with Joan's goals.

Groups for therapy and instant intimacy developed concurrently with the expansion of corporations and their practice of transferring personnel. That was probably no accident. Managers have been frequent participants in sensitivity-training groups sponsored by their corporations. The corporate life, by denying opportunities for gradually maturing relationships, creates a need to find quick ways to fulfill the functions of intimacy. As Goodwin Watson, who has participated in and led numerous groups from Esalen to T, writes:

> The anonymity of life in large cities, the mobility of persons, the instability of family ties, and the rapid changes in institutions have left many of us feeling alienated. This situation provides fertile soil for the growth of movements designed to provide quick and intense experiences of feeling accepted

> and cared for. Under a variety of names, groups have been designed to enable strangers to meet, to increase contacts with one another and to enjoy for a limited time the long-missing sense of incorporation within a warm social organism.[7]

The question, however, is whether in a short time it is possible to be accepted, cared for, and incorporated within a warm social organism, or whether strangers who meet for a limited time to spill out their deepest problems and thoughts are only playing at intimacy.

Time was when intimacy was for intimates; for persons who knew each other for a long time and intended to stay together; for those who had made some commitment to each other; who to a great extent shared the same fates; who felt affection for each other and shared a trust based on past experiences. Now it is not even considered bad manners to want "to get into somebody and know about all that they're thinking without having to entertain them"; without having to make even the small commitment of a shared meal. Once, only persons who had lost or given up their civil rights—religious novitiates, prisoners, mental patients—could be expected to forsake privacy. Even they are usually given sufficient institutional care to keep them alive in return for their loss of liberty.[8] Today groups of strangers call for a willing relinquishment of privacy and accept no responsibility for the individual in return. National self-improvement franchises like "est" now sell intimacy like hamburgers. They become a means to gemeinschaft with only the fleeting, cursory commitment of gesellschaft.

Whether it is a quick strike into the depths of another personality or (what is more common with GPIers and their friends) the sharing of some simple recreation, precipitate association prevents a sensitive knowledge or appreciation of another. This became apparent as GPIers talked about their friends. Beyond identifying friends with a place of residence, many GPIers could not differentiate among them. TC members, on the other hand, with hardly any prompting and often with much gusto, would launch into deep analyses of other TC members, friends and foes alike. For them each individual's biography—his or her idiosyncrasies, motivations, public utterances, and day-to-day activities—was worthy of much scrutiny and discussion. By contrast, for GPIers everyone was alike. Here is a typical comment made by one GPI wife:

> I think people are people regardless. Of course, it depends. I mean, if it's somebody from Denver, naturally most of the talk is going to be around things we did there. And if they happen to still be living there we find out what's going on and things like that. Of course, it varies in that respect.

Such lack of distinction hardly fits friendship. In friendship we are both chosen and choosing; we bestow unique identities upon each other.

Because friends are special to each other, they expect something special from each other. Simmel noted that one mark of friendship is "a readiness to sacrifice." That readiness is seldom called into play, but when it is we all take note. Thus is Dean Acheson's risk of his own reputation—"I will not turn my back on Alger Hiss"—remembered. There was no such drama about either the GPIers or the TC members; but the latter's willingness to put community before career and permanence before promotions, not for a particular friend but for the *possibility* of friendship, does capture something of a readiness to sacrifice.

Finally, we come back to the question of whether a relationship that is restricted to only one shared activity or one common interest can be called friendship. It was not so labeled by TC members, who, if all they did with another individual was play tennis, would call that person a tennis partner, not a friend. GPIers quite frequently did associate each Fairtown friend with a particular shared activity, just as they associated each friend they wrote to with the particular place where they had met. A manager who wanted to stay in Fairtown explained why:

> I now know where to go fishing in this area and I know about ten guys that are crazy enough to go fishing with me, because I'll wear all ten of them out. I'll call a different one each time, because I like to go and they just like to go now and then. I have three or four people that like to hunt that I can now do things with. Believe it or not, that's important. We have good friends that we can do things with that we don't feel the relationship is a very superficial one.

One man's denial of superficiality might be another man's definition of it. A GPIer who had not been transferred said he could satisfy all his needs with just one pair of good friends, and did—with his wife's sister and brother-in-law. He thought other GPIers who had been transferred needed many friends because:

> People who are transient, who move a lot, they jump into a group so the man can say, "I play golf with him, play tennis with him, maybe drink with him." What the guy can do is, he doesn't have to have one real close friend, but "Gee, I think I want to play golf, that's Joe." He can get on the phone and call Joe and say, "Hey, how about a game of golf?" Or he wants to fish or he wants to bowl or go out and have a couple of drinks. He knows to call that guy and not this guy.
>
> I think what they do is they fragment their needs. Yet they don't have to get that close to somebody. Maybe they don't want to. Maybe they do want to. But maybe they'd rather not create such a strong friendship because, "My God, he's going to be gone in a year and he'll be down in Atlanta, Georgia, someplace." I think after five or six moves or some-

thing they get a style and that style builds a barrier, maybe even unconsciously. They get just so friendly with everybody and not too friendly.

Of course, it's hard to tell whether some other pair of friends are "getting just so friendly and not too friendly." But there was one final, most significant clue that GPIers' friendships were not as close as those enjoyed by TC members; and that for all their fragmenting of needs, some needs were never satisfied: GPIers did not talk with their friends about politics and religion.

Taboo Topics

A few GPIers talked about politics and religion with their relatives; most did not. With friends there was an almost universal understanding that those two subjects were to be shunned. One woman said:

> We talk, once in a while, politics, but to be honest, we don't usually enjoy talking politics.

Similarly, from a manager:

> I don't talk much politics. I guess I have a point of view probably on who I'm going to vote for, or whatever the issue is. I wouldn't say it overly bugs me that people talk about political things, but neither am I overly interested in it.

Another woman reflected the general opinion that talk about such issues dragged on too long:

> I don't know, that really is just not my way of enjoying an evening—hour after hour of any particular subject, I don't care what it is.

Many managers echoed her comment. Here's one of them:

> The conversation goes on and on and on and on. Now I've been involved in them, needless to say, and maybe expressed

> my point of view, but it's not of interest to me to get involved in that; that's not a big thing.

Others, mostly men, complained about the lack of resolution of such discussions:

> I don't find it interesting or stimulating or whatever you want to call it to talk where people have really definite points of view on both sides. I guess the reason I don't enjoy it that much is that it's kind of a no-win thing anyhow—nobody wins in the end.

Another said:

> They're all somewhat arbitrary in their thinking and you can't really win. They've got their minds set and you've got your mind set and you don't really have enough time to develop the dialogue, to be in a position where you might influence someone.

Those who most carefully avoided talk of religion or politics were likely to remember the time they had failed to take such matters lightly. One woman made a point of assuring me that a discussion about religion she had been part of had "left no hard feelings," but it had been so distasteful that she remembered it a decade later and based her avoidance of such topics upon that experience:

> Most times we have heard conversations about politics and religion that have got so out of hand. I have seen it get into very deep, lengthy, hour-after-hour discussion. One night in New Jersey it was on religion and it went on and on and on and it was strictly a matter of opinion, that's all. So that's why it's very very seldom that we discuss those two subjects.

Under the categories of religion and politics, most GPIers would list any social issue; anything that might elicit disagreement. A man, the one who said he had no "close or even semiclose friends in Fairtown," recalled an argument he had had a few years earlier with his wife's friend:

> I think the only time I got in a controversy was with Barbara's girl friend over junior colleges, and it wasn't worth it. The generalization was that all junior college people couldn't get into four-year colleges. That was silly and I took great exception to it. That was a rip-roaring conversation.

And Lisa VanDyke carried the painful memory of a time that she had been particularly outspoken about her feelings toward the corporation:

> It seems to be this terrible thing of everybody has to be so careful and nobody really says what they think. One evening, in Houston, we were with friends, sitting around. And I had never spoken to a friend's husband the way I spoke to this man. We were in total disagreement (admittedly two little drinkies are too much). I had never spoken to another man like that and I felt really terrible, but in a way it was a very purging thing. I was so angry with him. I was just completely mad and everybody was upset. It was awful. I really said what I thought for the first time in a social situation without being careful of treading on somebody else's toes. I guess I was the one that was the most upset because I was really revealing myself. I told him exactly what I thought of the whole corporate setup and the moving—everything we've been talking about, the whole thing. And he just thought it was the silliest thing he'd ever heard. No one had ever spoken to him that way. The next day I talked to my friend Nancy and said, "Boy, I really made an ass out of myself."

Remembrance of controversies long past was fairly common among GPIers and almost nonexistent among TC members. One reason is that rare events are more easily remembered. TC members talked often about social issues but

GPIers and their friends considered controversy indiscreet or unpleasant, so issue-oriented conversation seldom occurred. The woman who could not forget that night in New Jersey when the conversation turned to religion described a much more common and pleasant occasion:

> We might say, "What do you think about this candidate or that candidate?" and have a little conversation about that; but as far as a deep discussion on it, it's very seldom. Maybe a few words said about something like Watergate. Like Sunday afternoon we were with friends up at their pool and I had noticed an advertisement for bumper stickers in *Cue* that said "Don't blame me, I voted for McGovern," and we were laughing at that. And maybe this conversation went on for three minutes and then that was it. And this is usually the way it is. Nobody really cuts it off.

Nobody really cuts it off, but somehow the subject does get changed, as the man who took a disagreeable tack on junior colleges explained:

> Normally the discussion flow is where everybody's agreeing that x is a bad thing or a good thing, and you don't get into too many major controversies. There's always opportunity for that to happen, but you usually don't let it—that normally doesn't come up too much.

Why didn't the GPIers let controversial subjects come up, while TC members seemed to thrive on them? The answer lies primarily in the transitoriness of the GPIers' social life compared with the permanence of place TC members enjoyed, coupled with the related condition that GPI friendships, no matter how close they might have been, were isolated—between two individuals or two couples—whereas TC members' friendships were enmeshed in the complicated web of relationships that constituted the Fairtown community.

* * *

Politics, religion, and all questions bearing on social issues require moral choices. They deal with human relations—what they should be, what they should not be. They have to do with values. Those who feel a part of a community will find discussion of values necessary while others will claim that values are personal, private, and off conversational limits. As Michael Walzer has written, moral choices "are not only personal, but also collective"; about them we need to "think out loud, to argue, to criticize, to persuade." [9] However, we are likely to expose our thoughts about values only where we feel secure. Better assume agreement than test it—unless the social environment has ways of making disagreements inconsequential, as in T groups; or of healing ruptures caused by disagreement, as in permanent communities.

What Greeley said about "the neighborhood" can be said as well about the TC members' Fairtown:

> It is a place where you can trust the people you meet. Not everybody, of course, is a friend, and not everybody can be called upon to demonstrate implacable loyalty, but the neighborhood is a place where friendship and loyalty are highly valued. . . . Without the giving and exchanging of commitments and more or less permanent fidelity, human social interaction becomes impossible, or so it seems to us in the neighborhood. The rational, formal, bureaucratic legalistic structures of society are simply not enough to sustain human interaction networks unless the lubrication of friendship, trust, fidelity, and loyalty is applied. If you don't have anyone you can trust or anyone you can count on, you become so anxious, so fearful, so threatened that you almost have to strike first before others strike at you. From the neighborhood perspective, personal commitment to one's friends is not an option but a necessity. As a young Irish lawyer in Chicago put it, "Someone who won't be loyal to a friend will never be loyal to an idea." [10]

GPIers did not strike first before others struck at them, they simply struck *ideas* from their discourse. It takes security to argue, security that though your ideas may be rejected, you will not be. TC members had that security. They talked about politics and political issues with friends who agreed with them and with friends who did not; even with persons who were not their friends. They discussed and they argued, and sometimes voices would be raised in living rooms or at dinner tables. They felt the questions were important, and they raised them to test the waters or to influence fellow citizens, but always with the shared assumption that both the issues and the discussants mattered.

Nor did it disturb TC members that discussion of moral issues was inconclusive. The GPIers were quite right: talk about religion and politics does go on and on, and no one wins. It is in the nature of moral questions that they cannot be "solved" but must be continually confronted. Stable groups return to these issues again and again. They thrive on inconclusiveness. Persons on their way somewhere else feel they must settle every argument at one sitting, for there may never be another.

Not surprisingly, the only GPIer who did talk about politics was Frank Auslander. Not only did he manage to stay in one house for more than twenty years, but he also was able to keep up with friends from high school:

> I have a group from high school. We try once a year to get together. It's funny, but we consider ourselves close friends and may not see each other for eighteen months. But this past year I was in the hospital and when they found out, the telephones were ringing. We try to get together, though we don't get together as often as we would like. Sixty miles is still a great distance, but we do. Actually they are probably my closest friends even though I don't see them as frequently

as people around here. They're the ones I grew up with. There's only two or three who don't still live in Brooklyn. One's in Cincinnati, one's in St. Louis, and the other one has died; he lived in Florida. There are about twelve, thirteen of us, I know it's just over a dozen, we consider ourselves the "dozen plus." All but one of us went to college. They're all engineers, doctors, dentists, all but one are professionals. We go to, say, the Poconos as a group for the weekend—an extended weekend.

Generally we talk politics. It's quite a split group. It always comes back to politics. We enjoy it because there's never complete agreement. In fact there's hectic arguments sometimes, but we never go away mad.

Talk about politics reinforces assumptions that an ongoing community life exists. Moreover, what was true about Frank Auslander and his friends was also true about TC members and their friends: they had a fairly long experience of each other, so that any argument raged before a backdrop of agreements and disagreements over dozens of other issues. No one discussion could be the basis of a friendship nor could it destroy sociability. Theirs was a complex social world filled with nuances in which agreement was not synonymous with affection, nor was disagreement tantamount to aversion.

More important, perhaps, than TC members' friendships, were their acquaintances within the community—with persons they might even dislike. As Greeley has noted, not everyone in a community is a loyal friend; what he left out was the quality of relationships between antagonists. TC members knew whom they could trust with their innermost thoughts because they knew whom they could not trust. And trust was not just something between friends; TC members knew just how far a foe might be trusted.

How antagonists join in community is probably just as important as how friends join together. Theodore White caught it well in a remembrance of the Boston Jewish ghetto where he grew up:

> Long before ethnicity became a fashionable political concept, we knew about each group living in its own community. But we were also all Americans, and even where the friction between groups was greatest—in my neighborhood, along its borders with the tough Irish—it was not intolerable. Our house sat on that border; our yard backed against the yards of Irish families on the next street, a line of fence dividing them. In the house across the fence from ours lived a boy my age, Johnny Powers, whom I had always considered my enemy.
>
> But the day my father died I climbed over the fence to call Johnny to come out—and he came out, bristling. I explained that my father had died that morning, and asked him if he could keep the kids in his street quiet for the rest of the day. Not to worry, Johnny said; he'd make sure there wouldn't be a sound from his block. He'd take care of his gang. And he did.[11]

Over the years, even enemies find opportunities to share favors, to learn what can be expected of the other, to discover something in common. They are "also all Americans," also all Fairtowners, also all parents whose children might strike up a close friendship, also all human.

It takes time, but sooner or later even those whose opinions are poles apart may find they agree on something and may have to work together if they are to get their way. It happened in Fairtown over a proposed town charter.

Not infrequently, arch-conservative libertarians will agree with staunch liberals when it comes to the rights of citizens to govern themselves. Both oppose an overbearing state. And so they did in Fairtown when a charter granting increased powers to the first selectman was proposed—and favored mostly by groups in the ideological center. Opponents to the charter were brought together by a Republican Town Committee member who, because their daughters were friends, had developed a close relationship with a woman on the Democratic Town Committee:

> That first meeting I put a bottle of scotch and a bottle of bourbon and an ice bucket and glasses on the table and laid down the one rule that the discussion would be nothing but charter. There would be no talk about anything else. And boy, we worked together! . . . Later, one after the other from each side came to me and said, "They really work. Aren't they good!" And several of them made friends among themselves.

Working together to promote a common interest gave persons in the TC members' world an opportunity to meet, a reason to submerge differences. Those in Fairtown who had fought both against and alongside each other could not objectify their opponents. Over the years they got to know each other well and a grudging fondness developed even among enemies. They knew what each had suffered; often, as in the case of the TC member whose son had died, personal tragedies brought people together. Moreover, TC members knew that matters of religion and politics were not always "no-win." Sometimes individuals did change their ideas. They also knew that what others thought mattered. For TC members shared a community with other Fairtowners and they expected to continue to do so. The ideas they debated would shape the community they shared. Most TC members could look to some part of the community—a school, a change in the government structure, a new organization—and remember their part in it. If the direction they suggested worked out well, they were proud of it. If it didn't, some admitted their mistake or there was someone to remind them of it. Whatever the outcome, most TC members expressed a sense of responsibility for whatever befell Fairtown. GPIers did not. Although a few managers were beginning to see that frequent transfers meant that managers were not in one job long enough to have to be accountable for their work-related actions, none saw that the same flight from responsibility occurred in their residential communities as they moved from one to another.

Moreover, every community activity TC members participated in—the dozens of voluntary organizations in town, where they might have lent a hand or contributed a word; the scores of governmental boards and commissions they might have served on—brought them into acquaintanceship, and sometimes friendship, with members of all the different social groups in town. Because membership in groups overlapped, so did the alliances formed within them. Friendships among GPIers, like the roads they lived on, led nowhere; but TC members' friendships were like intersections on the roads that crisscrossed the town: they made connections.

TC members' Fairtown was not a gemeinschaft of the medieval agricultural variety. Everyone did not have a face-to-face primary relationship with everyone else. But it was gemeinschaftlike, for they all did have a path through primary relationships to virtually everyone else residing in the permanent community. Friendships and family relationships could be used like steppingstones to get from one group in town to almost every other group.

Friendship, then, was the link between private and public relationships. It was the affective glue that held the community together. Most TC members' friends knew each other and they formed into clusters of mutual friends. The clusters were shifting and overlapping, so that individuals who were not friends were drawn together by others who were. And at the periphery of every cluster were individuals who were familiar but not intimate, friendly but not friends. Most relationships were neither gemeinschaft nor gesellschaft; they lay somewhere in between. TC members had scores of such associations. GPIers had few. Without such associations they could not be part of the Fairtown community. Thus their attachment to the center economy left them unattached to all other institutions except their family; central in the economic world, they were, perforce, peripheral in all other worlds.

CHAPTER 9

Politics in Fairtown

Not being part of the mesh of relationships that was the Fairtown community, most GPIers hardly ever became a part of the town's political life. For it was through local friends or acquaintances that most TC members had first been brought into the political mainstrcam, and that initiation generally did not occur until the TC member had been in town for at least two years—a length of time necessary to know and be known by those who were already active. That could not happen to GPIers until they too had stayed in town for a similar length of time; and it would not happen at all unless the GPIers expressed an interest in local affairs, as virtually all of the TC members had done. But, rationalizing their own lack of involvement, many GPIers spoke of local matters with cool disdain. As one woman said, "I don't like to talk about trivia, and most of the things in town seem sort of petty to me."

Did it matter that GPIers hardly ever participated in the political life of Fairtown? Not according to the GPIers; and not according to most TC members, who complained about the too active participation of transients, not about their apathy.

If we turn to the political theorists with whom we began, we see that only the pluralists would find managerial detachment from the political scene a cause for concern. Most elitists would argue that citizen activities at the local level are merely a smokescreen that conceals the true elite power structure of the polity; and the "elitist-democratic" theorists would argue that the managers' inactivity was itself a sign of their satisfaction with the polity.

This book does not address the question of a national elite

except to say that if the national government is dominated by a power elite, GPI's middle-ranking managers showed absolutely no signs of being included in it. Some elite theorists argue that local communities reflect the national power structure and that within each there is a small group that rules. Using a technique similar to that which the elitists usually employ in their community studies,[1] I tested for a covert Fairtown power elite and found none. This study gave more support to the "elite-democratic" view of power in local communities, which sees a system of "dispersed inequalities" in which no one group dominates all decisions. Power is spread among a number of individuals and groups, depending upon their interests and upon their control over resources such as time, money, and numbers of citizens in the community with similar backgrounds or opinions. So it was in Fairtown, where some active citizens concentrated on school issues, others on land use, and still others on taxes; and where some individuals gained influence because of wealth or large landholdings, and others because of a large ethnic following. On most public issues, however, it seemed as if winning depended more upon the amount of energy a group could exert than upon any other single factor. This is where the GPIers and managerial families like them were a crucial factor in Fairtown's politics. They were a reserve army of the unconcerned whose vote could be called out whenever a group wanting it strove hard enough.

An example of how that worked was the 1974 town budget. That year it took two votes to get the budget passed. In the first, two thirds of those who voted favored a reduced budget. So the budget was sent back to the Board of Finance, which cut that portion of the budget to be used for town expenditures but left the school budget intact. That angered a group in town called the Taxpayers. They petitioned for another referendum to cut the school budget. Supporters of the school budget then launched a vigorous telephone countercampaign, and in the second referendum the school budget survived by a small majority.

The way GPIers voted on that issue indicates that they and others like them tend not to vote at all when there is no concerted effort to attract their votes; but when an energetic campaign is undertaken by others, they will sometimes respond. Of the 72 GPIers, 10 were not registered; 7 of those 10 had been in town less than two years. (Although Connecticut has no length-of-residency requirement, most GPIers did not register until the first presidential election after their arrival.) Of the 62 others, 31 did not vote in either referendum, 8 voted in both, and 23 voted only in the second.

Those figures suggest a far greater difference in turnout between the first and second referenda among the GPIers than among the rest of the townspeople. Of all the registered Fairtown voters, 20 percent turned out for the first and 32 percent turned out for the second referendum; among the GPIers it was 13 percent for the first and 47 percent for the second. Virtually all the GPIers who voted in the second but not in the first referendum said they had voted in favor of the school budget and had gone to the polls at the urging of a friend, a neighbor, or someone on the telephone. "I have a friend who tells me when to vote," said one.

What this sort of voting does is strengthen the hand of any group willing and able to wage a vigorous campaign. Because those at the ideological extremes are often more passionate in their beliefs and therefore more willing to work for them, they can, in a community with a large contingent of transient managers, have an influence that far exceeds their numbers. Not that GPIers will respond to any message or vote for any group; but they do not have strong priorities and they are often ignorant of the full meaning of local issues—which means they can be swayed by a one-sided appeal if that is all they hear.

For the most part GPIers were Republican and moderate.

They generally opposed social welfare programs unless some personal experience led them in the opposite direction. For instance, almost all GPIers felt that a national health program was "socialistic," but one woman whose son required dialysis treatment thought *some* federal relief was necessary. Again, at the time of the study one issue current in Fairtown was subsidized housing. Almost all GPIers opposed it, but one man—whose mother was living in a federally supported old-age development—favored it. As for other local issues, most GPIers favored high-quality, somewhat liberal school programs, low taxes, and lax land-use regulations. This set of attitudes left GPIers open to appeals from both ends of the political spectrum. For instance, those who telephoned in support of the school budget stressed the need for quality education in Fairtown. However, had the Taxpayers group followed their referendum petition with a telephone campaign they could as easily have stressed the danger of higher taxes and perhaps have won as many votes from the GPIers as the other side did with its campaign.

In short, the managers, whose centrist views might have lent stability to local politics, became instead a missing middle, a moderate voice that did not express itself, but instead gave sporadic support to first one side and then the other. Hence, contrary to the contention of some political theorists that non-participation in politics aids and reflects stability in the American democratic system,[2] the nonparticipation of managers in Fairtown intensified instability in their local government.

Those active in Fairtown's politics tended to overlook the support *they* sometimes received from GPIers and other managers and to think only of the managers' aid to opponents. Therefore, TC members of every political persuasion were most likely to complain of the baneful effect transient managers had on the town. Conservatives blamed them for initiating and supporting expensive or ill-conceived projects and then leaving before the taxes had to be paid. Liberals, meanwhile, grumbled that transient managers rejected necessary improvements and then left before they would have to suffer the consequences of inadequate services. For instance, the day after the school budget referendum, one of those who had voted for reduction was quoted in the local paper as follows:

> People moving into town want what's best for them, which is understandable. However, if these people don't plan to stay in Fairtown, why do they even bother to vote? The problem arises when these people vote everything in and then all of a sudden move out of town. This is a transient problem and it is about time we responsible citizens sit down and analyze the situation a little better.

Many TC members felt that transient managers were without local commitment and were too easily swayed:

> The corporation people, they make no investment in the town. They're quick to take up a cause or a new group and then they cast it off just as quickly.

Some held that transients voted only on issues that directly pertained to themselves:

> They're not as active as they should be. They do tend to turn out on things that they are interested in. I noticed that anything affecting the Bonate developments, the people will turn out to vote. These developments have organizations and the people are instructed and told what the issues are.

A few figured, quite rightly, that transients were not much involved:

> I'm not sure that the kind of individual who works for these large corporations ever let themselves get involved. They protect themselves by not caring about the places they're living in. . . . But I don't think they have a very strong effect on the school because they don't get involved. I don't

know, but I would think that a corporate hotshot, he's here for a few years and it's time to move on. I would think he's more concerned with his work than with the community. I would think that moving up in a corporate echelon requires almost a total commitment from that guy. I think you have to sacrifice your family and I don't think that leaves very much room for anything else.

Finally, a woman on the Democratic Town Committee summed up what she thought was wrong with having the managers in town:

The trouble with transiency is that every time an issue arises you have to go back and recapitulate everything that over the years led up to it, but they don't really want to listen. So the community as a whole has no memory.

For their part, many GPIers knew what the more permanent residents of Fairtown were saying about them, and they didn't like it. A GPI woman said:

I can remember when we first came here and the people in our development were fighting this electric generator and we became tagged as "corporate gypsies" and they were saying, why should we really have anything to say about it because we'll be here today and gone tomorrow. I mean not just us but our type of people.

A few weeks ago I went to the garden shop and they must have thought I looked like a native because they were talking about how upset they were with these people moving into town and how it was becoming so built up and the population was increasing and they came up with the corporate gypsy thing too.

I didn't like it that much. Wherever I live it's home and I want to feel like I belong there, not that I'm just sort of renting a spot that really belongs to somebody else who has more right to live there than I do. Where would all these people be without corporations? Not everybody can be First

Selectman or own the art shop in town. There's just a limited number of people who can do that.

GPIers fought back by disparaging the active citizens. According to most GPIers, people who were active in local politics were motivated by a need for fulfillment and self-esteem that they could not get from their work. GPIers thereby justified their own lack of involvement by downgrading those who were involved. One man said:

> It would be hard for me to ever become a part of the political scene because my perception of that scene is that it is very superficial, that it's a lot of hail-fellow-well-met politics kind of stuff, and that just drives me bananas.

The form of government was held in no higher esteem by GPIers than were the individuals involved in it. Fairtown, like most small towns in Connecticut, is governed by a First Selectman and a town meeting in which all citizens may participate. Few GPIers had ever attended a town meeting but they had heard about them. Most said they would like to go to one someday because they had heard that the locals put on a good show:

> I've heard that the town meetings are wild. You really must go see one. But I haven't.

One man who did attend a town meeting was not highly impressed with what he saw. In the early 1970s an infestation of gypsy moth worms forced many New England towns to decide whether to institute massive spraying. The issue elicited strong feelings on both sides. This GPIer was against spraying:

> I attended a town meeting two years ago when they were discussing whether or not to spray the bugs and it looked more like a Shakespearean farce than a town meeting.

The town meeting ended with a voice vote in favor of spraying, a vote that this GPIer and several other Fairtowners thought

was unfairly counted. What was most revealing was the difference between the manager's reaction and the response to
that same meeting of a TC member who also opposed the
spraying. The GPIer said:

> We didn't have any form of representative government. It was
> a farce. That was the first and only and last town meeting for
> me. Why go?

The TC member, on the other hand, went on to fight in court
and won an injunction against the spraying.

When TC members lost, they might fight again. When
GPIers lost, they also lost interest and attacked the system.
It was as if they felt they had no part in it. While national
leaders and events did sometimes command their attention,
local events and candidates were so far beneath most GPIers'
concerns that even those who did vote in local elections could
not remember, a month or two later, whom they had voted for:

> I don't know who I voted for; I voted for somebody a friend
> of mine said I should vote for on the school board. I couldn't
> tell you who I voted for, I'm not close enough. Our friend had
> a strong opinion and they convinced my wife and me that that
> was a good way to vote. I wasn't enough involved to know
> who the hell I was voting for. . . . I have a kind of fleeting
> memory about things like that unless you're talking about the
> president, where I really get identified with it.

Nonetheless, most GPIers did reveal enough of an underlying belief in the importance of participation to claim to vote
at every election, although the records in Town Hall indicated
that most voted only in presidential elections. Most also
claimed to vote independently for the issue or the "man," not
for any political party. Yet a review of their votes in presidential elections indicated party regularity, usually Republican.
And most GPIers said they thought they ought to be more
active than they were. As one woman put it:

I'm not very active; it's terrible, I know.

But her self-criticism did not run very deep. When asked why she said her inactivity was terrible, she replied:

I think it's a habit. I don't really feel guilty that I'm not doing things.

Finally, to answer the question with which we began—did it matter that GPIers were not politically active?—we must return to the pluralists, for they alone, among all the political theorists, still hold to the belief that democracy is more than a dream; it is always a possibility. Whether citizen action is specifically political or not, participation in voluntary organizations has been judged a cornerstone of democratic government. Voluntary organizations are said to provide buffers between the individual and the state and to prevent the arbitrary exercise of governmental power. They school citizens in the fundamentals of group and political action, giving them both a feeling of community and an opportunity to make the rules by which they must abide. George Sabine has argued that "the extent to which freedom of association can be generally and effectively achieved, and the extent to which association can preserve individual spontaneity, are measures of liberty in any society." [3] Indeed, one of the crucial differences between democratic and totalitarian governments is that the former permits and the latter forbids freedom of association. [4] Yet it is not enough for the state to *permit* freedom of association: the citizen must *use* that freedom. Alexis de Tocqueville, no champion of democracy though he understood it well, argued that if power was to be diffused, then citizens must join together or lose both their liberty and their civilization:

If men living in democratic countries had no right and no inclination to associate for political purposes, their independence would be in great jeopardy, whereas if they never acquired the habit of forming associations in ordinary life, civilization itself would be endangered. A people among whom individuals lost the power of achieving great things single-handed, without acquiring the means of producing them by united exertion, would soon lapse into barbarism.[5]

The GPIers had the right to associate for political purposes, but they did not exercise it. They had the right to discuss political issues freely, but they did not use it. The GPIers were unconcerned, for they saw no connection between their own indifference and its dangers for society. They seemed unaware that rights, like muscles, will atrophy from disuse.

CHAPTER 10

Conclusion

Giant corporations, with their sophisticated technology and abundant production, promised more: mankind was to be set free from the struggle for survival, free to develop talents and powers other than the mastery of the material world. The social changes that came with the industrial revolution carried a similar promise. Mercantilism, feudalism, the guild system, the hierarchical church—all the old shackles on individuals were impediments to industrialization and eventually became obsolete. Unleashed from those restraints, men and women were presumed to be ready to enjoy freedom and independence.

Yet here was a sample of men and women closest to the corporation, persons who more than most others produced and shared in its wealth, and though they were surrounded by plenty in a material sense, they seemed impoverished in every other way. They were not grubbing for a subsistence, but they were so taken up by the demands of work that they had not the energy nor the time nor the heart for much else. For them, material abundance had brought only more of the same; it did not seem to be convertible into intellectual or emotional growth. Although they worked with persons, not with things, their experience did not quicken their sensitivities nor expand their understandings. Instead, their feelings were numbed and they had to deny sympathy even toward those they loved.

Still, they were not callous. If Mrs. Corelli judged harshly the woman whose near-collapse forced her husband to quit GPI and take the family back to California, it was not that Mrs. Corelli was hardhearted but that she sensed that indulgence would have uncovered in herself a confusion of unmendable injuries. If she tossed off the pains of leaving close friends and familiar places with "It was *just* emotion," it was not that her heart didn't ache at times, but that she couldn't afford to heed its promptings. She had come a long way from her girlhood days in Cleveland, where her unskilled parents had labored in a factory to feed her brother and herself. The way was lined with things her parents never dreamed possible for themselves—cars, appliances of every sort, bigger and bigger houses in ever-wealthier subdivisions. How was Betty Corelli to notice that very subtly and insidiously something she had never learned to value, her independence and Al's, was slipping away?

When Al joined GPI he seemed to be making the same sort of bargain at the corporation that their parents had made at the factory: so much time, so much money. At home, in the community, by himself, he was to be free from the corporation. After all, a crucial aspect of the new social order was that it separated the roles an individual played. No single institution, not the family, not the church, not the state, not the corporation, was supposed to be able to dominate a person's life.

But GPI was invading all spheres of its managers' lives. The exchange between it and the men was not merely an economic one. The managers received more than money and GPI demanded more than work. It exacted first claim on its managers' time and insisted that they give it in New York on Monday, in Detroit on Wednesday, and in Memphis on Friday, if that was what suited GPI. The corporation demanded also that its managers move their families wherever *it* found convenient. GPI could not tell a manager how to vote, but it did set conditions of employment that rendered active citizenship virtually impossible. It could not determine the relationships that existed between husbands and wives, but it manipulated them so that they pressured each other to be obedient to corporate demands. The corporation could not decide how many children they would have or what sort of parents they would be, but it did determine that those children would see little of their fathers and would grow up in many different places. GPI was not, then, all-powerful, but it did exert a strong dominance over its managers and their families.

It should be emphasized, however, that the corporation did not dominate the lives of *all* its managers. The ones who were already of the middle class before they came to GPI—men like Auslander, whose mother was an opera singer and whose father was such a successful contractor that the son "never knew in the nineteen thirties that there was a depression going on"—were able to keep a private family life inviolate and sealed off from the corporate influence. Though he had to lower his career sights in order to raise this personal barrier, Auslander knew how to tap GPI's largess without being captured. Men from the middle class could do that. First of all, they knew independence was important; they were sons of propertied, autonomous men, professionals, or businessmen who had no boss. Second, they usually came to the corporation with the kind of educational background that empowered them to choose among employers and employments. Third, having grown up in affluence, they knew that a superfluity of possessions was just that; it would not carry subtler goods in its wake. To them GPI could offer a good job but not passage into a higher class; and because the corporation was doing less *for* its middle-class managers it lacked the power to do more *to* them.

As for most of the managers, those from the working class, it was because they were in transit that they were so vulnerable. Existential philosophers, and sociologists such as Park and Simmel, have emphasized the freedom, the independence of mind and spirit that comes with breaking away from restricted communities. Nietzsche dreamed of a race of supermen who might soar beyond the downward pull of social institutions. And he was right, in the sense that it would take *super*men to be able to live without institutional sustenance. Ordinary men and women, it seems, must join others. Cut loose from their families, their communities, their old way of life, GPI's managers did not soar. Instead they quite naturally bound themselves over to the only available institution that offered them order and stability—their corporation. But the stability they found at GPI was thin. They had no vested interest in the corporation; their tenure there was at the pleasure of their superiors; and they could not pass on the positions they had gained there to their children.

Perhaps that is why they expressed a lack of concern for their children's future, rare in the middle class. Though the aspirations of their working-class parents had been the springboard from which many of the managers and their wives began their upward climb, and though it is common for parents to want to transmit their gains to their children, these couples were surprisingly free of ambition for their children. When asked what they wanted their children to be, most parents said they did not care, and many suggested that the country needed skilled tradesmen—plumbers, carpenters, and the like. Only a vice-president, who had been to Harvard and to Yale Law School, and the accountant, who told about the rapid rise of the Harvard Business School graduate, worried about the kind of college their children would attend, or whether they would attend college at all. From the rest was heard the easygoing refrain, "As long as they're happy, that's all that matters."

It was in some ways refreshing to hear. Suburban parents have a reputation for educational pushiness, for putting pressure on school systems to prepare children for admission to elite colleges, no matter the suitability of the child for the college or the college for the child. GPI's parents belied that reputation. Indeed, their relaxed attitude might have suggested that they had achieved a blessed end to striving, had there not been something in the tone of their parental nonchalance which prompted a different interpretation.

Most of the managers' children were too young to give any indication of the direction their adult lives might take. A few, however, were completing high school and entering college, and some of the career choices those youngsters were making bothered their parents. The children were not dropping out of school or running off to communes as young people a few years their senior had done;[1] but the paths they were taking still implied a rejection of the world of their fathers. One father, whose son had decided to become a dentist, explained his son's choice:

> Part of why he wants to be a dentist is that he said, "No company is going to tell me where to move or when to go." It wasn't that he minded the places where we lived, it was a matter of *having* to do it. He said, "I'm going to have greater control over my destiny than that."

Although this father understood his son's decision, he responded to it by rationalizing about his own career:

> That's fine for him. I've chosen my lot in life and I've got to sleep in the bed I made. He's going to have to do the same thing and it's not all a bed of roses, you know. I would not stand and look down somebody's throat for eight hours a day in a little office that's eight feet square.

A mother whose son had decided to become a geologist because he "didn't want to be an organization man like his father" said, "Well, if he wants to wander around in the woods all day looking at rocks, that's okay with me, but I wish he'd remember it's the organization that's paying his tuition."

These parents sounded hurt and defensive, as if their sons'

career choices were not a step in the right direction but a reproach. In truth, they seemed to be suffering reproaches from all sides. Hardly anybody praised them; hardly anybody accorded them the honor they had expected would come with promotions and raises. Their own children were critical rather than appreciative. The managerial couples could hardly open a newspaper or a magazine or go to the bookstore without reading warnings of the psychological wreckage careers like theirs might cause. For in the popular press, and in academic publications as well, managers and their suburbs have been the subject of scorn and the cause of much hand-wringing.

Yet the managerial couples were not complaining about their lives. Far from it, they were proud of their achievements. Life, most of them felt, had been good to them. Like the managers William H. Whyte interviewed two decades earlier, it could be said about the GPI managers that "they have no great sense of plight; between themselves and the organization they believe they see an ultimate harmony." [2] It seemed the same sort of self-satisfaction Herbert Gans had in mind when he observed, "If suburban life was as undesirable and unhealthy as the critics charged, the suburbanites themselves were blissfully unaware of it." [3]

What accounts for the chasm between the way managers see themselves and the way their critics see them? Perhaps, as Gans has suggested, the gap in outlook reflects a corresponding gap in social origins: the criticized and the critics are experiencing the same phenomena from different social vantage points. The managers and their wives know they have come a long way, and if they have had to pay a price, they have been willing. The critics often have as narrow a view as the managers'. They assume that the managerial life-style is freely chosen and they blame the managers for their good fortune. Instead, managers might be viewed as the latest in that long line of migrants who at the start of the industrial revolution began leaving rural villages to work in urban factories. If for the managers the transition is motivated by the carrot of high salaries and prestigious occupations rather than the stick of enclosure laws that forced the first industrial workers from their homes, so much the better. Yet the price paid in terms of their humanity may not be very much different. Training their eyes not on the benefits, but on the cost—on the nonmaterial price paid by managers for their material gain—outsiders often see only a bad bargain. Perhaps it is. But all sorts of groups make what appears to others as bad bargains without becoming the subject of such vehement attacks as are frequently leveled at corporation managers. Why should managers come in for special opprobrium?

Why, for example, do critics decry the self-denial of corporate families when they would probably praise a similar devotion to work on the part of musicians or ballet dancers? An obvious reason is that corporate products seldom approach the sublimity symphonies can reach. Even so, why not shrug off what appears to be the managers' misplaced sacrifice in words similar to those of the father of that aspiring dentist: "That's fine for [them]"? The answer probably lies not in the nature of corporate dominance but in its breadth. Corporate power seems to reach out into the noncorporate community, threatening all lives with its near-totalitarian control.

Persons who prefer to eschew the corporate way, who would like to choose independence over subservience to a large organization, political involvement with its frustrations over apathy with its moral insouciance, residential stability over career advancement, and work in the peripheral economy over work in the center economy—all at the cost of material gain—such persons find that they are increasingly deprived of such choices. When the TC member said, "Even as we remain, they're making transients of us," she was voicing a complaint that is well grounded in contemporary experience. For here was a woman who like many of her fellow Americans tried to avoid a corporate influence on her daily life but could not.

Whether it is through their managers, who as neighbors bring the corporate influence into the communities where they sojourn, or through their own invasion into commercial territories that may once have seemed necessarily local—such as luncheonettes, child-care centers, or real estate businesses [4]—giant corporations appear to be setting the style and dictating the terms of life for those they do not employ almost as much as they do for those in their pay. So critics worry not so much about what corporations do to their managers as about the possibility that what has happened to the managers might happen to the critics themselves.

Such worries are appropriate to a people whose forebears took great pains to limit the powers of their government; for institutional domination is to be feared whether it comes from the religious, the political, or the economic sphere. The nation's founders had experienced both religious and political tyranny. They successfully checked by revolution an overbearing monarchy. Then they set out to guard themselves against the domination of either church or state by writing a constitution that limited the state's powers, guaranteed rights and freedoms to citizens, and separated church from state in order both to protect and to restrain the religious order. The economic order did not loom as large then as it does today. It was not feared and therefore not restrained.

Thus today giant corporations enjoy rights appropriate to yeoman farmers. Before the law they are similar to persons, with virtually all the rights granted persons to keep them free from control by their government, but with virtually none of the restraints placed upon democratic governments to prevent oppression.[5] Hence, workers for giant corporations such as

GPI, though they may be citizens of a democracy, live most of their lives within a social structure that is not democratic but hierarchical; not open but secretive; a place where the higher one climbs the more protected and hidden one is and therefore the less answerable one becomes. Small wonder that GPI's managers were morally insensitive and politically mute when they spent most of their waking lives in a social structure where responsibility was so diffused and hidden that sometimes not even the managers knew who was making the decisions governing their lives. Jim VanDyke, for instance, had spent twenty years at GPI depending on "someone at the national level [who] had some kind of long-range plan for old Jim." When he got to headquarters he searched in vain for that person.

Small wonder, too, that those outside the corporation, those who must suffer its incursions into their communities and its creeping domination over their lives but who have no effective forum in which to complain—no vote with which to try to turn the tide, no living leader to topple, not even a human face to shake a fist at—small wonder that these outsiders point to the anonymity of power at the corporation as its most frightening aspect.[6] The corporation with the technology it has organized seems a headless monster on the loose. As Bruce Catton writes:

> We have set all our other qualities aside and have entrusted ourselves entirely to our mechanical ingenuity. Proud that we have escaped from age-old superstition, we have condemned ourselves to life in a world of our own creation. . . . The one impossibility now is to turn back, or to go at half speed. This machine operates only at full speed. Unfortunately it cannot be steered.[7]

But there is no reason to give in so easily. Like all social institutions, corporations are human creations that must be continually re-created through human action. If they have lately taken a turn we do not desire, we can summon the will to change their direction. The only impossibility is that corporations will be reformed from within. Persons trained to trivialize their own feelings as well as the political and moral climate in which they live are not likely to see the need for change nor to be strong enough to effect it.

But if insiders are impotent, outsiders need not be. Human beings made the rules that govern corporate structures, and human beings can change the rules. GPI's managers show us what life is like in the corporate world, and by inference what life will become for all of us should corporate power—faceless and unaccountable—engulf us. Surely people once able to establish rules that restrained kings and priests can now impose rules that will restrain corporate leaders. May our politics be equal to the task.

APPENDIX: CHARACTERISTICS OF THE MANAGERS AND THEIR WIVES

When the study began in the spring of 1973, 39 GPI couples were living in Fairtown. During the year at least 1 member of all but 4 of the couples agreed to be interviewed, resulting in 64 interviews—30 with men and 34 with women. Following is a description of their major characteristics:

Functions at GPI: Twelve of the men were sales managers, 10 were in finance, 6 provided GPI with special services such as engineering or legal counsel, 3 were in merchandising, and another 4 held jobs in production.

Positions at GPI: Five of the men in sales were regional division sales managers, 6 were sales planning managers, and 1 was a beginning salesman. The 10 in finance included 1 vice-president of a subsidiary, 1 controller, 7 middle-level managers, and 1 cost accountant. Among those providing professional services, there were 1 vice-president and general counsel, 2 personnel managers, 2 special projects engineers, 1 laboratory manager, and 1 insurance specialist. The 4 in production included 2 distribution administrators; 1 manufacturing manager, and 1 senior buyer; the 3 in merchandising included 1 marketing research manager, 1 product group manager, and an associate product manager.

Years at GPI: Nearly all the men had served in the military and about one third had, for a few years, held one job before starting work at GPI. Otherwise, the men's entire careers were spent at GPI.

Incomes: Except for the beginning salesman, none of the men earned less than $20,000, and 3 earned more than $50,000. Most had incomes between $30,000 and $45,000.

Transiency: Five of the managers had never been transferred, 2 had been transferred once, 11 had been transferred two to four times, and 17 had been transferred at least five or more times.

Number of years in Fairtown: Five of the couples had lived in Fairtown for more than five years; 22 had been there for less than two years; the other 8 had been in town between two and five years.

Moving within town: At the time of the interviews, 5 couples were moving to a different house in Fairtown and 2 were moving to a neighboring town. Four others had lived in more than one house in Fairtown.

Children: Two couples, both recently married, were childless; 1 couple had but 1 child. The rest had 2 or more. Most of the children were in grade school or high school. Eight families had at least 1 preschooler and 6 had at least 1 child in college.

Education: All but 1 of the managers held at least one college degree. (Many had worked their way through school.) Almost all had majored in business administration or engineering; 2 had majored in history and 1 in political science. Four men held master's degrees, 3 in business administration and 1 in industrial psychology. One held a law degree. Three had taken graduate courses but had not completed their work for higher degrees. (One man was never reached for an interview because GPI had sent him to Harvard Business School for a "master's.")

Three of the men had attended parochial schools and the rest had attended public schools; none had attended a private preparatory school. Two of the bachelor's degrees were earned at Ivy League schools. The rest came either from state colleges or from small, little-known colleges. The graduate degrees were generally earned at more prestigious schools. The law degree came from Yale and 1 of the 2 M.B.A.s came from Harvard.

While there were fewer college graduates among the wives, only 1 wife lacked some post-high school training.

Wives' activities: Three of the women held full-time secretarial jobs; 1 was a part-time secretary; 2 were salespersons for products sold door to door; 1 was on the board of directors of the League of Women Voters; 1 had helped form the local Women's Political Caucus; and 1 was actively pursuing a career as an artist. The other 26 women devoted themselves to their families.

Fathers' education: One woman was a doctor's daughter; 2 other women were schoolmasters' daughters. One man was the son of an engineer. Otherwise, the parents of the managers and of their wives did not hold college degrees; many had not completed high school.

Fathers' occupations: Two-thirds of the men and women were children of blue-collar workers—miners, factory workers, or small farmers. Three men were sons of small retailers; 3 others were sons of corporation managers. In all, 7 of the men and 6 of the women had fathers who were either professionals or substantial entrepreneurs.

Parents' standard of living: Half the men and women remembered being raised in straitened economic circumstances. Two men and 1 woman recalled hardship and poverty; 3 men and 3 women remembered having been better off than others in their towns or neighborhoods. Most of the others said they had been "just comfortable."

Region of origin: Five men and 3 women grew up in Connecticut, and 2 women were raised in other New England states. One man and 2 women were raised in the South. One couple grew up in Cuba and left during the Castro revolution; 1 of the women grew up in California. Among the rest, slightly more than half were raised in the Middle Atlantic states. The others grew up in the Midwest.

Age: Most of the couples were in their thirties. Six women and 3 men were younger; 11 men and 10 women were older.

Ethnic background: Twenty-six of the 35 couples were white Protestants of Anglo-Saxon background. The others included the Cuban couple, 3 Irish Catholics, 2 Italian Catholics, 1 black couple, 1 Jewish couple, and 1 mixed Jewish-Protestant couple. Ten of the 64 respondents had at least 1 parent who was not born in the United States.

1. In order to protect the anonymity of the respondents, names of persons, places, and institutions have been changed. In addition, and for the same reason, descriptive details about places and persons have also been altered in those instances where such changes would protect privacy without abusing the sense of the respondents' experiences or the meanings of their statements. Moreover, for the sake of clarity and brevity, some quotations have been edited.

2. In Connecticut, town committees function in much the same ways that precinct or ward organizations do in other parts of the country.

3. These background characteristics indicate that the GPI managers living in Fairtown came from somewhat lower-ranking families than the subjects of other studies of managers. Michael Maccoby, for instance, describes the managers he studied as follows:

> The typical manager grew up in a town or small city. About half went to little-known colleges and half studied at leading state universities or elite private institutions. (More of the top managers went to the leading state or private universities, especially to the graduate schools in business administration.) . . . His parents were middle-class (American-born or Northern Europe); his father was either a manager, a white-collar worker, or a skilled worker in some technical or technically related work such as railroading, engineering, surveying or technical sales. [*The Gamesman*, pp. 37–38.]

Whether the GPI managers are more typical of corporation managers in general is hard to tell. Although several surveys of the background characteristics of chief executives are available, I have been unable to find comparable material on the family backgrounds of middle-ranking managers. However, one indication that the GPI managers may be more representative of the nation's managers is that GPI is a corporation without extraordinary characteristics. For reasons that suited his study objectives, the companies Maccoby chose were outstanding. They "are among the most dynamic and successful billion-dollar-a-year multinational corporations . . . and are considered models of excellence . . ." (p. 19). If GPI's managers share many of the characteristics of Maccoby's "gamesmen," but are less dynamic, less willing to take risks, and more bland, it is probably in large part because they come from different backgrounds.

A more detailed description of the background characteristics of GPI's managers can be found in the appendix.

4. Maccoby, *op. cit.;* Rosàbeth Moss Kanter, *Men and Women of the Corporation*; C. Wright Mills, *White Collar*; J. M. Pahl and R. E. Pahl, *Managers and Their Wives*; John R. Seeley, R. Alexander Sim, and Elizabeth W. Looseley, *Crestwood Heights*; Robert Seidenberg, *Corporate Wives— Corporate Casualties?*; A. C. Spectorsky, *The Exurbanites*; William H. Whyte, Jr., *The Organization Man*; Michael Young and Peter Willmott, chapter 9, "Managing Directors," *The Symmetrical Family*, pp. 239–90.

CHAPTER 1: INTRODUCTION

1. C. Wright Mills, *The Sociological Imagination*, p. 7.

2. All the managers interviewed in this study were men. The method of selecting respondents turned up only male managers. At the time the interviews were conducted (1973–74), few women were employed at the managerial rank. The 1970 census showed that nearly 98 percent of all managers and administrators earning more than $30,000 yearly were men (U.S. Bureau of the Census, *Occupational Characteristics and Occupations of Persons with Higher Earnings*, Washington, D.C., U.S. Government Printing Office, 1973). It is pos-

sible, with affirmative-action programs, that more women will become managers. Then, it might be assumed, corporations will use the same training techniques with females that they use with males. However, high-ranking executives frequently argue that the reason they do not like to hire women is that women's family obligations preclude such training. Whether entrance of women into the managerial ranks will force corporations to modify their training practices or whether, because training is harder for women with families, it will create a cadre of women managers more narrowed even than the men, is yet to be seen.

3. Robert T. Averitt, *The Dual Economy,* pp. 1–2.

4. David Riesman, Nathan Glazer, and Reuel Denney, *The Lonely Crowd*; and William H. Whyte, Jr., *op. cit.*

5. Maccoby, *op. cit.*

6. John Kenneth Galbraith, *The Affluent Society*, p. 13.

7. Galbraith, *The New Industrial State*, pp. 71–83.

8. Daniel Bell, *The Coming of Post-Industrial Society.*

9. Alvin Toffler, *Future Shock.*

10. Maurice R. Stein, *Eclipse of Community*; Vance Packard, *A Nation of Strangers*; Philip Slater, *The Pursuit of Loneliness*; Ralph Keyes, *We, the Lonely People*; David Riesman, *Abundance for What?*

11. Andrew Hacker, "Introduction: Corporate America," in Hacker, ed., *The Corporation Take-over,* p. 2.

12. Hacker, "Politics and the Corporation," in Hacker, *op. cit.*, p. 250.

13. Gus Tyler, "The Other Economy: America's Working Poor," p. 7.

14. Hacker, *op. cit.*, p. 2.

15. Table 918, *Statistical Abstract of the United States, 1977*, U.S. Department of Commerce, Bureau of the Census.

16. "Money Income in 1971 of Families and Persons in

the United States," Current Population Reports, Series P-60, No. 85, Tables 3, 8, December 1972, U.S. Department of Commerce, Bureau of the Census.

17. *Survey of Consumer Finances*. Ann Arbor, University of Michigan Survey Research Center.

18. Patricia Cayo Sexton and Brendan Sexton, *Blue Collars and Hard Hats*; and Richard Parker, *The Myth of the Middle Class*.

19. *1970 Census of Population, Volume 1: Characteristics of the Population*, Washington, D.C.: Bureau of the Census, Part 8, Connecticut, Table 102, pp. 348–53, Table 82, pp. 208–14, Part 34, New York, Table 82, pp. 343–48, Table 102, pp. 463–74, March, 1973.

20. Stephan Thernstrom, *The Other Bostonians*, p. 224.

21. *Ibid.*, pp. 228–29.

22. Packard, *op. cit.*, pp. viii–ix.

23. Hacker, *op. cit.*, p. 256.

24. Vilfredo Pareto, *The Mind and Society*; Gaetano Mosca, *The Ruling Class*; and Robert Michels, *Political Parties*.

25. Thorstein Verblen, *The Engineers and the Price System*; James Burnham, *The Managerial Revolution*; and Galbraith, *op. cit.*

26. Mills, *The Power Elite*.

27. Even Robert A. Dahl, one of the leaders in elitist-democratic theory, subscribes to this assumption. His research in New Haven indicated that those he called economic and social notables tended to "escape to the suburbs," thereby reducing their influence on city politics. Without testing the notion, he assumes that "many of these business and professional emigrants, who might have participated in New Haven politics had they stayed, turned up in the suburban communities as party officials, selectmen, or members of the innumerable boards and committees characteristic of Connecticut govern-

ment" (*Who Governs? Democracy and Power in an American City*, pp. 76–77). As this study indicates, economic notability when it comes from the core economy tends to preclude, rather than promote, participation in local communities.

28. William Kornhauser, *The Politics of Mass Society*; and Arnold M. Rose, *The Power Structure.*

29. Alexis de Tocqueville, *Democracy in America*; and James Bryce, *The American Commonwealth.*

30. Charles R. Wright and Herbert H. Hyman, "Voluntary Association Memberships of American Adults;" and Herbert H. Hyman and Charles R. Wright, "Trends in Voluntary Association Memberships of American Adults."

31. Paul Lazarsfeld, Bernard Berelson, and Hazel Gaudet, *The People's Choice.*

32. Bernard Berelson, Paul F. Lazarsfeld, and William N. McPhee, *Voting.*

33. *Ibid.*, p. 314; Seymour Martin Lipset, *Political Man*, pp. 183–229; Francis G. Wilson, "The Inactive Electorate and Social Revolution"; Herbert Tingsten, *Political Behavior*; V. Lance Tarrance, "The Vanishing Voter"; Giuseppe Di-Palma, "Participation or Apathy"; and Stephen Yeo, "Apathy."

34. W. G. Runciman, *Social Science and Political Theory*, pp. 98–99.

35. Scott Greer, *The Emerging City*, p. 37.

36. Mills, *The Sociological Imagination*, p. 11.

CHAPTER 2: THE MAKING OF MANAGERS

1. A study by Frederick D. Sturdivant and Roy D. Adler of chief executives indicates that chief business executives "are a more homogeneous group than they were ten years ago" ("Executive Origins," p. 125). Earlier reports of executive homogeneity include G. William Domhoff, *Who Rules America?* and C. Wright Mills, *The Power Elite*, pp. 118–47.

2. Edgar H. Schein, *Organizational Psychology*, pp. 27, 40.

3. Rosabeth Moss Kanter, *Men and Women of the Corporation*, pp. 47–55.

4. I am following Peter Blau's distinction here. He states that the most basic difference between social and strictly economic exchanges is that "the obligations incurred in social transactions are not clearly specified in advance," while "in economic transactions the exact obligations of both parties are simultaneously agreed upon; a given product is sold for a certain price" ("Social Exchange," p. 454).

5. Peter L. Berger and Thomas Luckmann, *The Social Construction of Reality*, pp. 157–59.

6. Bernard Levenson, "Bureaucratic Succession."

7. Wilbert E. Moore, *The Conduct of the Corporation*, p. 114.

8. Arnold van Gennep, *The Rites of Passage*, pp. 3, 183. Although Gennep intended "rites of passage" to refer to "all the ceremonies which accompany the passage from one social and magico religious position to another" (p. 18), its present usage is generally restricted to ceremonies of passage into adulthood.

9. Herbert Kaufman, *Forest Service*, pp. 177–78.

10. Examples of the popular treatment are: Associated Press, "Executives Aren't Moving," *Argus Leader*, Sioux Falls, S.D., October 25, 1978, p. 1.; and "Mobile Society Puts Down Roots," *Time*, June 12, 1978, p. 73. Contradictory evidence comes from a study conducted by Raymond E. Hill and Edwin L. Miller, "The Structure of the Job Change Decision for Mid-Career Managers: A Factor Analytic Study."

11. Such long hours of work are not peculiar to GPI managers. Other studies of managers report similarly long work weeks. See, for instance, Kanter, *op. cit.*, pp. 63, 64, 119; Michael Young and Peter Willmott, *The Symmetrical Family*,

pp. 145, 146, 247; and William H. Whyte, Jr., "How Hard Do Executives Work?"

12. *The New York Times*, February 17, 1975, p. 20.

13. Gennep, *op. cit.*, p. 81.

14. Moore, *op. cit.*, p. 57.

CHAPTER 3: PRUNING AND PRESERVING

1. Peter L. Berger and Thomas Luckmann, *The Social Construction of Reality*, p. 159.

CHAPTER 4: EXCHANGE AND POWER IN CORPORATE LIFE

1. Peter M. Blau, *Exchange and Power in Social Life*, pp. 121–22.

2. E. M. Beck, Patrick M. Horan, and Charles M. Tolbert II, "Stratification in a Dual Economy," pp. 704–20.

3. Wilbert E. Moore highlights the importance of office decor not only in keeping managers tied to the corporation but in the competition between family and corporation as well. He writes: "Many managers cannot afford at home the kind of opulent comfort that they enjoy at work. . . . In the covert struggle between the employer and the home, . . . the corporate employer often holds the higher cards" (*The Conduct of the Corporation*, p. 102).

4. Blau, *op. cit.*, p. 119.

5. Moore, *op. cit.*, p. 114.

6. Recent court cases involving the rights of corporations to demand secrecy are reviewed by Lawrence Stessen in "Keep Your Eyes off My Paycheck."

7. J. M. Pahl and R. E. Pahl, *op. cit.*, p. 26.

8. Such independence is as much the ideal in Great Britain as it is in the United States. Young and Willmott found that "half the full-time male employees in the sample shared the aspiration to have their own business" (*The Symmetrical*

Family, p. 163), and in their study, Goldthorpe and his colleagues found that 73 percent of manual workers and 56 percent of white-collar workers had either thought about having a business of their own or had actually tried one (J. H. Goldthorpe, *et al.*, *The Affluent Worker*, pp. 131–36).

9. John R. Seeley, R. Alexander Sim, and Elizabeth W. Loosely, *Crestwood Heights*; William H. Whyte, Jr., *The Organization Man*, pp. 295–449; A. C. Spectorsky, *The Exurbanites*; and Maurice R. Stein, *Eclipse of Community*, pp. 199–304.

10. Fairfield and Westchester Counties are perhaps extreme, but housing costs are likely to rise rapidly in those metropolitan areas that harbor many corporate headquarters and are therefore subject to high rates of transiency. Because corporations usually guarantee that managers need not sell at a loss, the managers can hold out until they are offered a price for their houses that represents a profit over and above the increase caused by inflation.

11. John Bowlby, *Attachment and Loss*, vol. I, chapter 12, and vol. II, chapters 18 and 19; and R. D. Laing, *The Self and Others*.

12. Edward C. Banfield, *The Unheavenly City*, pp. 47, 53.

13. Richard Sennett and Jonathan Cobb, *The Hidden Injuries of Class*.

14. Robert K. Merton, *Social Theory and Social Structure*, p. 151.

CHAPTER 5: THE MIND OF THE MANAGER

1. Max Weber, *The Theory of Social and Economic Organization*, p. 364.

2. Adolf A. Berle and Gardiner C. Means, *The Modern Corporation and Private Property*, 1967.

3. Jacob Schmookler, *Invention and Economic Growth*;

John Jewkes, David Sawers, and Richard Stillerman, *The Sources of Invention*; Robert T. Averitt, *The Dual Economy*, p. 16.

4. Peter L. Berger and Thomas Luckmann, *The Social Construction of Reality*, p. 93.

5. Rosabeth Moss Kanter, *Men and Women of the Corporation*, pp. 59–63.

6. *The New York Times,* "Reynolds Added to Bribing List," September 12, 1976, 4:3.

7. W. Eugene Smith and Aileen M. Smith, *Minamata*; Joel Swartz, "Silent Killers at Work."

8. *The New York Times*, "47 Box Executives Draw Jail and Fines for Rigging Prices," December 1, 1976, A:1.

9. Robert L. Heilbroner, Morton Mintz, Coleman McCarthy, Sanford Unger, Kermit Vandivier, Sol Friedman, and James Boyd, *In the Name of Profit*.

10. Robert M. Smith, "Books."

11. *The Wall Street Journal*, October 17, 1975, p. 14.

12. Gerald Sykes, *Foresights*, pp. 7–8.

13. Karl Mannheim, *Ideology and Utopia,* p. 118.

14. Berger and Luckmann, *op. cit.*, p. 93.

15. Edgar H. Schein, *Organizational Psychology*, p. 23; Kanter, *op. cit.*, pp. 48, 59–63; James D. Thompson, *Organizations in Action*, pp. 115, 159.

16. Studies by Rosabeth Moss Kanter (*op. cit.*, pp. 55–59) and others indicate that about three quarters of a manager's time is spent talking. Writers such as Edwin Newman have complained that a good deal of that talk is in an English so packed with neologisms and incorrect usage that it often becomes incomprehensible. There is perhaps method in that muddiness; it is usefully equivocal.

17. Wilbert E. Moore, *The Conduct of the Corporation*, pp. 55–56.

18. Kanter, *op. cit.*, pp. 254–64.

19. Bertell Ollmann, *Alienation*, p. 144.

20. *Ibid.*, p. 131.

CHAPTER 6: MARRIAGE CORPORATE STYLE

1. Nechama Tec, in her study of illicit drug usage among adolescents living in a suburb populated largely by managerial families, found: "It is precisely because intimate friendships are progressively more difficult to form and maintain that the burdens of the family become greater, encompassing more numerous and demanding functions. In addition to fulfilling the functions of procreation, socialization and sexual gratification, the family is asked to take over the function of companionship and intimate friendship. Far from becoming superfluous, therefore, the family is becoming more important." (*Grass Is Green in Suburbia*, p. 225.) In his study, Maccoby reported similar marital stability (p. 37).

2. *The New York Times*, December 29, 1974, 3:5.

3. The restrictions and confinements of rural areas and small towns, especially their intellectual repressions as contrasted with the emancipation and freedom to be found in cities, is an outstanding motif in the sociological literature of the city. For instance, in his classic essay "The Metropolis and Mental Life" Georg Simmel writes: "The small-town life in Antiquity and in the Middle Ages set barriers against movement and relations of the individual toward the outside, and it set up barriers against individual independence and differentiation within the self. . . . Even today a metropolitan man who is placed in a small town feels a restriction similar, at least, in kind. . . . Today metropolitan man is 'free' in a spiritualized and refined sense, in contrast to the pettiness and prejudices which hem in the small-town man" (*The Sociology of Georg Simmel*, pp. 417–18).

4. Karl Marx, "The Class Struggles in France," p. 298.

5. Michael Young and Peter Willmott, *The Symmetrical Family*, pp. 28–31.

6. *Ibid.*, p. 20.

7. *Ibid.*, p. 260.

8. Most studies of social mobility indicate that mobility is typically between adjacent ranks and that access to the uppermost levels is rare. See, for example, Natalie Rogoff, *Recent Trends in Occupational Mobility*; Thomas Fox and S. M. Miller, "Intra-Country Variations: Occupational Stratification and Mobility"; Peter M. Blau and Otis Dudley Duncan, *The American Occupational Structure*; Stephan Thernstrom, *The Other Bostonians*; Robert Perrucci, "The Significance of Intra-Occupational Mobility"; Seymour Martin Lipset and Reinhard Bendix, *Social Mobility in Industrial Society*; and Erwin O. Smigel, *The Wall Street Lawyer*.

9. The pattern is similar among women married to elite men in the United States (Arlene Kaplan Daniels, "The Female Power Elite").

10. Charles Horton Cooley, *Human Nature and the Social Order,* p. 183.

11. There were few minority members in the sample —one black man and two Jews. Two of them were in merchandising, where, presumably, the corporation required creativity more than comformity; and all three were more highly qualified than others holding comparable positions. One, for instance, was the only salesman with an M.B.A. and, with the exception of a lawyer, he was the only manager whose degrees came from elite schools. His B.A. was from Yale and his M.B.A. from Harvard, but he had not experienced the rapid advancement typical of the careers of white Protestant males with elite educational backgrounds.

12. Studies of the emotional effects of transiency have so far produced contradictory findings. Reports of psychic damage include: Mildred Kantor, "Internal Migration and Mental

Illness"; K. Tooley, "The Role of Geographic Mobility in Some Adjustment Problems of Children"; Lionel Tiger, "Is This Trip Necessary?"; Vance Packard, *A Nation of Strangers*; William H. Whyte, Jr., *The Organization Man*; and Robert Seidenberg, *Corporate Wives—Corporate Casualties*? On the other hand, the *Journal of Marriage and the Family* devoted its May 1973 issue to studies of transiency, and most of the research reported in that volume shows that geographic mobility has few, if any, psychological ill effects. Reasons for these differences might include the following: First, managers and their wives, like the GPIers, are generally reluctant to discuss the problems of transiency. Evidence of difficulties usually emerges only after some probing. The first set of research findings more commonly came from in-depth interviewing techniques, while most of the research in the *Journal of Marriage and the Family* was based on survey data from questionnaires. Second, managers tend to emphasize the advantages of moving. And, third, most of the studies that reported no adverse effects of transiency were sponsored by moving companies.

13. The Pahls found that a similar assumption is commonly made by managerial couples in Great Britain (J. M. Pahl and R. E. Pahl, *Managers and Their Wives*, p. 138).

14. He was one of four men who were out of town so often that they could not be reached for an interview.

15. Betty Friedan, *The Feminine Mystique*.

16. Erik H. Erikson, *Identity: Youth and Crisis*.

17. Robert K. Merton and Alice S. Kitt, "Contributors to the Theory of Reference-Group Behavior," pp. 87–89.

18. Pahl and Pahl, *op. cit.*, p. 104.

19. *Ibid.*, p. 104

20. Erikson, *op. cit.*, p. 27.

21. One of the reasons books such as Alvin Toffler's *Future Shock* enjoy great popularity in corporate circles, even though

they include occasional criticisms of corporations, is that they feed this important part of the corporate ideology.

22. Larry H. Long, "Does Migration Interfere with the Progress of Children in Schools?"

23. Along with the notion that small towns are intellectually stultifying and cities are invigorating goes the equally widespread idea that movement and exposure to people of different cultural backgrounds brings with it personal growth. For instance, Robert Park writes: "It is now clearly recognized that what we ordinarily call a lack of intelligence in individuals, races and communities is frequently a result of isolation. On the other hand, the mobility of a population is unquestionably a very large factor in its intellectual development" ("Human Migration," p. 106). The contrast Robert Merton and Alvin Gouldner make between "locals," whose social contacts and mental outlook are directed inward toward a small local community, and "cosmopolitans," whose associations and perspective reach outward and beyond, lies within this theoretical framework. (Alvin W. Gouldner, "Cosmopolitans and Locals," *Administrative Science Quarterly*, vol. 2 (1957–58), pp. 281–306, 444–80; and Robert K. Merton, Patterns of Influence," chapter X, pp. 387–420, in *Social Theory and Social Structure*).

24. Robert Park, *op. cit.*, "Human Migration," p. 136.

25. Richard Sennett, *The Uses of Disorder*.

26. Max Weber, *The Protestant Ethic and the Spirit of Capitalism*, p. 182.

CHAPTER 7: TWO WORLDS

1. Ferdinand Toennies, *Community and Society*.

2. Philip Slater, *Footholds*, p. 13.

3. Quoted in Ralph Keyes, *We, the Lonely People*, p. 145, which he quoted from the *Los Angeles Times*, February 8, 1972, p. 5; and *Time*, February 21, 1972, p. 4.

4. Emile Durkheim, *The Division of Labor in Society*.

5. Louis Wirth, *On Cities and Social Life*, p. 71.

6. In the nineteen fifties, when a number of researchers began to discover gemeinschaftlike communities where they were least expected—in the city—social scientists began to challenge the old assumptions concerning the nature and inevitability of gesellschaft in industrial societies. What they saw in contemporary neighborhoods did not, of course, display precisely the gemeinschaft of folk communities or medieval estates. Theirs was a modified version based on relationships Herbert Gans has called "quasi-primary," and on a degree of commitment that Morris Janowitz has termed a "community of limited liability." The research and theoretical essays in this area are too extensive to list or summarize here. What I shall do instead is note those that most influenced my own thinking on this issue: Herbert J. Gans, "Urbanism and Suburbanism as Ways of Life;" Scott Greer, *The Emerging City* and *The Urbane View*; Morris Janowitz, *The Community Press in an Urban Setting*; William F. Whyte, *Street Corner Society*.

7. For instance, Louis Wirth writes: "The larger the number of persons in a state of interaction with another, the lower is the level of communication and the greater is the tendency for communication to proceed on an elementary level, *i.e.*, on the basis of those things which are assumed to be common or to be of interest to all" (*op. cit.*, p. 83).

8. Andrew Greeley, "Marginal but Not Alienated: Confessions of a Loudmouthed Irish Priest."

CHAPTER 8: FAST FRIENDS

1. Andrew Greeley, "Marginal but Not Alienated: Confessions of a Loudmouthed Irish Priest," p. 8.

2. Georg Simmel, *The Sociology of Georg Simmel*, pp. 325–26.

3. Richard Sennett, *The Fall of Public Man*, p. 221.

4. Charles Horton Cooley, *Human Nature and the Social Order*, pp. 95, 119.

5. I do not, of course, deny that community might have other than a geographical basis; that there might be something called a community of scholars held together by shared ideas; but even then occasional meetings seem necessary, or why would learned societies gather at regular intervals? I do not deny either that one can be deeply affected by the idea (and ideas) of imaginary persons or by persons long dead (as Cooley was by Emerson and Goethe). As Cooley argued, we can carry on imagined conversations with persons not present. But I do claim that such feelings and conversations are not the same as relationships and conversations with corporeal others. And it is odd that Cooley, the man who coined the term "primary group" because he recognized the importance of face-to-face intimacy and exchange, should have thought they were. For the difference between relationships grounded in place and those divorced from it has to do with the crucial characteristic of primary relationships: fusion of personalities. We can think of our friend often, but unless we communicate, he or she will never know; there will be no fusion of personalities, no reciprocal change.

6. Scott Greer, *The Emerging City*, p. 37.

7. Goodwin Watson, "Working with Groups: A Fifty-year Retrospective," p. 33.

8. Erving Goffman, *Asylums*, p. 76.

9. Michael Walzer, "Teaching Morality."

10. Andrew Greeley, *op. cit.*, p. 7.

11. Theodore White, "Growing Up in the Land of Promise," p. 39.

CHAPTER 9: POLITICS IN FAIRTOWN

1. Their approach is to determine the nature of a commu-

nity's power structure on the basis of judgments made by community members who are considered "knowledgeable" about community life. They are asked to select the names of the most powerful persons in town from lists that include holders of major governmental positions as well as business and society leaders. The persons most frequently selected are said to constitute the power structure. For the most part, I used the TC members as "knowledgeables," but because this "reputational" approach has been criticized for limiting the judges' choices, I did not supply my judges with a list; instead I let them suggest names of the persons they considered most powerful. If a judge named only political officeholders, I would suggest a name or two from other categories, such as business or society leaders to let him know that such persons were also to be considered. The result was that the persons most often mentioned either held or had once held political positions—although a few had political power based on their land holdings or social and business positions.

2. Seymour Martin Lipset, *Political Man*, p. 185.

3. George Sabine, "The Two Democratic Traditions," p. 470.

4. Carl J. Friedrich and Zbigniew K. Brzezinski, *Totalitarian Dictatorship and Autocracy*, pp. 22, 33.

5. Alexis de Tocqueville, *Democracy in America*, Vol. II, p. 107.

CHAPTER 10: CONCLUSION

1. Ralph Keyes writes: "Those studying communes have found a curious paradox. Experiments in communal living are top-heavy with the root-seeking children of nomadic corporation men" (*We, the Lonely People*, p. 18). He cites Keith Melville, *Communes in the Counter Culture*; and Robert Houriet, *Getting Back Together*.

2. William H. Whyte, Jr., *The Organization Man*, p. 4.

3. Herbert J. Gans, *The Levittowners*, p. xvi.

4. In an article entitled "Corporate Giants Invade the Residential Market," Peter T. Kilborn writes: "The metamorphosis in the residential real-estate business is already well at work in thousands of communities across the country. Southington is typical. . . . A few years ago, the real-estate business here was made up of a dozen brokerage offices and a few independent brokers who operated out of their homes. Most of the home-office agents have now disappeared. One of the established brokers has sold out to a West Hartford concern, . . . and several of the other leading offices have signed on with franchisers. . . ."

5. James S. Coleman, *Power and the Structure of Society*, pp. 13–18, 35–37; and John P. Davis, *Corporations*, Volume II, pp. 209–10. As we all do, Coleman and Davis embrace the same fiction the law does by reifying the corporation. We speak of corporations as if they were human, as if they could think and act and have a will and be held responsible. Of course we know they cannot.

6. For instance, Herbert Marcuse, *One-Dimensional Man*; and Bertram M. Gross, "Friendly Facism, A Model for America."

7. Bruce Catton, *Waiting for the Morning Train*, pp. 220, 222.

Averitt, Robert T. *The Dual Economy: The Dynamics of American Industry Structure*. New York: W. W. Norton, 1968.

Banfield, Edward C. *The Unheavenly City*. Boston: Little, Brown, 1968.

Beck, E. M., Horan, Patrick M., and Tolbert, Charles M., II. "Stratification in a Dual Economy: A Sectoral Model of Earnings Determination." *American Sociological Review* 43:5 (October, 1978) 704–20.

Bell, Daniel. *The Coming of Post-Industrial Society: A Venture in Social Forecasting*. New York: Basic Books, 1973.

Berelson, Bernard R., Lazarsfeld, Paul F., and McPhee, William N. *Voting: A Study of Opinion Formation in a Presidential Campaign*. Chicago: University of Chicago Press, 1954.

Berger, Peter L., and Luckmann, Thomas. *The Social Construction of Reality: A Treatise in the Sociology of Knowledge*. Garden City, N.Y.: Anchor Books, 1966.

Berle, Adolf A., and Means, Gardiner C. *The Modern Corporation and Private Property*. New York: Harcourt Brace & World, 1967.

Blau, Peter M. *Exchange and Power in Social Life*. New York: John Wiley & Sons, 1964.

———. "Social Exchange," in *The International Encyclopedia of the Social Sciences*, D. E. Sills, ed. New York: Macmillan, 1968.

———, and Duncan, Otis Dudley. *The American Occupational Structure*. New York: John Wiley & Sons, 1967.

Bowlby, John. *Attachment and Loss*. New York: Basic Books, 1973.

Bryce, James. *The American Commonwealth*. New York: Macmillan, 1907.

Burnham, James. *The Managerial Revolution.* New York: Putnam, 1942.

Catton, Bruce. *Waiting for the Morning Train.* Garden City, N.Y.: Doubleday, 1972.

Coleman, James S. *Power and the Structure of Society.* New York: Norton, 1974.

Cooley, Charles Horton. *Human Nature and the Social Order.* New York: Scribners, 1902. Reprint, New York: Schocken Books, 1964.

Dahl, Robert A. *Who Governs? Democracy and Power in an American City.* New Haven: Yale University Press, 1961.

Daniels, Arlene Kaplan. "The Female Power Elite." Paper presented to the Center for the American Woman and Politics, Rutgers University, 1975.

Davis, John P. *Corporations: A Study of the Origin and Development of Great Business Combinations and Their Relation to the Authority of the State.* New York: Capricorn Books, 1961.

DiPalma, Giuseppe. "Participation or Apathy: Toward Political Choice," in *New Patterns in American Politics,* Thomas A. Reilly and Michael W. Sigall, eds., pp. 143–74. New York: Praeger, 1975.

Domhoff, G. William. *Who Rules America?* Englewood Cliffs, N.J.: Prentice Hall, 1968.

Durkheim, Emile. *The Division of Labor in Society.* George Simpson, translator. Glencoe, Ill.: The Free Press.

Erikson, Erik H. *Identity: Youth and Crisis.* New York: Norton, 1968.

Fox, Thomas, and Miller, S. M. "Intra-Country Variations: Occupational Stratification and Mobility," in *Studies in Comparative International Development.* 1:1 (1965).

Friedan, Betty. *The Feminine Mystique.* New York: Norton, 1963.

Friedrich, Carl J., and Zbigniew K. Brzezinski. *Totalitarian Dictatorship and Autocracy*. Cambridge: Harvard University Press, 1965.

Galbraith, John Kenneth. *The Affluent Society*. Boston: Houghton Mifflin, 1958.

————. *The New Industrial State*. Boston: Houghton Mifflin, 1967.

Gans, Herbert J. *The Levittowners: Ways of Life and Politics in a New Suburban Community*. New York: Knopf, 1967.

————. "Urbanism and Suburbanism as Ways of Life: A Reevaluation of Definitions," in Peter I. Rose, *The Study of Society: An Integrated Anthology*. New York: Random House, 1972, pp. 424–38.

Gennep, Arnold van. *The Rites of Passage*, translated by Monika B. Vizedon and Gabrielle L. Caffee. Chicago: The University of Chicago Press, 1960.

Goffman, Erving. *Asylums: Essay on the Social Situation of Mental Patients and Other Inmates*. Garden City, N.Y.: Anchor Books, 1961.

Goldthorpe, John H., et al. *The Affluent Worker: Political Attitudes and Behavior*. Cambridge: Cambridge University Press, 1968.

Gouldner, Alvin W. "Cosmopolitans and Locals: Toward an Analysis of Latent Social Roles." *Administrative Science Quarterly* 2 (1957–58) 281–306, 444–80.

Greeley, Andrew. "Marginal but Not Alienated: Confessions of a Loudmouthed Irish Priest." *Social Policy* 5 (May 1964) 4–11.

Greer, Scott. *The Emerging City: Myth and Reality*. New York: The Free Press, 1962.

————. *The Urbane View: Life and Politics in Metropolitan America*. New York: Oxford University Press, 1972.

Gross, Bertram M. "Friendly Fascism, a Model for America."

Social Policy, November/December 1970, pp. 44–52.

Hacker, Andrew, ed. *The Corporation Take-over*. New York: Harper & Row, 1964.

Heilbroner, Robert L.; Mintz, Morton; McCarthy, Coleman; Unger, Sanford; Vandivier, Kermit; Freidman, Sol; and Boyd, James. *In the Name of Profit*. Garden City, N.Y.: Doubleday, 1972.

Hill, Raymond E., and Miller, Edwin L. "The Structure of the Job Change Decision for Mid-Career Managers: A Factor Analytic Study." Mimeograph, Ann Arbor: Graduate School of Business Administration, The University of Michigan.

Hillery, George A., Jr. "Definitions of Community: Areas of Agreement." *Rural Sociology* 20 (1955).

Hyman, Herbert H., and Wright, Charles R. "Trends in Voluntary Association Memberships of American Adults: Replication Based on Secondary Analysis of National Sample Surveys." *American Sociological Review* 36 (April 1971) 191–206.

Janowitz, Morris. *The Community Press in an Urban Setting: The Social Elements of Urbanism*. Glencoe, Ill.: The Free Press, 1952.

Jewkes, John; Sawers, David; and Stillerman, Richard. *Sources of Invention*. New York: Norton, 1969.

Kanter, Rosabeth Moss. *Men and Women of the Corporation.* New York: Basic Books, 1977.

Kantor, Mildred. "Internal Migration and Mental Illness." *Changing Perspectives in Mental Illness,* Stanley C. Plog and Robert B. Edgerton, eds. New York: Holt, Rinehart and Winston, 1969.

Kaufman, Herbert. *Forest Service: A Study in Administrative Behavior*. Baltimore: Johns Hopkins Press, 1960.

Keyes, Ralph. *We, the Lonely People: Searching for Community*. New York: Harper & Row, 1973.

Kilborn, Peter T. "Corporate Giants Invade the Residential Market," *New York Times*, February 4, 1979, section 3, p. 1.

Kornhauser, William. *The Politics of Mass Society*. New York: The Free Press, 1959.

Laing, R. D. *The Self and Others*. New York: Pantheon, 1970.

Lazarsfeld, Paul; Berelson, Bernard; and Gaudet, Hazel. *The People's Choice: How the Voter Makes Up His Mind in a Presidential Campaign*. New York: Columbia University Press, 1944.

Levenson, Bernard. "Bureaucratic Succession." *Comparative Analysis of Complex Organizations*, Amitai Etzioni, ed. New York: Holt, Rinehart and Winston, 1961.

Lipset, Seymour Martin. *Political Man: The Social Bases of Politics*. Garden City, N.Y.: Anchor Books, 1959.

————, and Bendix, Reinhard. *Social Mobility in Industrial Society*. Berkeley: University of California Press, 1959.

Long, Larry H. "Does Migration Interfere with the Progress of Children in School?" Paper delivered to the American Sociological Association, 1973.

Maccoby, Michael. *The Gamesman: The New Corporate Leaders*. New York: Simon & Schuster, 1977.

Mannheim, Karl. *Ideology and Utopia: An Introduction to the Sociology of Knowledge*. New York: Harcourt, Brace and World, 1936.

Marcuse, Herbert. *One-Dimensional Man*. Boston: Beacon Press, 1964.

Marx, Karl. "The Class Struggles in France." *Marx and Engels: Basic Writings on Politics and Philosophy*, Lewis S. Fever, ed. Garden City, N.Y.: Anchor Books, 1959.

Merton, Robert K. *Social Theory and Social Structure*. Glencoe, Ill.: The Free Press, 1949.

————, and Kitt, Alice S. "Contributors to the Theory of Reverence-Group Behavior." *Continuities in Social Re-*

search: Studies in the Scope and Method of the American Soldier, edited by Robert K. Merton and Paul F. Lazarsfeld. Glencoe, Ill.: The Free Press, 1950.

Michels, Robert. *Political Parties.* Glencoe, Ill.: The Free Press, 1958.

Mills, C. Wright. *The Power Elite.* New York: Oxford University Press, 1956.

————. *The Sociological Imagination.* New York: Oxford University Press, 1959.

————. *White Collar: The American Middle Classes.* New York: Oxford University Press, 1951.

Moore, Wilbert E. *The Conduct of the Corporation.* New York: Random House, 1962.

Mosca, Gaetano. *The Ruling Class.* New York: McGraw-Hill, 1939.

Ollmann, Bertell. *Alienation: Marx's Conception of Man in Capitalist Society.* Cambridge: Cambridge University Press, 1971.

Packard, Vance. *A Nation of Strangers.* New York: David McKay, 1974.

Pahl, J. M., and Pahl, R. E. *Managers and Their Wives: A Study of Career and Family Relationships.* London: Allen Laine, 1971.

Pareto, Vilfredo. *The Mind and Society.* New York: Harcourt Brace, 1935.

Park, Robert. "Human Migration." *Classic Essays on the Culture of Cities,* Richard Sennett, ed. New York: Appleton-Century-Crofts, 1969.

Parker, Richard. *The Myth of the Middle Class.* New York: Harper & Row, 1974.

Perrucci, Robert. "The Significance of Intra-Occupational Mobility: Some Methodological and Theoretical Notes, Together with a Case Study of Engineers." *American Sociological Review* 26 (1961) 874–83.

Riesman, David. *Abundance for What? And Other Essays.* Garden City, N.Y.: Doubleday & Company, 1964.

————. Glazer, Nathan; and Denney, Reuel. *The Lonely Crowd: A Study of the Changing American Character.* New Haven: Yale University Press, 1950.

Rogoff, Natalie. *Recent Trends in Occupational Mobility.* Glencoe, Ill.: The Free Press, 1953.

Rose, Arnold M. *The Power Structure: Political Process in American Society.* New York: Oxford University Press, 1967.

Runciman, W. G. *Social Science and Political Theory.* Cambridge: Cambridge University Press, 1963.

Sabine, George. "The Two Democratic Traditions." *The Philosophical Review* 61 (October 1944) 451–74.

Schein, Edgar H. *Organizational Psychology.* Englewood Cliffs, N.J.: Prentice-Hall, 1965.

Schmookler, Jacob. *Invention and Economic Growth.* Cambridge: Harvard University Press, 1966.

Seeley, John R.; Sim, R. Alexander; and Loosley, Elizabeth W. *Crestwood Heights: A North American Suburb.* New York: Basic Books, 1956.

Seidenberg, Robert. *Corporate Wives—Corporate Casualties?* New York: AMACOM, 1973.

Sennett, Richard. *The Fall of Public Man.* New York: Alfred A. Knopf, 1977.

————. *The Uses of Disorder: Personal Identity and City Life.* New York: Alfred A. Knopf, 1971.

————, and Cobb, Jonathan. *The Hidden Injuries of Class.* New York: Random House, 1972.

Sexton, Patricia Cayo; and Sexton, Brendan. *Blue Collars and Hard Hats: The Working Class and the Future of American Politics.* New York: Random House, 1971.

Simmel, Georg. *The Sociology of Georg Simmel.* Kurt H. Wolff, trans. New York: Free Press, 1950.

Slater, Philip. *Footholds: Understanding the Shifting Sexual and Family Tensions in Our Culture.* New York: E. P. Dutton, 1977.

————. *The Pursuit of Loneliness: American Culture at the Breaking Point.* Rev. ed. Boston: Beacon Press, 1976.

Smigel, Erwin O. *The Wall Street Lawyer.* Bloomington, Ind.: Indiana University Press, 1969.

Smith, Robert M. "Books: Business Corruption," *The New York Times,* October 10, 1975, F:8.

Smith, W. Eugene, and Smith, Aileen M. *Minamata.* New York: Holt, Rinehart and Winston, 1975.

Spectorsky, A. C. *The Exurbanites.* Philadelphia: Lippincott, 1955.

Stein, Maurice R. *Eclipse of Community: An Interpretation of American Studies.* Princeton: Princeton University Press, 1971.

Stessen, Lawrence. "Keep Your Eyes off My Paycheck." *New York Times,* June 13, 1976 3:1.

Sturdivant, Frederick D., and Adler, Roy D. "Executive Origins: Still a Grey Flannel World?" *Harvard Business Review* 54:6 (November–December 1976) 125–32.

Swartz, Joel. "Silent Killers at Work." *Crime and Social Justice* 3 (Spring–Summer 1975) 15–20.

Sykes, Gerald. *Foresights: Self-Evaluation and Survival.* Indianapolis: Bobbs Merrill, 1975.

Tarrance, V. Lance. "The Vanishing Voter: A Look at Non-Voting as a Purposive Act," in Jonathan Moore and Albert C. Pierce, eds. *Voters, Primaries, and Parties: Selections from a Conference on American Politics.* Cambridge: Institute of Politics, John Fitzgerald Kennedy School of Government, Harvard University, 1976.

Tec, Nechama. *Grass Is Green in Suburbia: A Sociological Study of Adolescent Usage of Illicit Drugs.* Roslyn Heights, N.Y.: Libra, 1974.

Thernstrom, Stephan. *The Other Bostonians: Poverty and Progress in the American Metropolis, 1880–1970.* Cambridge: Harvard University Press, 1973.

Thompson, James D. *Organizations in Action.* New York: McGraw-Hill, 1967.

Tiger, Lionel. "Is This Trip Necessary? The Heavy Human Costs of Moving Executives Around." *Fortune* XC:3 (September 1979) 139–41.

Tingsten, Herbert. *Political Behavior: Studies in Election Statistics.* New York: Arno Press, 1975.

Tocqueville, Alexis de. *Democracy in America.* New York: Random House, 1944.

Toennies, Ferdinand. *Community and Society (Gemeinschaft und Gesellschaft).* Charles P. Loomis, translator and editor. East Lansing: Michigan State University Press, 1957.

Toffler, Alvin. *Future Shock.* New York: Random House, 1970.

Tooley, K. "The Role of Geographic Mobility in Some Adjustment Problems of Children." *Journal of the American Academy of Child Psychiatry* (1970) 366–78.

Tyler, Gus. "The Other Economy: America's Working Poor." *New Leader* LXI:10 (May 8, 1978).

Veblen, Thorstein. *The Engineers and the Price System.* New York: Harbinger, 1963.

Walzer. Michael. "Teaching Morality." *The New Republic* (June 10, 1978) 12–14.

Watson, Goodwin. "Working with Groups: A Fifty-year Retrospective," *Social Policy*, 5:2 (July/August 1974) 33–38.

Weber, Max. *The Protestant Ethic and the Spirit of Capitalism.* New York: Charles Scribner's Sons, 1930.

———. *The Theory of Social and Economic Organization.* New York: The Free Press, 1964.

White, Theodore. "Growing Up in the Land of Promise." *Atlantic* (August, 1978) pp. 33–58.

Whyte, William F. *Street Corner Society: The Social Structure of an Italian Slum*. Chicago: University of Chicago Press, 1955.

Whyte, William H., Jr. "How Hard Do Executives Work?" *The Executive Life*. Garden City, N.Y.: Doubleday, 1956.

————. *The Organization Man*. New York: Simon & Schuster, 1956.

Wilson, Francis G. "The Inactive Electorate and Social Revolution." *South Western Social Science Quarterly*, 16:4 (1936) 73–84.

Wirth, Louis. *On Cities and Social Life*. Chicago: University of Chicago Press, Phoenix Books, 1964.

Wright, Charles R., and Hyman, Herbert H. "Voluntary Association Membership of Adults: Evidence from National Sample Surveys." *American Sociological Review* 23 (June 1958) 284–94.

Yeo, Stephen. "Apathy." *European Journal of Sociology*, 15:2 (1974) 279–311.

Young, Michael, and Willmott, Peter. *The Symmetrical Family*. New York: Pantheon Books, 1974.